Family in America

Family in America

Advisory Editors: David J. Rothman

Professor of History,
Columbia University

Sheila M. Rothman

THE FAMILY

American
Sociological Society

$\mathcal{A}$RNO $\mathcal{P}$RESS & $\mathcal{T}$HE $\mathcal{N}$EW $\mathcal{Y}$ORK $\mathcal{T}$IMES

New York   1972

Reprint Edition 1972 by Arno Press Inc.

Reprinted from a copy in
The University of Chicago Library

LC# 78-169370
ISBN 0-405-03846-1

Family in America
ISBN for complete set: 0-405-03840-2
See last pages of this volume for titles.

Manufactured in the United States of America

Reprinted from Papers and Proceedings
of the American Sociological Society,
Volume III (Third Annual Meeting held at
Atlantic City, N.J. December 28-30,1908)

PUBLICATIONS

OF THE

AMERICAN SOCIOLOGICAL SOCIETY

GENERAL TOPIC:

THE FAMILY

AMERICAN SOCIOLOGICAL SOCIETY
Organized at Baltimore, December, 1905

OFFICERS FOR THE YEAR 1909

President: WILLIAM G. SUMNER, Yale University
Vice-Presidents: FRANKLIN H. GIDDINGS, Columbia University
ALBION W. SMALL, The University of Chicago
Secretary and Treasurer: C. W. A. VEDITZ, George Washington University, Washington, D. C.

Executive Committee, in addition to the above officers:
FRANK W. BLACKMAR, University of Kansas
CHARLES H. COOLEY, University of Michigan
CHARLES A. ELLWOOD, University of Missouri
GRAHAM TAYLOR, Chicago Commons
LESTER F. WARD, Brown University
U. G. WEATHERLY, University of Indiana
D. COLIN WELLS, Dartmouth University

Communications regarding membership, meetings, and the general affairs of the Society should be addressed to the Secretary at Washington, D. C., care of the George Washington University. Orders for publications should be addressed to the University of Chicago Press, Chicago, Ill., and 156 Fifth Avenue, New York City.

NATURE AND PURPOSES OF THE SOCIETY

The American Sociological Society was organized at Baltimore in 1905 at conferences which were held there in conjunction with the annual meetings of the American Economic Association, the American Historical Association, and the American Political Science Association. Among those who atended these conferences there was an almost unanimous opinion that the interests of sociologists were sufficiently important and sufficiently distinct to warrant the creation of a new organization which would bring together at regular intervals those interested in the promotion of sociological studies.

Quite as much as the economists, who formed a national association twenty-one years ago, or as the political scientists, who formed the Political Science Association four years ago, American sociologists, like their European colleagues, have need of the stimulus and the mutual criticism which would come from an organization that is national, permanent, and scientific in character. Such an organization would, it was felt, bring historical, theoretical, and practical sociologists together in helpful co-operation and exalt sociology in the eyes of the general public.

It is the purpose of the society, therefore, to include in its membership all those who recognize the importance of the scientific aspects of sociology—scientific philanthropists as well as teachers of sociology, sociological workers as well as sociological writers. The membership fee is Three Dollars a year, or Fifty Dollars for Life Membership. Each member will receive a copy of the current publications of the Society, and *The American Journal of Sociology.* Application blanks, as well as further information concerning the Society, may be obtained of the Secretary, PROFESSOR C. W. A. VEDITZ, GEORGE WASHINGTON UNIVERSITY, WASHINGTON. D. C.

PAPERS AND PROCEEDINGS

THIRD ANNUAL MEETING
AMERICAN
SOCIOLOGICAL SOCIETY

HELD AT ATLANTIC CITY, N. J.
DECEMBER 28–30, 1908

———

VOLUME III

———

Published May 1, 1909

Composed and Printed By
The University of Chicago Press
Chicago, Illinois, U. S. A.

TABLE OF CONTENTS

THE FAMILY AND SOCIAL CHANGE*

PROFESSOR WILLIAM G. SUMNER
Yale University

We currently speak of the "institution" of marriage. We also use marriage instead of wedding, nuptials, or matrimony. The result is confusion. A wedding or even nuptials occur as a ceremony or festival, on a day, and as the commencement of wedlock or matrimony. Wedlock may be an institution, but a wedding is not. A wedding lacks the duration or recurrence which belongs to an institution. It does not provide for an enduring necessity. It has no apparatus for the repeated use of the same couple. Wedlock is a permanent relation between a man and a woman which is regulated and defined by the *mores*. It brings the pair into co-operation for the struggle for existence and the procreation and nurture of children. Wedlock therefore forms a family, and a family seems to satisfy our idea of an institution far better than marriage or matrimony. The family institution existed probably before marriage. A woman with an infant in her arms is what we see as far back as our investigations lead us. She was limited and burdened in the struggle for existence by her infant. The task of finding subsistence was as hard for her as for a man. The infant was another claimant of her time and labor. Her chance of survival was in union and co-operation with a man. Undoubtedly this gives us the real explanation of the primitive inferiority of woman. They needed the help of men more than men needed women and if a union was made it was made on terms of which the woman got the disadvantage. It certainly is a great mistake to believe that the women were put down because the men were physically stronger. In the first place the men are not always stronger; perhaps it is, as a rule, the other way.

*Address of the president of the American Sociological Society at its third annual meeting in Atlantic City, N. J., December 28–30, 1908.

Mr. H. H. Johnstone says of the Andombies on the Congo that the women, though working very hard as laborers in general, lead a very happy existence; they are often stronger than the men and more finely developed, some of them having splendid figures. Parke, speaking of the Manyuema of the Arruwimi in the same region, says that they are fine animals, and the women very handsome. They are as strong as the men. In North America an Indian chief once said to Hearne, "Women were made for labor; one of them can carry, or haul, as much as two men can do." Schellong says of the Papuans in the German protectorate of New Guinea that the women are more strongly built than the men.[1]

Kubary[2] says that a man has the right to beat his wife but the women are so robust that a man who tries to do it may well find that he will get the worst of it. Fights between men and women are not rare in savage life and the women prevail in a fair share of them. Holm mentions a case where a Greenland Eskimo tried to flog his wife but she flogged him.[3] We hear of a custom in South Eastern Australia that fights between the sexes were provoked when

there were young women who were marriageable but were not mated, and when the eligible bachelors were backward. The men would kill a totem animal of the women or the women would kill a totem animal of the men. This led to a fight of the young men and young women. Then, after the wounds healed they would pair off and the social deadlock would pass away.[4]

Another case, from higher civilization, shows how the woman was weakened by considerations of another kind. Sieroshevski, a Pole, who lived for twelve years among the Yakuts, says that he knew a Yakut woman who was constantly abused by her husband although she was industrious and good-natured. At last the European asked her why she did not fight. He assured her that she would succeed and he argued with her that if she would once give her husband a good beating he would not misuse her any more. She, however, answered that that would never do. Her husband's companions would deride him as the man whose wife beat him and their children would be derided by the other children for the same reason. She would not do any-

[1] H. Ellis, *Man and Woman*, p. 4.

[2] *Nukuoro*, p. 35.

[3] *Angmagslikerne*, p. 55.

[4] Howitt, *South Eastern Australia*, p. 149.

thing which would produce that consequence and would make her worse off. This case has many parallels. A characteristic incident occurred at the Black Mountain station on the Snowy River about the years 1855–56.

A number of Theddora (Ya-itma-thang) black's had come across from Omeo and there met a woman, known to me as Old Jenny, of their tribe, who had broken their law by becoming the wife of a man to whom she stood in the tribal relationship of *Najan* (mother). She had been away for some years, and this was the first time that her kindred had encountered her. The wife of one of them attacked her first with a digging-stick, but she defended herself so well with the same weapon that the woman had to desist, and her husband continued the attack on Old Jenny, who had divested herself of all but one small garment. He commenced with a club, but finding he could not hit her, changed it for a curved club with which he tried to "peck" her on the head over guard. After a time he also had to give it up, and they had to make friends with the invincible woman. This is an instance of the manner in which the women are able to defend themselves with their weapon, the "yam-stick," being no mean opponents of a man armed only with a club.[5]

The status of women was generally sad and pathetic in savage life but we may accept it as an established fact that that was not because she was physically inferior to man but that it was due to inferiority in the struggle for existence on account of maternity. In the family the man often tyrannized over the woman, and the woman came into the family unwillingly, driven by a greater necessity, but the family was not a product of force. It was a product of contract. It was controlled by the *mores* which soon established notions of the right way to behave and of rights and duties which would be conducive to prosperity and happiness.

In this primitive society the family became the arena in which folkways were formed and taught, traditions were handed down, myths were invented, and sympathies were cultivated. The mother and the children were in the closest association and intimacy. The instruction of example was the chief instruction, without spoken command or explanation. It makes little difference whether we think of a family in a horde or of a monandrous family of Australians or Bushmen. The children learned from

[5] Howitt, p. 197.

their mothers the usages which were domestic and familiar, which underlie society and are moral in their character. At puberty the boys went with their fathers into the political body and became warriors and hunters. Then they were disciplined into the life of men and left the family. They got wives and founded families, but the father, in his own family, was an outsider and a stranger with few functions and little authority.

Mohammed gave approval to the father-family which seems to have been winning acceptance in his time. Islam is founded on the father-family. In the Koran women are divided into three classes in respect to marriage: First, wives, that is, status-wives with all the rank, honor, and rights which the name implies; second, concubines, that is, wives of an inferior class, in a permanent and recognized relation but without the rank and honor of wives; thirdly, slaves, whose greatest chance of happiness was to "find favor" in the eyes of their master or owner. This classification of the wives was also a classification of the mothers and it produced jealousy and strife of the children. Only men of rank and wealth could have households of this complex character. Those of limited means had to choose which form of wife they would take. The full status-wife could make such demands that she became a great burden to her husband and it appears that the Moslems now prefer concubines or slaves. In Mohammedan royal families the jealousies and strifes of children, where the son of a slave might be preferred and made heir by the father, have reduced kingdoms and families to bloodshed and anarchy.

In general, in the mother-family, the family must have lacked integration and discipline. The Six Nations or Iroquois had the mother-family in well-developed form. Each woman with her husband and children had a room about 7 feet square in the "long house." This room was separated from others inhabited by similar families, not by a partition but only by a pole three or four feet from the floor over which skins were hung. Each family shared fire with another family opposite. Evidently privacy was only imperfectly secured. Any man who did not bring in what was considered his fair share of food-supply could be expelled at any time. A husband had to satisfy not only his wife but all her female relatives if he was to be in peace and comfort. He could withdraw when he chose but he must leave his children which belonged to his wife. He must also keep the peace with all the other husbands in the house while it is easy to see that frequent occasions of quarrel would occur. In short, the man had constant and important reasons to be dissatisfied with the mother-family. He always had one alternative; he could capture a woman outside the group. If he did this he distinguished himself by military prowess and the woman was a trophy. He was not limited in his control of her or their children by any customs or traditions and he could arrange his life as he pleased. We should expect that great numbers of men would try this alternative but it does not appear that many did so. If they had done so they would have speedily introduced man-descent and the father-family. As we well know uncivilized men do not freely reflect on their experience or discuss reforms or speculate on progress. They accept custom and tradition and make the best of it as they find it. The change to the man-family was brought about by some great change in the conditions of the struggle for existence or by the invention of a new tool or weapon used by the men or by war with powerful neighbors. This much, however, can be said with confidence about the family under woman-descent: It was the conservative institution of that form of society in which traditions were cherished and education was accomplished. It did not encourage change or cherish reforms. It preserved what had been inherited and protected what existed.

Probably the change from mother-family to father-family was by far the greatest and most important revolution in the history of civilization. This was so because the family, especially in primitive society, is such a fundamental institution that it forces all other societal details into conformity with itself. Miss Kingsley, speaking of the negroes of West Africa, describes societal details as follows:

The really responsible male relative is the mother's older brother. From him must leave to marry be obtained for either girl or boy; to him and the mother must the present be taken which is exacted on the marriage of a girl, and should the mother die, on him and not on the father, lies the responsibility of rearing the children. They go to his house and he treats and regards them as nearer and dearer to himself than his own children, and at his death, after his own brothers by the same mother, they become his heirs.[6]

These details are all consistent with the mother-family and perfectly logical deductions from its principles. There never was any such thing as woman-rule if by that it should be understood that women administered and conducted in detail the affairs of house or society, directing the men what they should do or not do, but the women of the Iroquois regulated the house life, they owned the land, in the only sense in which Indians could conceive of land-owning, because they tilled it, they established the reputation of warriors and so determined who should be elected war chief in any new war, and they decided the treatment of captives. Women, however, never made a state, and war, so long as the woman-family existed, was always limited and imperfect. It was never decided whether a man must fight with his wife's people or go back to the clan in which he was born and fight with that. War was oftenest about women, or about blood-revenge. It was, as among our Indians, a raid and not a persistent campaign. It was mean, cowardly, savage, and marked by base bloodshed.

Much of this seems strange and inverted to us, because our society has long been on the father-family. The state has long been the institution, or set of institutions, on which we rely for our most important interests and our notions of kinship, of rights, of moral right or wrong, and our ways of property, inheritance, trade, and intercourse have all been created by or adjusted to the system of man-descent. We can see what a great revolution had to be accomplished to go over from woman-descent to man-descent. Christian missionaries now often find themselves entangled in this transition. In West Africa the native tie between mother and children is far closer than that between father and children. The negro women do not like the

Travels in West Africa, p. 224.

change which white culture would bring about. In native law husband and wife have separate property. If white man's law was introduced, the woman would lose her property and would not get her husband's. The man also objects to giving his wife any claim on his property. At the same time he does not want the children saddled on him. It seems to him utter absurdity that it should be his duty to care more for his wife than for his mother and sister.[7] At every point, in going over to the father-family, there is a transfer of rights and power and a readjustment of social theory.

In the long history of the man-family men have not been able to decide what they ought to think about women. It has been maintained that woman is man's greatest blessing and again that she is a curse. Also the two judgments have been united by saying that she is a cheat and a delusion. She looks like a blessing while she is a curse. Each of those exaggerated views supported the other. Every blessing may appear doubtful, under circumstances; every curse will sometimes appear to be a blessing. What was most important about both these views was that man was regarded as independent and complete in the first place and the woman was brought to him as a helpmeet or assistant; at least as an inferior whose status and destiny came from her position as an adjunct. That was the position of woman in the man-family. We have abandoned part of the harshness of this construction of the status of woman and all the unkind deductions from it. The moral inferences, however, remain, and we regard them as self-evident and eternal. Loyalty to her husband is the highest virtue of a woman and devotion to her family and sacrifice for it are the field of heroism for her. We speak of the Christian family as the highest form of the family and, in our literature and our current code the Christian family is considered as furnishing women with their grand arena for self-culture and social work. I cannot find that Christianity has done anything to shape the father-family. The Old Testament tells us hardly anything about the Jewish family. In Proverbs we find some weighty statements of general truths, universally

[7] Kingsley, *West African Studies*, p. 377.

accepted, and some ideal descriptions of a good wife. The words of Lemuel in chap. 31 are the only didactic treatment of the good wife in the Old Testament. She is described as a good housekeeper, a good cook, and a diligent needlewoman. Such was the ideal Jewish woman. In the New Testament there is no doctrine of marriage, no description of the proper family, and no exposition of domestic virtues. Down to the time of Christ it appears that each man was free to arrange his family as he saw fit. The rich and great had more than one wife or they had concubines. The Talmud allowed each man four wives but not more. In fact at the birth of Christ among Jews, Greeks, and Romans, all except the rich and great had one wife each, on account of the trouble and expense of having more. Yet, if circumstances, such as childlessness, seemed to make it expedient, anyone might take a second wife. Therefore it became a fact of the *mores* of all but the rich and great that all practiced pair-marriage and were educated in it.

Christianity took root in the lowest free classes. It got the *mores* from them and in later centuries gave those *mores* authority and extension. This is the origin and historical source of the Christian family. The Pharisees are credited with introducing common-sense into domestic relations. They made the Sabbath an occasion of "domestic joy," bringing into increasing recognition the importance and dignity of woman as the builder and guardian of the home. They also set aside the seclusion of women at child-birth, in spite of the law.[8] A leader of the Pharisees introduced the *Ketubah,* or marriage document, "to protect the wife against the caprice of the husband." The Shammaites would not allow a wife to be divorced except on suspicion of adultery, but the Hillelites allowed more easy divorce for the "welfare and peace of the home."[9] The ancient Romans practiced pure monogamy but after they developed a rich leisure class, in the second century B. C., they practiced luxurious polygamy. The traditions which came down into the Christian church were confused and inconsistent and

[8] Lev. 12:4–7; 15:19–24.

[9] *Jewish Encyclopedia*, Vol. IX, pp. 663 f.

various elements have from time to time got the upper hand in the history of the last 1,900 years. Gide says:

> In a word, the law of the gospel accomplished a radical revolution in the constitution of the family. It broke domestic tyranny and recomposed the unity of the family by uniting all its members under mutual duties. It elevated and ennobled marriage by giving it a heavenly origin, and it made of marriage a union so intimate and so holy that God alone can break it.[10]

This is a good literary statement of what is generally taught and popularly believed, but it is impossible to verify it. We cannot tell what was the origin of our modern pair-marriage, but it grew up in the *mores* of the humble classes in which Christianity found root. In the first centuries of the Christian era the leading classes at Rome went through rapid corruption and decay, but the laboring classes had little share in this life. Christian converts could easily hold aloof from it. During the first four centuries Christians believed that the world was about to perish. Evidently this belief affected the whole philosophy of life. Marriage lost sense and the procreation of children lost interest. This may be seen in I Cor., chap. 7. It also helps to explain the outburst of asceticism and extravagant behavior such as the renunciation of conjugal intimacy by married people.

> Paul also, as is well known, discusses the renunciation of marriage, but he speaks with remarkable restraint, and urges objections. John of Asia Minor appears in tradition as the apostle of virginity, and the glorification of virgins [11] confirms this view of his. But it is something quite different from this when false teachers are said in the Pastoral Epistles to hinder marriage.[12] Procreation as such was considered sin, and the cause of death's domination. Christ came to break away from it[13] Hence, on the other hand, we have the idealizing of Christian motherhood.[14] Woman fell into sin but shall be saved through child-bearing. Sexual impulse is a foul frenzy, something devilish.[15] Stories of the lust of the devil and his companions after beautiful women make up the gnostic romances. The horribleness and insatiableness of the sensual passions are illustrated by all sorts of terrible tales.[16]

[10] *Condition privée de la femme,* p. 195.
[11] Apoc. 14:4.   [12] I Tim. 4:3.
[13] Satornil *apud* Iren., i, 34. 3; Tatian, *ibid.,* 38. 1; Gospel of the Egyptians.
[14] I Tim. 2:15.   [15] Act Joh., 113, p. 213.
[16] Dobschütz, *Christian Life in the Primitive Church,* pp. 261, 262.

It may indeed have happened, as the Acts of Thomas report, that bride and bridegroom from the very marriage-day renounced wedlock, and man and wife separated from one another. In particular, the continually recurring narratives of a converted wife avoiding common life with her unbelieving husband seem to be taken from life. We have the express witness, not only of Christian apologists, but also of the heathen physician Galen, that among the Christians many women and men abstained all their life from the intercourse of sex. It is not possible for us to estimate the actual spread of this kind of absolute renunciation.[17]

On the one hand the women are little thought of. In the Clementine homilies (3:22) it is expressly declared that the nature of woman is much inferior to that of man. Women, except the mother of Clement, play almost no rôle in this romance.[18]

Professor Donaldson[19] shows the error of supposing that Christianity raised the status of women.

It is rather a formulation due to dogmatic than historical interests to assert that the worth of women came to recognition first in Christianity and in Christianity from the very beginning.[20]

Renan says that Christianity, in the second century of the Christian era, "gave complete satisfaction to just those needs of imagination and heart which then tormented the populations" around the Mediterranean. It offered a person and an ideal. It made no such demand on credulity as the old mythologies which had now lost their sense. It joined stoicism in hostility to idols and bloody sacrifices and the faith in Jesus superseded ritual. Renan thinks it a wonder that Christianity did not sooner win control, but at Rome, all the civil maxims were against it.[21] The latest scholars also recognize the strong rivalry between Christianity and Mithraism.

Tertullian (born A. D. 160) was an extremist among Christian ascetics, but he was one of the ablest and most influential men of his time. Addressing women he says:[22]

---

[17] *Op. Cit.*

[18] *Ibid.*, 263.

[19] *Contemp. Rev.*, September, 1889.

[20] Tscharnak, *Der Dienst der Frau in den ersten Jahrhunderten der christlichen Kirche*, p. 5.

[21] Renan, *Marcus Aurelius*, pp. 582–85.

[22] *De Cultu Feminarum*, i, 1.

Woman, thou shouldst always be dressed in mourning and in rags, and shouldst not offer to the eyes anything but a penitent drowned in tears and thus shouldst thou pay ransom for thy fault in bringing the human race to ruin! Woman, thou art the gate by which the demon enters! It was thou who corruptedst him whom Satan did not dare to attack in face [man]. It is on thy account that Jesus Christ died.

It was the doctrine of the church fathers who lived about 400 A. D. that marriage is a consequence of original sin, and that, but for the first sin, God would have provided otherwise for the maintenance of the human species.[23] "Let us cut up by the roots," said Jerome, "the sterile tree of marriage. God did indeed allow marriage at the beginning of the world, but Jesus Christ and Mary have now consecrated virginity." Virginity thus furnished the ideal in the church and not honest wedlock.

Juvenal and Tacitus give us pictures of Roman (heathen) society in the first centuries of the Christian era which would make us doubt if there was any family at all, but some of our later historians have well pointed out that we ought not to take the statements in Juvenal and Tacitus as characteristic of all Roman society.

Let me quote two or three passages from Dill about Roman women of the empire:

Tacitus, here and there, gives glimpses of self-sacrifice, courageous loyalty, and humanity, which save his picture of society from utter gloom. The love and devotion of women shine out more brightly than ever against the background of baseness. Tender women follow their husbands or brothers into exile, or are found ready to share their death. Even the slave girls of Octavia brave torture and death in their hardy defense of her fair fame. There is no more pathetic story of female heroism than that of Politta, the daughter of L. Vetus. . . . . Vetus himself was of the nobler sort of Roman men, who even then were not extinct. When he was advised, in order to save the remnant of his property for his grandchildren, to make the emperor chief heir, he spurned the servile proposal, divided his ready money among his slaves, and prepared for the end. When all hope was abandoned, father, grandmother, and daughter opened their veins and died together in the bath. . . . .

The bohemian man of letters (Juvenal) had heard many a scandal about great ladies, some of them true, others distorted and exaggerated by prurient gossip, after passing through a hundred tainted imaginations.

[23] See Chrysostom, *De Virginitate,* i, 282.

In his own modest class, female morality, as we may infer from the *Inscriptions* and other sources, was probably as high as it ever was, as high as the average morality of any age. There were aristocratic families, too, where the women were as pure as Lucretia or Cornelia, or any matron of the olden days. The ideal of purity, both in men and women, in some circles was actually rising. In the families of Seneca, of Tacitus, of Pliny, and of Plutarch, there were not only the most spotless and high-minded women, there were also men with a rare conception of temperance and mutual love, of reverence for a pure wedlock, to which S. Jerome and S. Augustine would have given their benediction. Even Ovid, that "debauchee of the imagination," writes to his wife, from his exile in the Scythian wilds, in the accents of the purest affection. . . . .

Dion Chrysostom was probably the first of the ancients to raise a clear voice against the traffic in frail beauty which has gone on pitilessly from age to age. Nothing could exceed the vehemence with which he assails an evil which he regards as not only dishonoring to human nature, but charged with the poison of far-spreading corruption. Juvenal's ideal of purity, therefore, is not peculiar to himself. The great world was bad enough; but there was another world beside that whose infamy Juvenal has immortalised. . . . .

From the days of Cornelia, the mother of the Gracchi, to the days of Placidia, the mother of Honorius, Roman women exercised, from time to time, a powerful, and not always wholesome, influence on public affairs. The politic Augustus discussed high matters of state with Livia. The reign of Claudius was a reign of women and freedmen. Tacitus records, with a certain distaste for the innovation, that Agrippina sat enthroned beside Claudius on a lofty tribunal, to receive the homage of the captive Caractacus. Nero emancipated himself from the grasping ambition of his mother only by a ghastly crime. The influence of Caenis on Vespasian in his later days tarnished his fame. The influence of women in provincial administration was also becoming a serious force. . . . . Thus Juvenal was fighting a lost battle, lost long before he wrote. For good or evil, women in the first and second centuries were making themselves a power.[24]

The Christian emperors made the dower of the wife not simply the property of the two spouses. It was the endowment of the new household, a sort of reserve fund which the law assures to the children which they would find intact in spite of the ruin of their family, if it should occur. The dower was offset also by the gift *propter nuptias* which the man must give. The law also provided that the dower and the gift *propter nuptias*

[24] Dill, *Nero to Marcus Aurelius*, pp. 48, 49, 76, 77, 81.

should be equal and that the spouses should have the same rights of survivorship.[25] These seem to be distinct improvements on the dotal system, but that system has dropped out of popular use in modern times and the advantage of this legislation has been lost with it.

The family was more affected by the imperial constitutions of the fourth century which enacted the views and teachings of the clergy of that time. Constantine endeavored to put an end to concubinage, and the power of mothers over their children as to property and marriage was made equal to that of fathers.[26] It appears that the collapse of the ancient society and the decay of the old religion with the rise of Christianity and Mithraism with new codes of conduct and duty produced anarchy in the *mores* which are the every-day guides of men as to what they ought to do. On the one side we find asceticism and extreme rigor and then by the side of it, in the Christian church, extravagant license and grotesque doctrine. What element conquered, and why, it seems impossible to say. The society of western Europe emerged from the period of decay and rejuvenation in the twelfth century with some wild passions and dogmas of commanding force. Over-population produced social pressure and distress with the inevitable tragedy in human affairs. The other world was figured by unrestrained imagination and religion went back to primitive demonism.

Out of this period came the canon law.

Of all civil institutions, marriage is the one which the canon law most carefully regulated, and this is the idea from which all its prescriptions were derived; viz., marriage is a necessary evil which must be tolerated, but the practice of which must be restrained.[27]

The doctrine of this law is that "woman was not made in the image of God. Hence it appears that women are subordinated to men and that the law meant them to be almost servants in the household."[28] From this starting-point the law went on rationally although it contained two inconsistent ideas, the merit of

[25] Gide, 215.   [26] Cod. Theod., iv, 6.
[27] Gide, *Condition pricée de la femme*, p. 202.
[28] *Can.* 13–19, caus. xxxiii, qu. 5.

wedlock and the merit of celibacy. The product of such inconsistency was necessarily base. Some parts of the literary record which remain to us would lead us to believe that the whole society was brutal and vicious, but when we think of the thousands of families who died without ever making a mark on the record we must believe that domestic virtue and happiness were usual and characteristic of the society. The best proof of this is presented by the efforts at reform throughout the fifteenth century and the vigor of the reformation of the sixteenth century. The hot disputes between Protestants and Catholics turned chiefly on the doctrine of the mass and on sacerdotal claims but they contained also an element of dissatisfaction with inherited *mores* about marriage and the family. The Protestants denounced the abuses which had grown up around the monasteries and the gratuitous misery of celibacy. They, however, lost the old ideas about marriage and divorce and the Catholics denounced them for laxity and vice. At the Council of Trent, in 1563, the Catholics made a new law of marriage, in which they redefined and strengthened the ritual element.

Out of all that strife and turmoil our modern family has come down to us.

The churches and denominations are now trying to win something in their rivalry with each other by the position they adopt in regard to marriage and divorce and the family. The family in its best estate, now among us, is a thing which we may contemplate with the greatest satisfaction. When the parents are united by mutual respect and sincere affection and by joint zeal for the welfare of their children the family is a field of peace and affection in which the most valuable virtues take root and grow and character is built on the firmest foundation of habit. The family exists by tradition and old custom faithfully handed down. Our society, however, has never yet settled down to established order and firm tradition since the great convulsion of the sixteenth century. Perhaps the family still shows more fluctuation and uncertainty than any other of our great institutions. Different households now differ greatly in the firmness of parental authority and the inflexibility of filial obedience. Many nowadays have abandoned the old standards of proper authority and due obedience. The family has to a great extent lost its position as a conservative institution and has become a field for social change. This, however, is only a part of the decay of doctrines once thought most sound and the abandonment of standards once thought the definition of good order and stability. The changes in social and political philosophy have lowered the family. The family has not successfully resisted them. Part of the old function of the family seems to have passed to the primary school, but the school has not fully and intelligently taken up the functions thrown upon it. It appears that the family now depends chiefly on the virtue, good sense, conception of duty, and spirit of sacrifice of the parents. They have constantly new problems to meet. They want to do what is right and best. They do not fear change and do not shrink from it. So long as their own character is not corrupted it does not appear that there is any cause for alarm.

HOW HOME CONDITIONS REACT UPON
THE FAMILY

MRS. CHARLOTTE PERKINS GILMAN
New York City, N. Y.

Discussion of social processes, to be fruitful, must rest on some hypothesis as to the nature and purpose of society. It is here assumed that society is a life-form in course of evolution, that its processes are to be measured like those of other life-forms, as they affect the three main issues of existence—being, reproduction, improvement.

In so far as social processes are genetic they interest us as students and critics; in so far as they are telic they form the most practical and important subjects of study. The family has its origin in the genetic process of reproduction; but is modified continually by telic forces. In its present form it is an institution of confused values, based on vital necessity, but heavily encumbered with rudiments of earlier stages of development, some beneficent, some useless, some utterly mischievous; and showing also the thriving growth of new and admirable features.

We must consider it first on its biological basis, as a sex-related group for the purpose of rearing young; and the effect of conditions upon it should be measured primarily by this purpose.

Next we find in the existing family clear traces of that early long-dominant social unit, the woman-centered group of the matriarchate. Our universal and deep-seated reverence for the mother-governed home, with its peace, comfort, order, and good-will, has survived many thousand years of patriarchal government, and refuses to be changed even by innumerable instances of discomfort, discord, waste, and unhappiness.

Superimposed upon this first social group comes the establishment of the patriarchate, the family with the male head, based upon the assumption by the male of sole efficiency as transmitter of life. In this form the family enters upon an entirely new phase, and includes purposes hitherto unknown. It becomes a vehicle of masculine power and pride—was indeed for long their sole vehicle: it produces its ethics, its codes of honor, its series of religions, its line of political development through tribe and clan, princedom and monarchy, its legal system in which all personal and property rights are vested in the man, and its physical expression in the household of servile women. It is from this period that we derive our popular impressions that the family is the unit of the state, that the man is the head of the house, and other supposedly self-evident propositions. The patriarchal family, even in its present reduced and modified form, is the vital core and continuing cause of our androcentric culture.

Fourthly, we must view it as an industrial group of self-centered economic activities, the birthplace of arts and crafts as well as of persons. While the natural origin of these industries is in maternal energy, the voluntary efforts of the mother being the real source of human production, yet the family, as an economic group in the modern sense, is also an androcentric institution. Besides the mother's work for her children, the patriarchal family required the service of the man by his women—a claim which has no parallel in nature.

There is nothing in maternity, nothing in the natural relation of the sexes which should make the female the servant of the male. This form of economic relationship was developed when the man learned to take advantage of the industrial value of the woman and added to his profitable group as many women as possible. Moreover, when the masculine instinct of sex-combat swelled and broadened, blended with the hunter's predatory appetite, organized, and became war, then in course of time male captives were compelled to labor as the price of life, and set to work in the only social group then existent. It is to this custom, to this remote and painful period, that our institution owes its present name. Not father, mother, nor child, but servant, christens the family.

Further than this we find in our family group the development of a new relation, a new idea as yet but little understood, that which is vaguely expressed by the word marriage. Monogamy, the permanent union of one male and one female for reproductive purposes, is as natural a form of sex-relation as any other, common to many animals and birds, a resultant of continued and combined activities of both parents for the same end. This natural base of a true marriage should be carefully studied. Continued union in activity for a common purpose necessarily develops ease and pleasure in the relationship. The same couple can carry on these activities more easily than a new combination; hence monogamy.

In our human family we find many forms: androgyny, polygyny, and then the slow and halting evolution of monogyny. Monogynous marriage should include sex-attraction, romantic love, and a high degree of comradeship. It is now our common race ideal, recognized as best for the advantage of the child and the individual happiness of the parent; also, through greater personal efficiency, for the good of society. This form of marriage is slowly evolving in the family, but is by no means invariably present.

Lastly we must bear in mind that the family is our accepted basis of mere living; it, and its outward expression, the home, are so universally assumed to be the only natural form of existence, that to continue on earth outside of "a family," without "a home," is considered unnatural and almost immoral. In this regard the family must be studied as ministering to the health, comfort, happiness, and efficiency of adult individuals, quite aside from parental purposes, or those of marriage; as for instance in the position of adult sons and daughters, of aged persons no longer actively valuable as parents; or of coadjacent aunts, uncles, and cousins; as also in relation to the purely individual interests of members of the family proper.

When we now take up our study of home conditions, we have definite ground from which to judge and to measure them. How do they react upon the family in regard to those three major purposes of life—being, reproduction, improvement? Do they best maintain human life? Do they best minister to the reproduction of the species? And to the evolution of monogyny? Above all do they tend to race improvement?

Mere existence is no justification, else might we all remain Archaean rocks. Reproduction is not sufficient, else the fertile bacterium would be our ideal. All social institutions must be measured as they tend not only to maintain and reproduce, but to improve humanity. We will make brief mention of our essential home conditions and examine their reaction on the family as touching (*a*) marriage, (*b*) parentage, (*c*) child-culture, (*d*) the individual and social progress. What are our essential home conditions?

Here we are confronted with so vast and tumultuous a sea of facts; noisy, painful, prominent facts; that proper perspective is difficult to obtain. Here we are confronted also with the most sensitive, powerful, universal, and ancient group of emotions known to man. This complex of feelings, tangled and knotted by ages of ironbound association; fired with the quenchless vitality of the biological necessities on which they rest; intensified by all our conscious centuries of social history; hallowed, sanctified, made imperative by recurrent religions; enforced with cruel penalties by law, and crueller ones by custom; first established by those riotous absurdities of dawning ethics, the sex-tabus of the primitive savage, and growing as a cult down all our ages of literature and art; the emotions, sentiments, traditions, race-habits, and fixed ideas which center in the home and family—form the most formidable obstacle to clear thought and wise conclusion.

Forced by increasing instances of discontent, inefficiency, and protest within the group, we are beginning to make some study of domestic conditions; but so far this study has been on the one hand superficial; and on the other either starkly reactionary or merely rebellious.

The first home conditions forced upon our consideration are the material. Here we note most prominently the effects of economic pressure in our cities; the physical restriction of the home in the block, the tenement, the apartment house; the devastating effects of the sweatshop; the tendency toward what we call "co-operative" housekeeping.

As far as mere physical crowding is a home condition we may find that as far back as the cliff-dwellers, find it in every city of the world since there were cities, find it consistent with any form of marriage, with families matriarchal, patriarchal, polygynous, and monogynous. The Jew throughout Christian history has suffered from overcrowding as much as any people ever did; but he has preserved the family in a most intense form, with more success than many of the races which oppressed him. Even the sweatshop, while working evil to the individual, does but draw tighter the family bond.

Therefore we are illogical in our fear of the city-crowding as the enemy of the home, the destroyer of family life.

Others, identifying family life with the industries so long accompanying it, disapprove of that visible and rapid economic evolution in which the "domestic industries" as such dissolve and disappear. Yet if these observers would but study the history of economics they would find the period of undisputed "home industries" was not that of high development in family life, but rather of the mixed group of women slaves and male captives, when marriage in our sense was utterly unknown. The attempt to "revive home industries" is not difficult, since our modern family still maintains that primitive labor status; but it is reactionary, and tends to no real improvement.

"Co-operative housekeeping," as a term, needs brief but clear discussion. The movement to which the phrase is applied is a natural one, inevitable and advantageous. It consists in the orderly development of domestic industries into social ones; in the gradual substitution of the shirt you buy for the shirt your wife makes, of the bread of the public baker for the bread of the private cook, of the wine of known manufacture and vintage for the wine made for you by your affectionate great-aunt. All industry was once domestic. All industry is becoming social. That is the line of industrial evolution. Now what is "co-operative housekeeping"? It is an attempt to continue domestic industry without its natural base. The family was for long the only economic unit. The family is still, though, greatly reduced and wastefully inefficient, an economic unit. A group of families is not a unit at all. It has no structure, no function, no existence. Individuals may combine, do combine, should combine, must combine, to form social groups. Families are essentially uncombinable.

Vintner, brewer, baker, spinner, weaver, dyer, tallow-chandler, soapmaker, and all their congeners were socially evolved from the practicers of inchoate domestic industries. Soon the cook and the cleaner will take place with these, as the launderer already has to a great degree. At no step of the process is there the faintest hint of "co-operative housekeeping." Forty families may patronize and maintain one bakeshop. They do not "co-operate" to do this; they separately patronize it. The same forty families might patronize and maintain one cookshop, and never know one another's names.

If the forty families endeavored to "co-operate" and start that bakeshop, or that cookshop, they would meet the same difficulty, the same failure, that always faces illegitimate and unnatural processes.

The material forms of home life, the character of its structure and functions depend upon the relation of the members of the family. In analyzing home conditions therefore we will classify them thus:

A. *Ownership of women.*—It is to this condition that we may clearly trace the isolation of the home, the varying degree of segregation of the woman or women therein. The home is inaugurated immediately upon marriage, its nature and situation depending upon the man, and in it the man secludes his wife. In this regard our home is a lineal descendant of the harem. It is but a short time since the proverb told us "the woman, the cat, and the chimney should never leave the house;" and again, "A woman should leave the house but three times—when she is married, when she is christened, when she is buried." In current comment upon modern home conditions we still find deep displeasure that the woman is so much away from home. The continued presence of the woman in the home is held to be an essential condition. Following this comes—

B. *Woman-service.*—The house is a place where the man

has his meals cooked and served by the woman; his general cleaning and mending done by her; she is his servant. This condition accompanies marriage, be it observed, and precedes maternity. It has no relation whatever to motherhood. If there are no children the woman remains the house-servant of the man. If she has many, their care must not prevent the service of his meals.

In America today, in one family out of sixteen, the man is able to hire other women to wait upon him; but his wife is merely raised to the position of a sort of "section-boss;" she still manages the service of the house for him. This woman-service has no relation to the family in any vital sense; it is a relic of the period of woman-slavery in the patriarchal time; it exhibits not the evolution of a true monogamy, but merely the ancient industrial polygamous group shorn down to one lingering female slave. Under this head of wife-service, we must place all the confused activities of the modern home. Reduced and simplified as these are, they still involve several undeveloped trades and their enforced practice by nearly all women keeps down the normal social tendency to specialization. While all men, speaking generally, have specialized in some form of social activities, have become masons, smiths, farmers, sailors, carpenters, doctors, merchants, and the like; all women, speaking generally, have remained at the low industrial level of domestic servants. The limitation is clear and sharp, and is held to be an essential, if not the essential, condition of home life; the woman, being married, must work in the home for the man. We are so absolutely accustomed to this relation, that a statement of it produces no more result than if one solemnly announces that fire is hot and ice cold.

To visualize it let us reverse the position. Let us suppose that the conditions of home life required every man upon marriage to become his wife's butler, footman, coachman, cook; every man, all men, necessarily following the profession of domestic servants. This is an abhorrent, an incredible idea. So is the other. That an entire sex should be the domestic servants of the other sex is abhorrent and incredible.

Under this same head we may place all the prominent but

little understood evils of the "servant question." The position is simple. The home must be served by women. If the wife is unable to perform the service other women must be engaged. These must not be married women, for no married man wishes his private servant to serve another man. When the coachman marries the cook, he prefers to segregate her in the rooms over the stables, to cook for him alone. Therefore our women servants form an endless procession of apprentices, untrained young persons learning of the housewife mainly her personal preferences and limitations. Therefore is the grade of household services necessarily and permanently low; and household service means most of the world's feeding, cleaning, and the care of children. The third essential home condition is:

C. *The economic dependence of women.*—This is the natural corollary of the other two. If a man keeps a servant he must feed him, or her. The economic dependence of the woman follows upon her servitude. The family with the male head has assumed that the male shall serve society and the female shall serve him. This opens up an immense field of consequences, reacting most violently upon the family, among which we will select here two most typical and conspicuous. Suppose that the man's social service is of small value as we measure and reward our laborers. His return is small. His wages we will roughly estimate at $600 a year, a sum the purchasing power of which is variable. In our present conditions $600 is little enough for one person. For two it allows but $300 each. For six, if they have four children, it is $100 a year apiece—less than $2.00 a week for each, to pay for food, clothes, shelter, everything. This visibly spells poverty. While one man's production is worth to society but so much, and while that one man's production is forced to meet the consumption of six; so long, even without any other cause, the resultant is general poverty—a persistent condition in the majority of homes. To segregate half the productive energy of the world and use it in private service of the crudest sort is economic waste. To force the low-grade man to maintain an entire family is to force a constant large supply of low-grade men.

The second of these consequences is the unnatural phenomenon of the idle woman. The man, whose sex-relation spurs him to industry, and whose exceptional powers meet special reward, then proceeds to shower gifts and pleasures upon the woman he loves. That man shall be "a good provider" is frankly held to be his end of the family duty, a most essential condition of home life. This result, as we so frequently and sadly see, is the development of a kind of woman who performs no industrial service, produces nothing, and consumes everything; and a kind of man who subordinates every social and moral claim to this widely accredited "first duty;" to provide, without limit, for his wife and children.

These two home conditions: the enormous tax upon the father, if he is poor, together with the heavy toil of the mother, and the opposite one of the rich man maintaining a beautiful parasite, have visible and serious results upon the family.

The supposedly essential basic relations, the ownership of woman, the servitude of woman, and the economic dependence of woman, with their resultants, give rise to the visible material conditions with which we are familiar. The predominant concerns of the kitchen and dining-room, involving the entire service of the working housewife, rigidly measure the limitations of such families; while the added freedom of the woman whose housework is done vicariously seldom tends to a nobler life. Our insanitary households, our false and shallow taste, our low standard of knowledge in food values and nutrition, the various prosaic limitations within which we are born and reared are in the main traceable to the arrested development of the woman, owing to the above major conditions of home life.

Let us now show the reaction of the conditions above stated upon the family in modern society, in the order given, as they affect (a) marriage. (b) maternity, (c) child-culture, (d) the individual and society.

We are much concerned in the smooth and rapid development of a higher type of marriage, yet fail to see that our home conditions militate against such development. The effect of the modern home, even with its present degree of segregation of women, with its inadequate, confused, laborious industrial processes, and with its overwhelming expenses, is to postpone and often prevent marriage, to degrade marriage when accomplished through the servile and dependent position of the wife, and also to precipitate unwise and premature marriage on the part of young women because of their bitter dissatisfaction with the conditions of their previous home. This last gives an advantage in reproduction to the poorer types. The wiser woman, preferring the ills she has to those she foresees only too clearly, hesitates long, delays, often refuses altogether; not from an aversion to marriage, or to motherhood, but from a steadily growing objection to the position of a servant.

The man, seeing about him the fretful inefficiency of so many misplaced women, hearing *ad nauseam* the reiterant uniform complaints on "the servant question," knowing the weight of the increasing burden for which the man must "pay, pay, pay," waits longer and longer before he can "afford to marry;" with a resultant increase in immorality.

This paradoxical position must be faced fully and squarely. The industrial conditions of the modern home are such as to delay and often prevent marriage. Since "the home" is supposed to arise only from marriage, it looks as though the situation were frankly suicidal. So far, not seeing these things, we have merely followed our world-old habit of blaming the woman. She used to be content with these conditions we say—she ought to be now—back to nature! The woman refuses to go back, the home refuses to go forward, and marriage waits. The initial condition of ownership, even without service, reacts unfavorably upon the kind of marriage most desired. A woman slave is not a wife. The more absolutely the woman is her own mistress, in accepting her husband and in her life with him, the higher is the grade of love and companionship open to them. Again the economic dependence of the woman militates against a true marriage, in that the element of economic profit degrades and commercializes love and so injures the family. It may be said that the family with the male head cannot exist in a pure form without its original concomitants of absolute personal ownership and exploitation of woman. When the ownership is no longer that of true slavery but enters the contract stage, when marriage becomes an economic relation, then indeed is it degraded. Polygyny is a low form of marriage; but, as modern polygynists have held, it at least tends to preclude prostitution. The higher marriage toward which we are tending requires a full-grown woman, no one's property or servant, self-supporting and proudly independent. Such marriage will find expression in a very different home.

Next comes the reaction upon motherhood, the most vital fact in the whole institution. Our home conditions affect motherhood injuriously in many ways. The ownership of the woman by the man has developed a false code of morals and manners, under which girls are not reared in understanding of the privileges, rights, and pre-eminent duties of motherhood. We make the duty to the man first, the duty to the child second—an artificial and mischievous relation. There is no more important personal function than motherhood, and every item of arrangement in the family, in the home, should subtend its overmastering interests.

Ownership of women first interferes with the power of selection so essential to right motherhood, and, second, enforces motherhood undesired— a grave physiological evil. The ensuant condition of female servitude is an injury in demanding labor incompatible with right maternity, and in lowering the average of heredity through the arrest of social development in the mother. It is not good for the race that the majority of its female parents should be unskilled laborers, plus a few unskilled idlers.

In poverty the overworked woman dreads maternity, and avoids it if she can. If she cannot, her unwelcome and too frequent children are not what is needed to build up our people. In wealth, the woman becomes a perpetual child, greedy and irresponsible, dreads maternity, and avoids it if she can. Her children are few and often frail. Neither the conditions of the poor home nor of the rich tend to a joyous and competent maternity.

In this one respect the home, under present conditions, is proven an unfit vehicle for the family. In itself it tends to reduce the birth-rate, or to lower the quality of the most numerous children; and all of them inherit the limitations of a servile or an irresponsible motherhood.

As regards child-culture, our home conditions present a further marked unfitness. Not one home in a thousand even attempts to make provision for child-culture. If the home has but one room that room is a kitchen; but few indeed are the families who can "afford a nursery." Child-care is wholly subordinate to kitchen service; the home is a complicated, inconsistent group of industries, in which the child must wait for spare moments of attention; which attention when given is that of a tired cook, or a worried housekeeper. No clearer comment can be made on the inadequacy of home conditions to serve their natural ends than in this major instance; they do not promote, but on the contrary they prohibit the development of higher standards of child-culture.

As to mere maintenance of life, our children die most numerously during the years of infancy, when they are most wholly at home. As to reproduction, we have shown the effect on that; and as to improvement, it is a general admission that the improvement of the human stock does not keep pace with material progress. We need here a wise revision of domestic conditions in the interests of the child. At present any man who has a home to let, be it room, apartment, or house, prefers his tenants to be without children. The home, the birthplace, the rearing-place, is not built, fitted, nor managed for the benefit of children.

What is its further effect on the individual, and through him on society? Do the common home conditions of our time promote health, insure peace and comfort, tend to that higher development of the individual so essential to social progress?

Here we find another large ground for criticism. Modern society calls for individuals broad-minded, public-spirited, democratic, courageous, just, intelligent, educated, and specialized for social service. The family with the male head and its accompanying conditions of woman-ownership, service, and dependence tends to maintain in our growing democracy the grade of development, the habits of mind, the childish limitations of its remote past.   In it is a masculine dominance which finds expression in our political androcracy.   In it is a degraded womanhood which not only limits individual development in the mother, but checks it in the father through heredity and association, and acts powerfully to keep back the progress of the child.   Because of the low grade of domestic industry, the food habits of humanity have remained so long what they are, tending to self-indulgence and excess, to extravagance, to many forms of disease.

Mere confinement to a house is in itself unwholesome, and when that house is a cookshop and laundry, it is further disadvantageous.

The man, bound in honor (in his androcentric code of honor) to provide at all costs for his dependent family, has saddled himself with the task of making the product of one meet the consumption of many; and in making the woman a non-productive consumer, he has maintained in half the world the attitude of the child—the willingness to take, with no thought of giving an equivalent.

The social processes, left wholly to the male, are necessarily belligerent and competitive; and in the resultant turmoil, each man must needs strive to maintain his little island of personal comfort rather than to do his best work for the world.

Home conditions which tend to results like these require most serious consideration.   They react upon the family in general as tending to restrict its natural evolution toward higher forms.   They react upon it specifically as we have seen, precipitating injudicious marriage, postponing marriage, degrading marriage; similarly do they affect motherhood, enforcing it where the woman is not free to choose, and where she is free to choose tending to postpone and prevent it because of its difficulties.   The mechanical and industrial conditions of our homes, with their reaction upon character, lie at the base of that artificial restriction of motherhood so widely lamented.

Again they react upon child-culture, in age-long suppression of that greatest of sciences, in confining the care of little children to the ignorance of incompetent mothers and less competent servants. While the home enforces the condition of female servitude our children must continue to be born of and reared by servants.

Finally, these same conditions, these limitations in structure and function, this arrested womanhood and low-grade child-culture do not tend to develop the best individuals nor to promote social progress. Such as we are we are largely made by our homes, and surely we do not wish to remain such as we are. Our average health, longevity, efficiency, standard of comfort, happiness, and pleasure do not show the most wholesome influences.

The work of the constructive sociologist in this field is to establish what lines of change and development in our homes, what broad and hopeful new conditions, will act in harmony with social processes, will tend to a better marriage, a higher grade of motherhood, a freer and nobler environment for the individual. We need homes in which mother and father will be equally free and equally bound, both resting together in its shelter and privacy, both working together for its interests.

This requires structural and functional changes that shall eliminate the last of our domestic industries and leave a home that is no one's workshop.

The woman, no longer any man's property, nor any man's servant, must needs develop social usefulness, becoming more efficient, intelligent, experienced. Such women will bring to bear upon their proper problems, maternity and child-culture, a larger wisdom and a wider power than they now possess.

The home, planned, built, and maintained by men and women of this sort, would react upon its constituent family in wholly advantageous ways.

THE EFFECT ON WOMAN OF ECONOMIC DEPENDENCE

CHARLES ZUEBLIN
Boston, Mass.

The most famous description of a virtuous woman, and one accepted equally by both sexes, is that which has been attributed to Solomon:

"Who can find a virtuous woman? for her price is far above rubies." The patriarchal estimate of virtue is thus evident.

"The heart of her husband shall safely trust in her so that he shall have no need of spoil." Thus removing the temptation which confronts the modern money king, who must provide for his ambitious wife's "conspicuous consumption."

"She will do him good and not evil all the days of her life. She seeketh wool and flax and worketh willingly with her hands. She is like the merchant-ships. She bringeth her food from afar." Thus she not only tends the cattle and the fields, for the sake of both clothing and food, but she goes to the distant market.

"She riseth also while it is yet night and giveth meat to her household, and a portion to her maidens." Early hours are quite indispensable considering the extent of her labors.

"She considereth a field and buyeth it. With the fruit of her hands she planteth a vineyard." Her economies are not only sufficient for the needs of the household, but provide a surplus for investment.

"She girdeth her loins with strength and strengtheneth her arms." She has neither the time nor the need for the physical culture or the medical aid demanded by the prosperous woman of today.

"She perceiveth that her merchandise is good, her candle goeth not out by night." Obviously because of her addiction to heavy work, not light literature.

"She layeth her hands to the spindle and her hands hold the distaff." Thus finding occupation for the winter as well as for the summer.

"She stretcheth out her hands to the poor, yea, she reacheth forth her hands to the needy." Even in those early and active days she found leisure for charity.

"She is not afraid of the snow for her household, for all her household are clothed with double garments. She maketh herself coverings of tapestry, her clothing is silk and purple." She was able to provide not only comforts for her family but luxuries for herself.

"Her husband is known in the gates when he sitteth among the elders of the land." All this time her husband seems to have been absent at the legislature, representing, as women might have thought, in anticipation of Matthew Arnold, "that power not ourselves that makes for" unrighteousness.

"She maketh fine linen and selleth it and delivereth girdles unto the merchants." She not only dispenses with the need of a husband's support, but also has such excess of product that she can engage in a mercantile occupation, which helps to account for her ability to buy fields and to permit her husband to spend his time among the elders.

"Strength and honor are her clothing and she shall rejoice in time to come." Presumably she did not have much time to rejoice while engaged in these various occupations.

"She openeth her mouth with wisdom and in her tongue is the law of kindness. She looketh to the ways of her household and eateth not the bread of idleness." In fact, even from the masculine point of view she seems industrious.

"Her children arise up and call her blessed. Her husband also, and he praiseth her." Praise seems to have been an afterthought on the part of husband, but certainly creditable considering his preoccupation with the statesmen.

"Many daughters have done virtuously." The marginal reading is "have gotten riches" which throws light on the attitude of both the original author and the King James translators, after an interval of twenty-five centuries.

"But thou excellest them all. Favor is deceitful and beauty is vain, but the woman that feareth the Lord she shall be praised. Give her the fruit of her hands and let her own works praise her in the gates." This condescending attitude of the philosopher king, while characteristic of chivalry in all ages, seems not to have been followed to its logical conclusion. While her works are still allowed to praise her in the gates, or among the elders of the legislature, in lieu of any voice in her own government they still refuse to give her of the fruit of her hands.

There has been skepticism in an unbelieving generation as to the riches of Solomon, and comparisons to his disadvantage have been made with the money kings of today. But the riches of Solomon are easily understood when one reads the description, credited to him, of a virtuous woman and remembers that in addition to 300 concubines, he was said to have 700 such virtuous wives. The higher criticism may rob Solomon of the authorship of the Proverbs or the possession of one thousand wives, but it cannot dispute the continued acceptance of this ideal of a virtuous woman of three thousand years ago. She is still allowed to rejoice in the fact that "virtue is its own reward."

This hypothetical paragon of Solomon would have been an economic dependent, legally subject to man, gaining spiritual ends by circumlocution and hypocrisy, as truly as her leisured and less mythical sisters of today. In the course of the ages it has become less necessary to pursue this Solomonic inquiry than to join the search of Diogenes. Woman has been emancipated from most of these industrial obligations. With relief from them there has come increasing leisure, education, social activity, and economic freedom, but as yet no relation between services and income.

In spite of these advances, which are almost exclusively modern, the majority of women remain economically dependent. A woman's intellectual and social possibilities are conditioned primarily by her husband's income. The million-dollar wife married to the thousand-dollar man may be uncommon, but less striking discrepancies to her disadvantage are usual. Even the wife of little capacity united to the man of wealth is unable to lead her normal life because she is usually regarded as a toy or drudge. The difficulty is not only that woman is dependent upon man, nor that each woman is dependent on one man, but all of a woman's rich nature, the sum total of her personality, is dependent upon one man's income.

Men are paid a certain amount of money for specific labors. But their wives have no claim upon any definite sum; they are dependent upon the generosity of the husbands. Happily this seems adequate in most cases. Indeed it is quite the custom among workingmen to turn over all the family revenue into the hands of the wife. Among educated people generally it is customary to determine the disposition of the purse beforehand, that disposition to remain through life. But the husband is the "treasurer," doling out the amount which may be at any time at his command or convenience, thereby controlling not only the economic but the spiritual life of his wife.

The expression of this subjection, which is the most degrading, comes in the appeal which seems to be increasingly made, or receives increasing publicity in the United States—the appeal to the unwritten law. When man's choicest piece of property is violated, he avenges himself. The appeal to the unwritten law is the appeal to a law which he dare not put in the statute books, where nearly all the laws are concerned with property, although in Oklahoma it has been proposed to legalize the unwritten law, so that it may be frankly and brutally written. For the most part where the unwritten law is most often appealed to, it is associated with the lowest depths of immorality. Only in the most barbarous parts of the United States would a jury acquit a man for the murder of his wife or her lover, but anywhere a jealous brute may in a fit of passion commit murder. It is never, however, because of love for his wife. No man ever kills his wife for love. He may die for love or live for it; sometimes a woman kills herself for it, but she does not want that kind of defense from any man. Men with their property instincts have for the most part not yet learned that the inviolability of a woman's personality transcends in ethical importance that self-esteem which a property-loving man calls "honor." Even refined men who love the objects of their devotion, still often feel instinctively that they would, under provocation, take the law into their own hands, and use violence. But it is not an attribute of affection to do this, it is the property instinct which is stung.

However, there is a subtler expression of economic mastery in the men of today—the grandiloquent attitude of the courtly gentleman who says, "Are not the American women the best, the most beautiful, the most versatile in the world? Have they not everything they want, and if there is anything they would like will we not give it to them? We care not how much these American queens take or get, so long as they recognize the source of their power."

It would be unfair to say that most marriages are deliberately commercial; but most marriages will necessarily result in the dependence of woman until the equality of the sexes is recognized. As Havelock Ellis puts it, there is no hope for woman as long as she is looked upon "as a cross between an angel and an idiot." The age of chivalry has passed; woman is more respected and less worshiped, but she cannot lead her own life until she has an equal chance with man. Even the main function of woman, maternity, and the chief end of marriage which makes the female conservative, while the male is aggressive, cannot result happily for offspring or parents, until the woman is granted the same control of her life as man enjoys. Edward Carpenter says:

> No effectual progress is possible until the question of her capacity for maternity is fairly faced—for healthy maternity involving thorough exercise and development of the body, a life more in the open air than at present—some amount of regular manual work, yet good opportunity for rest when needful, knowledge of the laws of health and physiology, widened mental training and economic independence.

We may learn the wisdom of requiring caution in assuming the responsibilities of marriage and multiplying the examples of domestic bliss, but we cannot attain justice for women and children, nor the full benefits of sex-differentiation until women are given control of their incomes, and hence, their destinies. The wage-earning woman of today is in a superior position to command just treatment from her prospective spouse, and she brings to the marriage-state a greater capacity for the management of the family income; but there are still left the millions of women whose capacity is never tested, because whatever be their intellectual, spiritual, or social possibilities, they are the recipients of charity. The charity may be disguised by the love of the devoted husband, but they are still stunted by subservience to a patriarchal administration.

It is not the province of this paper to discuss the methods of securing economic independence, but it may be suggested briefly that the entrance of woman into the actual economic struggle, while it must be granted to any individual woman who chooses it, seems undesirable for the race because of the value of the prolongation of infancy and the constant availability of a mother's care. A system of pensions for mothers might be devised, which would recognize their services to the state, and which in spite of possible pauperizing effects would be unquestionably superior to the present disregard of woman's economic rights. The best proposal, however, seems to have been made by Mr. H. G. Wells, in demanding that upon marriage, and subsequently on the birth of each child, the father be required to take out an insurance policy providing annuities for wife and children.

What are some of the spiritual consequences of woman's economic dependence? The majority of women have to marry. They have no other alternative. Most of them, happily, wish to marry and many of them find appropriate husbands, but there is not sufficient opportunity for deliberate choice. The consequence is that quite innocently, having been trained from infancy to take the step, multitudes of women marry and live with men whom they do not love, whom they sometimes have never loved. It is a hard thought that this is legalized prostitution, and it need not carry the stigma which is often unjustly associated with professional prostitution. There can scarcely be a stigma when the victims are innocent. The fact remains and its moral consequences are unavoidable. It means that a woman has sold herself, although her early training and conventional morality may keep her pure in mind and otherwise blameless in conduct. There is no escape from the distorted view of life which this entails. One of its inevitable consequences is the subjection of woman to the physical mastery of man in ways in which untutored woman freely acquiesces, but not without moral anguish which would be quite incomprehensible to the unsophisticated husbands, who regard themselves as wholly generous. If for no other reason, legalized remuneration for housekeeping, child-birth, and child-rearing, is necessary, to remove the temptation of a virtuous woman to sell herself for life to one man. While thus escaping promiscuity, they still relinquish the control over their own bodies.

Another spiritual result of economic dependence is even more conspicuous because ubiquitous. Woman's chief moral defect is her method of circumlocution, forced upon her by her being compelled to make sex functions economic functions (as Mrs. Gilman has so forcibly stated). Whether it is during the courting illusion or in rifling her husband's pockets (which a sober American judge justifies) or in accomplishing benefits for him in subtle ways beyond his dull masculine comprehension, she is all the time perfecting the arts of hypocrisy. It is sufficiently serious that woman's character should bear this blemish, without a premium being put upon it by having it regarded as her chief charm. This method of indirection is becoming increasingly obnoxious as the larger social opportunities today demand for their satisfactory performance political activity. Women are not only engaged in innumerable social labors made possible by their advancing education and leisure, but they are now expected to perform many social obligations in spite of the constant difficulty of social reconstruction without political expression. In this country this handicap is due of course in part to the confused conception of the state in the untrained political minds of men. So long as the state is considered a thing apart, political action will be differentiated from social action. Aside from this, woman's social labors are doubled by the expectation that she will either accomplish them by clumsy and laborious voluntary means, or persuade men to aid her through their exclusive political prerogatives. The evidence that this political limitation is due in part to economic dependence, is shown in the frequent argument that tax-paying women should vote. It is manifest that if women were economically independent, political independence could not be delayed.

The handicap on fellowship of economic dependence is another of its defects. There is little *camaraderie* between men and women, even when married. This is partly temperamental; some people cannot be confidential with one another, but it is primarily due to the husband's having economic functions, the wife sex functions. The beginnings of marital unrest are found chiefly in the concealment of a man's thoughts due to his conviction that the dependent domestic creature who shares his home has had no training to share his larger economic experiences. Even the problems of sex, the right of a woman to control her life, the preparation of children for the revelation of the mysteries of life, are discussed with less frankness because of the instinctive feeling of the economic master that new and unconventional modes of thinking disturb the economic and social order. The consequences of economic freedom, of which every man dreams, cannot be less for woman than for man. They would in fact be of mutual benefit. If man can be brought to see the undesirability of the power of man over woman, a power enjoyed by the possession of money, we may then bring him to desire the removal of the power of money over man.

> The woman's cause is man's: they rise or sink
> Together, dwarfed or godlike, bond or free:
> For she that out of Lethe scales with man
> The shining steps of Nature, shares with man
> His nights, his days, moves with him to one goal,
> Stays all the fair young planet in her hands—
> If she be small, slight-natured, miserable,
> How shall men grow?
>   Let her make herself her own
> To give or keep, to live and learn and be
> All that not harms distinctive womanhood.
> For woman is not undeveloped man,
> But diverse: could we make her as the man,

Sweet love were slain: his dearest bond is this,
Not like to like, but like in difference.
Yet in the long years liker must they grow;
The man be more of woman, she of man;
He gain in sweetness and in moral height,
Nor lose the wrestling thews that throw the world;
She mental breadth, nor fail in childward care,
Nor lose the childlike in the larger mind.
And so these twain, upon the skirts of Time,
Sit side by side, full-summed in all their powers,
Dispensing harvest, sowing the To-be,
Self-reverent each, and reverencing each,
Distinct in individualities,
But like each other, even as those who love.

DISCUSSION

Dr. I. M. Rubinow, U. S. Bureau of Labor

Perhaps it may be best to begin by stating that I was asked to discuss not so much the interesting papers which were read this afternoon, as one special aspect of the home problem as it may affect present family relations—the so-called problem of domestic service. I hope it may be unnecessary for me to argue before a sociological assembly that the organization of domestic service is very closely connected with the organization of the home; that this problem therefore is not beneath the dignity of sociological inquiry; and I venture to hope that this time my audacity in approaching it will not call forth that scarcely flattering outburst of levity which was my fate on a previous occasion.

It may be argued that after all the home containing domestic servants is the abnormal home, and that it therefore does not throw very much light upon the general problems: how the present home and how the progressive changes in its organization influence family relations. It is true that in only one out of fifteen or sixteen homes, are the burdens of the home shifted upon the shoulders of hired assistants. But only thirty or forty years ago the proportion in this country was a much greater one, perhaps one out of every eight or nine families, and it may be said without exaggerations that the change expressed in these figures is one of the most important changes in modern home life.

Evidently the change is one that has taken place in the homes of the middle class. But that is true of most changes that are taking place in our home life at present. And more than that, if I may be pardoned for a seemingly too sweeping generalization, most of the tendencies which may be embraced in that comprehensive term of modern feminism, including the protest against the home and the modern family and the economic subjugation of woman, and even our suffragette movement, most of these are palpably middle-class movements. I am not stating this in any spirit of criticism. I am simply stating a fact which may be established by statistical analysis. Our literary woman, our club woman, is a middle-class woman, and even in the woman's invasion of the productive field it is in the genteel middle-class occupations that the tendency is most noticeable. It is in teaching and other liberal professions, among typewriters and stenographers, clerks and saleswomen, for example, that woman has begun to overcrowd the market. It is in the middle class, not in the upper leisure class, and not among the proletarians, that the protest against the old home, and woman's position in it, has become strongest. The problem of domestic service is back of a great part of this movement.

For what is this so-much-ridiculed problem of domestic service? It is the labor problem of our homes. The difficulty of solving this problem for the employer, the difficulty of obtaining efficient and cheap help (with the emphasis upon cheap), has attracted the attention of our women to the unsatisfactory organization of the home. The sad necessity of performing this labor, the inability of shifting it to other hired shoulders, drives the middle-class woman away from home, and creates the middle-class ideal of the independent spinster. In general it may be stated that the technical organization of the home has improved vastly during the last half century for the proletarian woman, while it has not been quick nor great enough to compensate the middle-class woman for the shifting of the burden back upon her own shoulders.

One patent fact which makes a "problem" of the recalcitrant servant girl is the peculiar condition of labor in this particular field. The demand is greater than the supply, even when the labor market is as overcrowded as it was during the recent crisis. Of course there is an adjustment of demand and supply by means of a constantly rising wage, but the constant complaint of our housewives amply demonstrate that the adjustment is far from a satisfactory one.

Now, what is the cause of this maladjustment? The differential advantage of the house-slave in her pay as compared with other more genteel occupations is greatly exaggerated. Yet some differential exists. Nevertheless, it is increasingly difficult to keep back the current which drives the working-woman from domestic employment into the factory, shop, or store.

The so-called social stigma which attaches to domestic service has often been pointed out as the main cause of the dislike for the employment. But this social stigma is itself the result of the material conditions of domestic service: the indeterminate and excessive working hours; the forced attachment of the servant to the employer's household, and the resultant deprivation of personal liberty, and the impossibility of personal life. The working-girl prefers the factory to the kitchen for the reason that, paradoxical as it may seem, employment in the factory may lead sooner to marriage, a home, and a family, while employment in a stranger's home is an efficient barrier and not a step to a home of one's own.

It has been well said that these peculiar conditions are themselves the results of an underlying cause—that in domestic service it is the *person* who is hired and not distinctively the *labor* of the person. In this feature domestic service differs radically from other fields of wage-work. Yet it must not be forgotten that this distinctive characteristic of the wage-contract in domestic service is not new. It is simply the survival of a labor-contract which was universal before the advent of modern capitalism, and which continued even during the earlier stages of that era. If it has survived longer in domestic service than in industry or commerce, it was because of the lack of technical progress in the organization of the home, in the methods of home life. The care of the home is proverbially a matter of such difficulty that, as the old saying goes, a woman's work is never done.

The truth of this scarcely needs any demonstration. The suggestion which I dared to make a year ago, that the problem of domestic service will never be solved until we have a legal regulation of the hours of domestic servants, called forth a storm of protest in the metropolitan press, the tenor of which was that it is impossible to squeeze all housework within the compass of eight hours. Some thirty or forty years ago a twelve or fourteen hours' limit would have been considered just as impossible.

Now, then, why has there been insufficient technical progress in the organization of the home? The answer is not at all difficult. The home has for many centuries had the enormous supply of labor-power of almost the entire female population for which there was no demand in the industrial field. A cheap supply of labor has always been the greatest obstacle to technical progress. As the *New York Tribune* has put it: "While our wives, mothers, sisters, and unappropriated aunts did all our domestic work, there was no need to think of technical progress." But conditions are changing rapidly. The increased demand for industrial and commercial female wage-labor has shortened the supply of female energy in the kitchen, and as a result we have the problem of domestic service, which thus appears simply as a phase in the larger problem of woman-labor—aye, of the entire organization of modern industry and commerce. Fewer women are ready to enter domestic service.

Now, what are the social influences of these conditions? In other words, what is the influence of the despised servant girl upon the evolution of the home? First, as already pointed out, an increasing number of women of the middle class are forced to remain in, or go back to, the kitchen. Probably a greater proportion of middle-class women are forced to get along without domestic help in this country than in any other civilized part of the world. The domestic virtues, arts, and accomplishments of the average American middle-class woman are perhaps greater than those of women of other nationalities. But to a great extent they are due to the recalcitrant servant girl; or rather, to her absence. Of course this does not fail to call forth considerable protest. The growing intellectual development of the middle-class woman makes her find the eternal drudgery of the home more objectionable. Hence the discussion of the organization of the home. If our own wives and sisters find this meeting so very interesting, it is not with them (nor with us, for that matter) a problem of purely academic interest. It is the expensive servant girl, more than any other factor, that gives rise to the complaining middle-class wife.

Complaints, provided they are reasonable, are a truly progressive power. They will force, they are even now forcing, inventive genius into the virgin field of domestic work, of home life organization; and under the influence of this new stimulus the home life of tomorrow will be as unlike the home life of yesterday as the twentieth-century flyer is unlike the methods of transportation of a hundred years ago.

Of course, a sociologist appreciates the danger of foretelling the future of any institution. But Mrs. Gilman has pointed out some very plausible and necessary changes. It is almost a self-evident proposition that the elimination of the so-called "home industries" will continue. The middle-class woman who, when deprived of the domestic servant, forces this process, is the first to profit by it. But the advantages of industrial progress finally percolate to all industrial groups. While the total elimination of all home work may perhaps be relegated to the dim future, speculations upon which are not profitable, surely the technical progress of the home (a point which Mrs. Gilman has seemingly missed) does not consist entirely in the elimination of home work. Certain functions are, on the contrary, reaching back to the home for the sake of comfort and economy of time. They are enabled to enter the home because of the work of inventive genius, for instance, the bathtub, the chafing-dish, the safety razor, the patent shoe polish. Besides, in constructing the picture of the future home, a large cosmopolitan city must not be taken as a standard. What is possible in New York will appear a complete utopia in a rural community. This is especially true of the pet ideal of Mrs. Gilman—the complete elimination of food-preparation from the home.

Nothing appeals to me more strongly than Mrs. Gilman's eloquent plea for the neglected child in the modern home. Perhaps her pessimism is somewhat exaggerated. Our institutions for orphans do not show any smaller infant mortality than our homes. Nor are the causes of this infant mortality essential to the principles of our home organization. Better wages for the father, better education for the mother would save millions of children's lives. Nevertheless, Mrs. Gilman's plea is a strong and a convincing one.

What is the logical outcome of the plea? It is true that the child is the central purpose of the home. The home is not, nor will it be in the future, mainly "a place where the man has his meals cooked and served by a woman." There are thousands of married couples who purchase their meals and wait for a home until there is a child. But the necessities of child-rearing demand a home of some sort. Thus a home will ever mean a place or rather an institution, where the interests of the child will be paramount—an institution requiring a considerable amount of effort, and let us hope that it will be an institution that is self-sufficient, without the wasteful employment of domestic help. I am speaking of the normal home, and not the exceptional one. Who then will contribute the necessary effort of that home? In pursuit of that evanescent ideal of absolute equality of man and woman, it may be urged that the effort should be divided between both parties to the marriage contract. But the demand for woman's economic independence as made by the feminist movement of today is a demand for independence under present economic conditions.

Let us then deal with stern reality and see what the demand means to the working-class woman, the working-class child, and the working-class family. To the middle-class woman it means a profession, a scientific or a literary career, social life, the possibility of earning fame or at least a reputation, and last but not least, the possibility of transferring the drudgery of the home upon other shoulders. To the working-woman it means none of these desirable things. It may mean very long hours, unhygienic work, low wages—many of these things in addition to the required minimum of housework—and it certainly means neglect of children, even more than the neglect of the husband's comfort. For this very good reason the working-woman, the working-man's wife, refuses to grow enthusiastic over the middle-class ideal of economic independence. It is a grave question whether on the whole those families are better off financially where the wife is forced to sell her labor-power. And I dare say economists are agreed that if the man's wages were not required to carry the entire burden of the support of the entire family, they would correspondingly fall. None of the members of the southern negro's family are better off because the woman is economically independent. And above all, the child-mortality is greater. Under the present industrial organization, the proletarian woman has nothing to gain and the proletarian child a great deal to lose, by this sort of economic independence.

Mrs. Gilman declares it is a productive waste "to segregate half of the productive energy of the world and use it in private service of the crudest sort." It is with this point of view that I must take issue, and defend the married woman against the accusation of the feminists. Do we think of the services of the trained nurse as services of the crudest sort? Is the proper independent care of the individual child—care that cannot be given without proper knowledge and proper love—an economic waste? Or is it not the greatest economic service? It is a serious economic fallacy to speak of the married woman and mother as only a consumer. The working-man's wages do not even now pay the entire cost of supporting the family. His earnings do not even now pay for all the consumption goods needed in the household. They are enough to purchase the raw materials out of which the consumption goods are manufactured and services such as cleanliness and comfort are created. While these are not paid for, they have a distinct commercial value. They need not be paid for, simply because we are supposed to have in the family a social unit of voluntary co-operation, based upon mutual affection or at least attachment, and common love of offspring. In short, we cannot claim in one and the same breath that the woman is overworked, and that she is not a productive worker, as long as the work she does is socially necessary.

To sum up: It seems to me there is now a plain tendency not to have a home unless there are children in the family, or rather, unless there is a family—for a family without children is a family in name only. And as all other economic functions of the home are gradually reduced, to give more space to child-culture, to intelligent, efficient child-culture, the woman will stay in her home to fulfil her natural function; and when I say, "natural function," I am simply following Mrs. Gilman in reducing the social problems to their original biological elements. For far back of the human race the female has been not only the main genetic factor of repro-duction, but also the social factor of child-rearing.

All women are not mothers; and for those who are, the period of child-rearing is limited. But while there are children to rear, and, with the decreasing birth-rate, no children to lose, society has nothing to gain by forcing the mother to add to the wealth of marketable goods. The dearth of marketable goods is not the great problem of modern industrial society. What we need is a standard of earnings which will enable a man to support a family, a standard of home-organization which will enable us to reduce the necessary work so that one person can do it pleasantly and intelligently, a standard of education for the mother which will make her efficient in home-building and child-culture, and perhaps a standard of training for the man which will teach him to appreciate the important work of child-culture, and the joys of parental success.

PROFESSOR MARION TALBOT, UNIVERSITY OF CHICAGO

I wish to call to your attention certain modifications in education which I believe are demanded if the home and the family are to fulfil their true function.

When the home was the skilled workshop, when father, mother, and children jointly contributed to the making of the home in its material aspect, there was constant opportunity for the training of the child in many of his activities. The child now has to leave his home for a large part of his training, physical, mental, social, and religious. With the disappearance of household industries or their relegation to the hands of the unskilled foreigner, we are compelled to introduce into the school curriculum matter and methods which will give the child some degree of command over his physical environment and we have as yet only made a beginning in filling up the gap. In spite of the satisfaction and comfort which come with the modern city house, heated, lighted, drained, furnished with water, food, and clothing at cost of little effort, many a parent longs for the "chore," the household industry, as a means of training his child in usefulness and efficiency. The gymnasium, the dancing school, the club, the Sunday school, and various outside agencies have come to take the place vacated in the child's life through the changes wrought in the home by the conditions of modern life.

The removal of household industries has changed the members of the family from producers to consumers, but education for the latter function is not yet generally recognized as necessary. Even the colleges are very reluctantly opening their curricula to courses for women bearing on this extremely important modern function of the housekeeper.

Under the former industrial system the father shared much more largely than at present in the life and training of the child. The part which he now plays is often so small as to give rise to a series of humorous tales with the child's ignorance of his father as the central theme. A lessening of the so-called feminization of the schools by replacing women with men teachers is but a sorry remedy for the difficulty. Under that system also community of interest and occupation served to develop in the group a sense of the value of the family as an agency for the protection and care of the young and for the growth of the more personal moral characteristics of the human being.

With fathers absent from the home and with communal control of sanitary and civic matters have gone many opportunities for training children to assume responsibility in matters leading to the good citizenship demanded in public affairs. Obedience to law, respect for authority, intelligent interest in impersonal activities find little opportunity for expression and what little there is is seldom used.

These aspects of the subject are important and are fortunately receiving the attention of students of society, of teachers, and, in some few cases, of the parents themselves. There is, however, another aspect which though more important is receiving the attention of but few people.

As has been pointed out, "the family has two functions, to afford an opportunity for eliciting the qualities of affection and character which cannot be displayed at all in the larger group, and it is a training for future members of the larger group in those qualities of disposition and character which are essential to citizenship." Mrs. Gilman has rightly stated that the father and mother must work together for its interests. Her plea for enriched intellectual life, larger social usefulness, and economic independence for women has as its aim not only to secure greater happiness and satisfaction for the individual herself, but to enable her to bring "to bear upon her proper problems, maternity and child-culture, a larger wisdom than she now possesses." I would add to this the imperative social demand that men be fitted for the duties of husband and father. The wife and mother alone cannot secure the permanence and well-being of the family in all its many essentials besides pecuniary prosperity, even if she is given intellectual opportunity and economic independence. I believe that quite as many American homes are suffering from the incapacity of husbands and fathers to contribute their share to the family life as from the attempt of wives and mothers to develop their individuality. Race suicide and divorce are symptoms of a social disorder, doubtless very grave and certainly very evident, whose remedy, in my opinion, lies in the direction of training both boys and girls for parenthood.

Modern pedagogy is urging the enrichment of the school curriculum for boys by teaching them social and industrial history, practical economics, civics, the organization of society, and financial methods, even if this involves the withdrawal of the older disciplinary and cultural studies. Business success is the aim in view. Is it not true that we should declare that the boy should be trained for his other duties in life? In spite of the pronunciamentos of chief executives and the higher clergy, I am firmly persuaded, on the evidence of physicians and of social investigators, that men are more responsible than women for the decline in the birth-rate. If boys were taught the principles of social hygiene and their part in maintaining life upon high levels, I can but believe that with this increased knowledge their moral natures would be aroused and strengthened and the difficulties by which all teachers who deal with young boys are baffled would largely disappear.

Without analogous training for girls we cannot expect that even those conditions for which Mrs. Gilman pleads will necessarily produce good mothers. In a condition of economic independence and intellectual and social freedom, maternity will claim its just place in the interests of a liberated woman only if, as a child, she is made to understand what the end of this function is and its dignity has been impressed upon her mind. Wifehood and motherhood are too often now the price of escape from a certain kind of slavery to parents and from bondage to conventionality.

It is needless to say that I realize how wise and sympathetic the parents and teachers who give this knowledge must be. It is time, however, for the student of the family to say to the educator that the data for this kind of instruction are available and must be put to use. It is no longer sufficient to think of the boy in the light of his future trade or profession, or even as a citizen, nor of the girl simply as a married woman, or even trained in some independent vocation. Throughout all their training must run the idea of their high function—that of parenthood.

THE RELATIONS OF SOCIAL DISEASES TO THE FAMILY

PRINCE A. MORROW, A.M., M.D.
66 W. Fortieth Street, New York City, N. Y.

It is but a truism to state that the welfare of the family underlies the welfare of society: Whatever injuriously affects this unit of our social organization, reacts unfavorably upon the collective social body.

Marriage was instituted for the purpose of regularizing sexual relations between men and women, and the creation, care, and maintenance of children. However individualistic the motives that influence men and women to matrimony, the civil object of marriage is the creation of the family—the raising of children. From the socio-political standpoint children are the only excuse for marriage—not offspring merely, but children born in conditions of vitality, health, and physical vigor, and capable of becoming useful citizens to the state.

Since the most valuable asset of a nation consists in healthy, capable citizens, the conservation of the health and productive energy of the family is essential to the prosperity, and existence even, of human society. The question of health and disease as affecting the family has never received adequate consideration. The state recognizes the fundamental importance of this institution as the condition of social preservation, and has surrounded marriage with the safeguards of law and morality; but the state takes no cognizance of the health of the contracting parties: it makes no provision against the introduction of diseases which may wreck the health of the wife and mother and engender a vast mass of disease and misery in the descendants.

Modern science has shown us that most diseases are of germ origin, and are spread by contact of individuals. The ordinary relations of family life afford exceptional opportunities for contagious contacts. So common is this mode of spread that certain

46

diseases such as tuberculosis, leprosy, etc., are often spoken of as "family diseases."

The class of diseases which form the subject of this paper, I have termed "social diseases" from their origin in the social evil. While they are commonly communicated in that relation between the sexes ordained by nature for the continuation of the race, they may be spread in the ordinary intimacies of family and social life—a syphilitic child in a household, for example, may be the source of numerous contaminations: It may infect its nurse and other members of the family, and they in turn may infect others; veritable epidemics of syphilis have originated in this way.

A case of gonococcus infection in the family may likewise be the source of multiple contagions; the ophthalmia, which blots out the eyes of babies, may be communicated to other children, the nurse, or attendants. Another specific infection of young girls, due to the gonococcus, often takes on the proportions of extensive epidemics. In the Hebrew Orphan Asylum of New York, in 1896, 65 cases of infection were traceable to one child. In the Babies Hospital of New York in 1903, 55 children were infected, and in 1904 there were 46 cases. In the epidemic of Posen, 236 schoolgirls from 6 to 14 years were infected from a bathing-house where two or more children used the same bathtub. It is this quality of expansiveness, this capacity of morbid irradiation through family and social life, that gives to these diseases their superior significance as a social danger.

The significance of disease in general is measured by its effect upon the health and life of the individual; but the dangers of this class of diseases are not limited to the individual, nor yet to the parents; they extend to the children, and through them to society at large.

The special significance of social diseases as a peril to the family comes from the fact that they specifically affect the system of generation, sterilizing the procreative capacity, or so devitalizing the primordial cells that the product of conception is blighted in its development, and the office of maternity desecrated by the bringing forth of tainted, diseased, or dead children. The physical interests of the race demand that the springs of heredity be kept pure and undefiled. Certainly no more important problem can engage the thoughtful attention of sociologists than the protection of the family from diseases which damage or destroy that function to which the life of the human race is entrusted.

In the further consideration of this subject, reference will be made to the introduction of these diseases into the family, the frequency of marital contamination, and the resulting dangers to the wife, to the offspring, to society, and finally, remedial measures.

1. *How are these diseases introduced into married life?*— At first glance it would appear somewhat incongruous to associate a class of infections which in popular estimation always bear the stamp of immorality, with a social institution which typifies our highest conception of virtue. Unfortunately marriage does not always prove that "asylum pure and chaste," into which diseases of vice cannot enter. On the contrary, thousands of pure young women find in this relation, legitimatized by the state and sanctioned by the church, as honorable and virtuous, not a safeguard against these infections, but a snare for their entrapment. The explanation is not far to seek.

A large proportion of men contract these diseases either before or after marriage, and carry the infection into the family. The conditions of married life render the wife a helpless victim. To quote a paragraph from my book on *Social Diseases and Marriage:*

> *The Vinculum Matrimonii* is a chain which binds and fetters the woman completely, making her the passive recipient of the germs of any sexual disease her husband may harbor. On her wedding night she may, and often does, receive unsuspectingly the poison of a disease which may seriously affect her health and kill her children; or by extinguishing her capacity of conception, may sweep away all the most cherished hopes and aspirations of married life. She is an "innocent" in every sense of the word. She is incapable of foreseeing, powerless to prevent this injury. She often pays with her life for her blind confidence in the man who, ignorantly or carelessly, passes over to her a disease he has received from a prostitute.

The only plea that can be urged in extenuation of these crimes against pure women is that the men who commit them are, for the most part ignorant that they are bearers of contagion, and especially ignorant of the terrible consequences to their wives and children. For, it is to be understood, these infections are markedly accentuated in virulence and danger to the wife and mother in fulfilling the functions for which marriage was instituted.

2. *The frequency of marital contamination.*—This frequency does not admit of exact mathematical expression. The amount of venereal infection in marriage is an unknown and unknowable quantity. Few of the innocent victims know or even suspect the name or nature of the disease which transforms them from healthy women into suffering invalids. The social sentiment which ignores the existence of these infections, and professional ethics which draws around them the sacred circle of the medical secret, unite in protecting them from exposure.

The proportion of women infected in marriage has been variously estimated by different authorities. Whether this proportion be 5, 10, or 15 per cent., considering the number of married women in this country, either of these percentages totals up an enormous aggregate. However startling the statement, it is nevertheless true, that there is, in the aggregate, more gonococcus infection among virtuous wives than in professional prostitutes in this country.

Since the discovery of the gonococcus—the causal agent—statistics bearing upon this point have the value of scientific accuracy. The specific germ may be identified in the inflammatory lesions it occasions.

An investigation of the amount of venereal morbidity in New York City was undertaken by the Committee of Seven, appointed by the New York County Medical Society in 1901. This investigation had among other objects the tracing of the sources of the contagion. From the reply to the circular letters sent out to all regular physicians in Greater New York, it appeared that 30 per cent. of all the women treated for venereal disease in private practice in 1900, were contaminated in marriage. The source of the infection in those treated in dispensaries and public institutions could not be traced—doubtless among the poorer and more ignorant classes who are treated in these institutions the proportion is larger.

A similar investigation undertaken by the Committee on Sanitary and Moral Prophylaxis, appointed by the Maryland State Medical Society in 1907, showed that nearly 40 per cent. of the cases of gonococcus infection in women treated in private practice in Baltimore, were contaminated in marriage.

Fournier's statistics of over 10,000 cases of syphilis, including women from every walk in life, showed that 20 per cent., or one in every five syphilitic women, received the infection from their husbands.

The president of the Gynecological Society, at the meeting of the Congress of American Physicians and Surgeons in Washington, 1907, stated that about 70 per cent. of all the work done by specialists in diseases of women in this country, was the result of gonococcus infection.

Brief reference may now be made to the specific effects of these diseases upon the family.

3. *Dangers to the wife.*—We are indebted to gynecologists for our knowledge of the specific dangers to the wife and mother, from gonococcus infection. To present the most salient of these facts in concrete form; 80 per cent. of all deaths due to inflammatory diseases peculiar to women, practically all purulent inflammations of the tubes and ovaries, and 75 per cent. of all special surgical operations performed upon women, are the result of gonococcus infection. This does not take into account the large number of infected women who are not operated upon, but drag out a miserable existence of semi- or complete invalidism.

One of the most common and characteristic results of this infection in women is sterility—50 per cent. of these infected women are rendered absolutely and irremediably sterile, while a much larger proportion are sterile after the birth of the first child; so that one child represents the total fecundity of the family. A large proportion of sterile marriages, contrary to the popular view, is from incapacity and not of choice.

The dangers of syphilis to the wife are too numerous and

varied to admit of detailed mention. Her personal risks from the disease are all the more serious as her health and resisting capacity are impaired by the bearing of dead or diseased children, and in addition she is often denied the benefit of prompt specific treatment. Incredible as it may appear, many men who infect their wives, employ every means to prevent their consulting a physician, from the fear that they may in some way learn the nature of the infection. The opinion of all specialists is concurrent upon this point, that women syphilized in marriage are not, as a rule, sufficiently treated, and it is probably on this account that so large a proportion of these women suffer from severe tertiary manifestations.

4. *Dangers to the offspring.*—While gonococcus infection is not susceptible of hereditary transmission, it often carries with it infective risks to the offspring. From 70 to 80 per cent. of the ophthalmia which blinds babies is due to this cause—besides other dangers to the children, one of which has already been referred to.

Syphilis is the only disease transmitted to the offspring in full virulence—killing them outright or so vitiating the processes of nutrition that they come into the world with the mark of death upon them, or, if they survive they are condemned to carry through life the stigmata of degeneration and disease. Moreover they are capable of transmitting the same class of organic defects to the third generation. Syphilis thus represents the most potent factor in the degeneration of the race. From 60 to 80 per cent. of syphilitic children die before being born or shortly after birth; only one in three or four finally survives; in some cases the mortality is 100 per cent., absolutely extinguishing the productivity of certain families. And here I may allude to the view which looks upon the destruction of these physical weaklings as Nature's process for the elimination of the unfit. There is no worse sophistry than to attribute to Nature what is clearly due to man's criminal ignorance. But for the fact of the syphilis of the parents these children might have been born in conditions of vitality and physical vigor.

5. *The personal risk of the husband from his disease.*— There are various complications or sequelae from gonococcus

infection which may seriously compromise the health of the husband, but which will be passed over in this paper. There is, however, one disability created by the disease, which, by destroying his procreative power, may defeat the object for which marriage is instituted. Sterility in the male is not an infrequent result of this infection. The proportion of non-premeditated childless marriages directly due to the husband's incapacity from this cause is variously estimated at from 17 to 25 per cent., and, as he is also responsible for the sterility of his wife, about 75 per cent. of all sterility in married life which is not of choice but of incapacity may be traced to the fault of the husband. Lier-Ascher's careful statistics place this proportion at 71–2 per cent.

Another danger to the family comes from the incapacitating effect of syphilis upon the husband in his character as head and support of the family. The dangers of syphilis to the individual are measured by its remote rather than by its immediate effects. The dreaded manifestations of the disease—the implication of organs essential to life and, especially, affections of the central nervous system, may not develop until 5, 10, 15, or even 20 years later. So it often happens that long after the follies of youth have been forgotten, and the man has become a husband and father, he must pay the penalty for his misdeeds in loco-motor-ataxia, tumor of the brain, paralysis, blindness, or other affections which are incurable for the most part, entirely incapacitate him as the breadwinner of the family, and may render him a charge upon friends or the community. So frequent are these delayed penalties that the French have a proverb: *C'est le mari qui paie la dette du garçon.* Unfortunately the wife and children are drawn into this vicious circle, and must share the punishment.

6. *Social misery and unhappiness.*—This review of the relations of social diseases to the family would be incomplete without reference to the domestic misery and unhappiness which flow from the introduction of these diseases into married life. Enforced childlessness from extinguishment of the procreative capacity is often a source of marital unhappiness. The instinct of maternity has been implanted, by nature, in every normally

constituted woman, and many women experience the keenest suffering when realizing that all the hopes and aspirations which center in motherhood and children are doomed to disappointment.

Social diseases are a frequent cause not only of domestic dissension, but of disunion of the family. Notwithstanding the conspiracy of concealment between the husband and physician, women often learn the name and nature of their trouble, which not infrequently leads to the breaking-up of the family. The number of applications for divorce from this cause, especially in the middle and upper classes of society is much larger than is commonly supposed. In divorce proceedings, the cause of action usually appears under some non-compromising name, such as "cruelty," "non-support," "desertion," while the true cause is never made public.

Time will permit only the briefest reference to the economic significance of social diseases—the blindness, the deaf-mutism, the idiocy, and other organic defects engendered by these diseases impose an enormous charge upon the state and community for the care and maintenance of those afflicted—the elimination of these diseases would render one-third, possibly one-half, of our institutions for defectives unnecessary.

From this cursory survey of the subject, it is evident that social diseases have most important relations with the family. They are directly antagonistic to all that the family stands for as a social institution—they are destructive to its health, its productivity, and its social efficiency. They occasion an enormous sacrifice of potential wealth from the loss of citizens to the state. Moreover, they distil a double venom, they poison not only the health, but the peace, honor, and happiness of the family. Their prevention is one of the most pressing problems of social hygiene that confronts us at the present day.

WHAT ARE THE REMEDIAL MEASURES?—If I have succeeded in interesting you in this recital, probably the dominant feeling excited is one of surprise that these abuses against the innocent and helpless members of society should be possible, and the great body of humane people in this country remain indifferent to their significance, ignorant of their existence even. Ignorance is the cause, and at the same time the explanation of this indifference. Men carry these infections into the family because they do not know; women suffer ill health, sterility, and mutilation of their bodies, because they do not know; society is insensible to their sufferings because it does not know; the saving hope of the situation lies in letting people know. Publicity of these evils, education of the public to their significance, are the prime indications.

The importance of this enlightenment is emphasized by the fact that this danger to the family and society has always been covered up and concealed. Social diseases furnish the most conspicuous example in human history of an evil which flourishes in disguise and darkness, and which owes its chief potentiality to the very obscurity to which it has been relegated by traditional prejudice. This social pestilence has been for centuries installed in our midst—poisoning the sources of life, sapping the foundations of our national vitality and vigor, ravaging the home and family—while society, behind "its seven-folded veil of prudery and false modesty," refuses to recognize its existence.

John Stuart Mill declared that "The diseases of society can no more be checked or healed than those of the body, without publicly speaking of them." But social sentiment has decreed that the "holy silence" upon everything relating to sex or its diseases must not be broken. And yet all experience shows that diseases communicated in the ordinary relations of family and social life cannot be prevented without the co-operation of the public, and that the first essential in securing this co-operation is the general dissemination of knowledge respecting their extent and dangers, and the means by which they are spread.

This has been signally shown in the present warfare against tuberculosis. We have recently witnessed the assemblage in Washington of a Congress of Tuberculosis, in which every civilized country of the globe was represented. Eminent scientists, distinguished specialists, prominent laymen, brought the results of their studies, their experience, and their wisdom for the discussion of the most effective ways and means of exterminating this scourge. I need not remind you that less than two decades ago, this "great white plague" existed in our midst, claiming its victims by tens and hundreds of thousands, ignored by the sanitary officials, disregarded by the public, or stoically accepted as an evil against which it was vain to contend.

What has wrought this wonderful change in the attitude of the profession and the public—transforming apathy into interest, converting inaction into earnest effort, substituting the energy of hope for the impotence of despair? Certainly advances in medical science and the more aggressive policy adopted by the sanitary authorities have contributed to this change. But it is undeniable that the brilliant results thus far achieved in the campaign against tuberculosis, would have been impossible without the enlightened aid and helpful co-operation of the public.

Physicians have been censured, and perhaps with some justice, for their silence in regard to matters which so vitally concern the interests of the family; but a change has come over the spirit and practice of the medical profession. The genius of modern medicine is essentially in the direction of popularizing hygienic knowledge; the medical profession is perfectly willing to share its knowledge, but it cannot reach the public to any effective extent. The channels of communication with the public which serve for its enlightenment are closed against this knowledge. The responsibility now rests with those who control the educational agencies of our social life.

Other measures for safeguarding the family from these diseases may be briefly referred to.

1. *Sanitary safeguards.*—Although social diseases are due to microbic invasion, their prevention is not a purely sanitary problem. Sanitary measures are directed to the correction of the causes of disease and their modes of spread. The causes of social diseases reside in social conditions which lie entirely without the pale of sanitary control and their communicative mode, entrenched in the stronghold of privacy, cannot be reached. Besides, sanitary measures are chiefly concerned with environmental conditions which cannot be controlled by the individual. The distinctive peculiarity of this special class of diseases is that they are communicated by the voluntary acts of individuals. But

while they are essentially *voluntary* infections, they are for the most part, *ignorant* infections.

It might at first glance appear that the most effective preventive would be the enlightenment of the individual patient by his physician; but as a matter of fact comparatively few men consult physicians as to their physical fitness for marriage and parentage, so that the opportunities for this prophylactic work are comparatively restricted. Besides, many men, to the discredit of human nature be it said, when warned by the physician of the danger of marrying with an uncured sexual disease, nevertheless for sordid or selfish reasons, take the risk, or, rather, subject the women they marry to the risk of infection. Some men are utterly unteachable, while others, being taught, are flagrantly careless in the matter of spreading disease. Evidently if enlightenment is to have its full force and efficacy as a preventive measure, it must be general; it must extend to the collectivity.

2. *Legal safeguards.*—Since experience shows that the enlightenment now available will not prove an infallible corrective of these crimes against the family, the question arises whether the state, through its instrument, the law, can more effectively intervene in their prevention.

Medical examination of the contracting parties, and the furnishing of a certificate of freedom from contagious sexual disease as a condition of license to marry, has been proposed as a solution of the problem. To many not familiar with the practical difficulties in the way, this measure commends itself. It would be difficult to enact a law which does not apply to both sexes, but so far as the woman is concerned such examination is entirely unnecessary, as women almost never introduce these infections into marriage; besides, many sensitive, refined women would rather forego marriage than be subjected to a physical examination which they would regard as an outrage upon their modesty, and an indignity to their persons.

Further, such a law, to be effective, must be general in all the states, otherwise couples wishing to marry would cross over the borders of a neighboring state where this law was not in force. There are other practical objections arising from the oftentimes latent character of these diseases, and the impossibility of making a diagnosis without prolonged observation, which, with other defects that cannot be here considered, would defeat the purpose of such a law.

Another proposed measure is the enactment of a law imposing penal responsibility for the introduction of these infections into marriage. Such a law would be equitable and just, as there can be no greater injury to the corporeal integrity of an individual than infection with venereal disease. Unfortunately the essential condition of the law's intervention is that the injury shall already have been received; besides, the injured party must be the complainant, appear in open court, and if the charge is substantiated, be publicly branded as the bearer of a shameful disease. It is evident that few self-respecting women would avail themselves of its doubtful benefits. The only advantage of such a law upon the statute books would be its educational value, rather than its frequent enforcement.

Eminent jurists who have studied this subject declare it doubtful whether additional legal guarantees for the safeguarding of marriage can be furnished by the state.

3. *Ethical safeguards.*—The family is not only the source of the life of the nation, but the conservator of the morality of the race. The moral element in this problem of prevention cannot be ignored. Observation shows that men are the responsible authors of these social crimes—women the victims. The root of the evil is grounded in the double standard of morality.

In legalizing marriage the law has placed man and woman upon the same moral plane of equality, the infidelity of either party constitutes a sufficient ground for divorce; but social convention has created one standard of morals for men, another for women. This code which was constructed to conform with man's sensual inclinations, while allowing him the largest sexual liberty, requires of the woman chastity before marriage, and absolute fidelity after marriage. This disparity in moral obligations has been justified by tradition on the ground of a physiological difference between men and women. In the opinion of the wisest and best men of the medical profession, the double standard of morality rests upon a false physiological foundation. The doctrine of the so-called "sexual necessity" for men, is a physiological fallacy; it receives no shadow of support from the teachings of science, and is disproved by the experience of thousands. From a purely physiological standpoint there is no more necessity for a young man to "sow his wild oats" than for his sister to do the same. There is every reason to believe that the relative chastity of men and women is due, not to a physiological difference, but to a difference in education and moral training.

These crimes against the family will continue until women know, as they have a perfect right to know, the facts which so vitally concern their own health and the health and lives of their children. When they know that the standard of morality they now tolerate in the men they marry is the responsible cause, the woman will demand of the man she receives as her husband and the potential father of her children, the same moral standard which the man has always required of the woman he takes as his wife. The emancipation of woman will never be complete until she is freed from the shackles of a traditional code, based upon the ethical heresy that one half of humanity has imperious duties which the other half may repudiate or disclaim. The result will be not to debase woman, but to uplift man to her higher standard.

Personally I believe that women will not be left to work out their own salvation alone. Every moral reform comes from the exposure of human suffering. We have seen that the practical effect of this unilateral code is, that in condemning the innocent to suffer for the sins of the guilty, it violates the principles of justice and humanity. Considerations of humanity demand that women, in fulfilling their mission as child-bearers of the race, should not be exposed to diseases which soil them, which poison them, and which kill them; justice to the unborn demands that they should not be robbed of their rightful heritage of vitality, health, and vigor. When the public is fully enlightened as to the significance of these dangers to the family, and their injury to the highest interests of human society, I believe that public opinion, which is the strongest force in the evolution of the conscience of the race, will no longer tolerate these evils, nor sanction the standard of morals of which they are the outgrowth.

A final word upon the relations of social diseases to the disunion of the family. These diseases play the sinister rôle of detectives in the household—they are *les maladies révélatrices*, often furnishing positive proof of infidelity, which otherwise might never have been revealed. The frequency of separation or divorce from this cause is far from being suspected by the public. It is one of the hidden, unavowable causes, "the shame that cannot be named for shame." No other commentary upon the intolerable situations created by the introduction of these diseases into the family is needed than the fact that so many women, loyal to the highest ideals of marriage, devoted to home and family, are driven to the divorce courts as a refuge. No one can condemn a self-respecting woman for separating from a man who has dishonored her with a shameful disease.

The evils that result from divorce have been fully exposed; it is time to expose evils that cause divorce; to endeavor to prevent divorce by correcting one, at least, of its most fruitful causes. While the interests of the social welfare demand the conservation of the integrity of the family, it is vain to attempt to preserve intact this corner-stone of our social fabric if we neglect the destructive forces at work undermining its foundation.

DISCUSSION

PROFESSOR SELIGMAN spoke of the economic aspects of the evil and called attention to the great need of publicity.

PROFESSOR A. B. WOLFE, OBERLIN, OHIO

Dr. Morrow's paper is a terrible revelation of the sinister hypocrisy of men in their relation to women and in particular to the women they promise to love, honor, and cherish; a proof positive, if any were needed, that our ideals both of what is manly and womanly need at some points violent revision. The problem of the family is in more ways than one the problem of women. The ideal we hold of woman and the ideal we hold of the family will develop *pari passu*. So long as our ideal of the strength and worth of woman is a low one—as I do not hesitate to say it was until Mary Wollstonecraft, John Stuart Mill, and the modern feminists forced upon us the beginnings of a reluctant revision—as it is yet in fact with the great masses of men—so long as woman was regarded mainly as a vehicle for sex gratification and a cheap housekeeper combined, so long as it is thought that "the noblest thing *any* woman can do is to be a good wife and mother," so long as women are not gladly and consciously recognized by men to be a part of the human race as well as bearers of it, that long will the ideal of the family leave much to be desired and the actual family remain a heavy sociological problem.

Much has been said in this discussion concerning publicity and education. The problem of venereal diseases, and of the social evil at large, will never approach a solution until men fully recognize that the wife or the prospective wife—that any woman—is entitled to just as complete a knowledge of these matters as is the male. But so long as women are regarded with a vestige of the old "clinging-vine" ideal, as beings who are to be "protected" (note the pungent irony of that term in this connection) and carefully guarded from knowledge of the world's hard facts, so long as women themselves fondly place a blind faith in a masculine "chivalry," the condescension and subtle contemptuousness of which many of them are at present incapable of perceiving, just so long will they be incapable of protecting themselves from their male protectors. It will in the future be one of the gravest charges the defenders of western civilization will have to meet that with all the civilizing and enlightening agencies it had at its command it so long allowed its ideal of womanhood to remain so purely a negative ideal. Let woman be only "pure" and "innocent," let her only guard her "virtue" (or have it guarded for her) against the wiles and attacks of the predatory male, let her at the same time have a pretty face, a lithe figure, and a "charming" way, and she was essentially the ideal woman. No woman whose chief ideality or virtue consists in purity or "innocence" can ever be other than an obstacle in the way of the solution of the twin problems of marriage and prostitution.

When we talk about publicity and education we mean that the social consciousness should be opened to these social dangers of contagious vice and disease. When, as in this case, the matter in hand concerns women as well as men, it behooves us, both men and women, to include women in that social consciousness, to recognize that they should have equal part with men in the formation and direction of the social consciousness. No recent writer on sociology has said a thing more pregnant with significant truth than Professor Thomas when he says that women are in the white man's world but not of it, and nowhere have I seen that fact more vividly illustrated than by the acknowledged effects of the "medical secret" of the physician, a man-made bit of professional ethics that sacrifices everything —wife, children, honor, health, and social welfare—to the supposed interest of the libertine male, even though he be "to a radiant angel linked." Whatever the present legal status of the medical secret, it seems clear that that institution could not long survive under the light and fire of a public opinion which women had equal part with men in shaping. For no sane woman would consent to the fallacious belief that the sanctity and unity of the home is to be maintained on the basis of collusion of husband and physician to deceive an ignorant though suffering wife. It may be necessary that women live more than men in what Professor Patten has called a pain-economy, but surely to ask them to live in a fool's paradise at the same time is to add insult to injury. There are other stagnant pools than simply that of male disease upon which the searchlight of inquiry should be turned. It would be well to turn it oftener and with greater intensity upon male egotism—upon the androcentricity of society, the root evil of which maladjustments in family and sex life are only too often the specific manifestations. Even the American Sociological Society, while it is extremely fortunate in having women as well as men speakers on its programmes, has not entirely escaped the androcentric world-view.

MRS. ANNA GARLIN SPENCER, NEW YORK CITY, N. Y.

Two things are most encouraging to note in connection with this subject. One is that the members of the medical profession have for the first time come fairly upon the platform of social responsibility in respect to these social diseases. Their oath, their tradition of care for the individual patient, the sanctity of the medical confessional, have all bound the doctors until lately to a purely personal duty in this regard. Gradually the idea of saving the social cost of other preventable diseases has deepened and grown, until we have boards of health and medical officials of various kinds at work to prevent typhoid and other scourges, to segregate and radically treat, even at public expense, those ill of contagious disease, in order that they may not help to spread the evil; and now tuberculosis is to be brought under control. The physician has fallen heir to the position of social command once held by the priest; and for the reason that we are all so concerned now-a-days with the physical basis of life and of well-being. The valuable paper by Dr. Morrow shows us that the "great black plague," a preventable and terrible scourge of humanity, is to be proceeded against and to be brought under control. And the encouraging thing is that the doctors, now recognizing their responsibility of leadership in this matter, are giving the public the facts they alone can give and assuming their proper place in preventive as well as in ameliorative effort. One can hardly realize how great an advance in the sense of social duty this marks in the medical profession, unless he remembers that great struggle in England over the Contagious Diseases Acts, and the attitude which the doctors took in that seven years' fight against the state legalization of prostitution. The physicians then generally took the ground of duty to try and save men from the consequences of sexual irregularity, while condemning women prostitutes to a slavery the most hopeless and most degrading that any class of human beings has ever suffered. The position now taken by Dr. Morrow and other physicians in the Society of Sanitary and Moral Prophylaxis is that all means for cure and amelioration should be freely accessible to all, men and women alike; that the home and innocent wives and children should be protected as far as possible; but that the final and most effective measures for wiping out this evil are moral and educational. We may congratulate ourselves on this great movement forward of the medical profession as one of the largest of social gains.

The second thing that is cause for congratulation and for hope in regard to the curbing of social diseases is the new solidarity of women, and the way in which that is working for the protection of the poorer and weaker womanhood. Social diseases imply prostitution, and it is the ignorant and poor among women who furnish the larger portion of prostitutes. The one most effective way to lessen the social evil, and the diseases that it causes, would be to make every young girl self-supporting with a living wage. And the best, the strongest, the most fortunate womanhood is at work to secure that end. By means of trade schools and welfare work and leagues of protection and help for the working girl, they are seeking to make girls too strong and too fairly paid to be such easy victims as they have been. There is a new sex-consciousness, which sometimes shows itself in unlovely forms, but which is really a testimony to social growth, which is making women help women. They are no longer willing that the sacred, seamless, robe of womanhood shall be torn asunder and one part dedicated to honor in the home and the other part given over to dishonor in the dark places of sin. This sense of belonging together is new among women but it is working toward a higher estimate of potential motherhood and a deeper sense of responsibility toward all the weak and poor and ignorant girlhood on the part of the women of character and social power. This will mean that while the doctors are working in the noble way indicated in Dr. Morrow's paper to lessen social diseases, the best womanhood will be working more and more to lessen the supply of "abandoned" women whose degradation is concerned in those diseases. We ought to protect the home. We ought also to protect all youth from that which hurts the home.

THE INFLUENCE OF INCOME ON STANDARDS OF LIFE

PROFESSOR R. C. CHAPIN
Beloit College, Beloit, Wis.

It goes without saying that the standard of living attained does not depend simply upon income. The natural environment—climate, the free gifts of nature—the social environment, whether urban or rural, the efficiency of government, the opportunities for recreation and education which are provided gratuitously—all these have a marked influence upon the plane of life that men attain. Furthermore, the actual comfort enjoyed by a given family depends hardly less upon the amount of its income than upon the wisdom displayed in applying it to the diverse wants which it may be made to meet. The woman who "looketh well to the ways of her household" is as important a factor in our time as she was in the days of King Lemuel.

But into these wide aspects of the question it is not my business to enter. I shall deal with the influence upon the standard of living of income alone, and I purpose to consider the effect upon the standard, first, of variations in amount of income; second, of variations in sources of income. I shall draw for illustration largely upon the results of an investigation into the standard of living in New York City carried on in 1907 under the direction of a committee of the New York State Conference of Charities. Returns were compiled from 391 families of four, five, and six persons each, 318 having incomes between $600 and $1,100.

I. Variations in amount of income.—It is plain that the larger the income, the larger are the possibilities of satisfaction. One of the evidences of a general rise of real wages in the nineteenth century is the increase in the number and kind of good things that are within reach of the ordinary man, and actually in his possession. We know, that is, that the rise of the standard of living so as to include trolley-rides and daily newspapers and silver-plated ware must be the result of a general increase in family income. But we can go farther than this. Ernst Engel has taught us to look at the apportionment of income among the principal objects of family expenditure, and to see just how changes of income work out in changes in the elements of the standard of living—what kind of things are added as income increases, what are omitted as income falls.

On the basis of returns from 199 Belgian families, gathered in 1855 by Ducpetiaux, Engel made out his familiar table of percentage expenditures for Saxon families of three income-grades. He found that the poorest families, whose income was under $300 of our money, gave for food 62 per cent. of all that they spent. Families having from $450 to $600 spent 55 per cent. for food, and those with from $750 to $1,000 spent 50 per cent. for this purpose. Hence he made his generalizations that, as income increased, a less and less part of it was needed for food, and that the percentage of expenditure for food was therefore an index of the degree of prosperity attained. He applied this standard in a later work to the wretched English peasants whose budgets had been collected by Eden in 1797, and found that the average of their food-expenditure was 73 per cent. of their total expenditures. The generalization regarding the tendency of the food-percentage to diminish as the income increases has been verified in many later compilations of family budgets. The *Report of the United States Bureau of Labor* for 1903, for instance, finds a decline in food-expenditure from 47 per cent. among families having incomes between $400 and $500, to 40 per cent. for families with incomes between $900 and $1,000. Colonel Wright's Massachusetts investigation of 1875 showed a decline from 64 per cent. for families having less than $450 a year to 51 per cent. for families having over $1,200 a year.

As the demands of the stomach are more easily met out of the larger income, what expenditures are increased to correspond? Engel's Saxon tables show a constant percentage for housing and for fuel and light, a slight increase for clothing, and a rise in the percentage allotted to expenditures outside of immediate physical necessities from 5 to 10 and from 10 to 15 per cent. as we ascend the income-scale. This indicates that, along with somewhat better provision for food and shelter, it is possible for the family to indulge in more attractive clothing and household furnishings, and to spend something for amusement, for reading-matter and for minor personal indulgences.

All reports agree as to the broadening of the plane of living, with rising income, in regard to expenditure for the satisfaction of these culture-wants. Not all, however, coincide with Engel's data in regard to a constant percentage for rent and for clothing. Colonel Wright's figures for the United States at large in 1901 show a nearly constant percentage for rent (17 to 18 per cent.), but his Massachusetts report of 1875 shows a decline in the first three income-groups from 20 to 15.5 and then to 14 per cent., followed by a rise to 17 per cent. and a drop to 15 per cent. Recent investigations in New York, that of Mrs. More in her *Working-men's Budgets,* and that of the Committee of the New York Conference, agree in showing a steady falling-off in percentage expenditure for rent with each increase of one hundred dollars in income. The percentages found in the latter inquiry were 24 for incomes between $600 and $700, and for successive income-groups, rising by hundred-dollar stages, 22, 20 19, 18, 16—the last for incomes over $1,100. The congestion of population in New York, fortunately exceptional, doubtless accounts in part for the fact that in that city house-rent claims one-quarter of the six-hundred-dollar incomes.

An examination of the percentages expended for food, housing, and other purposes suggests that the proportion of income devoted to each of them may not always move in the same direction as we pass from one income-group to the next higher. The $400 families in the *Labor Report* of 1903 spend a higher percentage for food than the $300 families. If the comparison is carried far enough upward in the scale of incomes, a point is reached in New York where rent ceases to fall off in percentage expenditure, and clothing ceases to demand a larger proportion than in the group preceding. The fact seems to be that each of the three primary wants takes its turn in urging its claims most

vociferously and when these have been pacified the desires for the
things that make life worth living begin to be heard. In regard
to each class of wants in turn a point of relative saturation is
reached, and a more adequate satisfaction of the next one becomes
possible.

In New York City the most imperative need on the lowest
incomes is for housing. Some place of shelter must be provided,
and, however wretched, it will not be cheap. Thirteen dollars a
month was the average rent paid by seventy-two families whose
average income was $650. But this amounts to $156 a year, or
24 per cent. of the total income. When the cost of shelter
demands a quarter of the whole income, food and clothing must
take what is left. But the accommodations obtained as the minimum that can be lived in by the families with $650 a year are
practically good enough for those with an income one and two
hundred dollars greater. Seventy-three families whose income
averaged $846, spent only fourteen dollars a week on the average
for rent. But this was only 21 per cent. of their larger total
expenditure. Meanwhile their food percentage was practically
as high as that of the $650 group (44.3 per cent.), representing
an increase in average amount expended from $290 to $360.

In food the point of diminishing percentage was not reached
until after the one-thousand-dollar line was passed. The food-
percentage increased, as with the families in the *United States
Labor Report* of 1903, on passing from $400 to $500, and from
$500 to $600. This may be due in part to exaggeration in the
returns of expenditure for food. In part it was due to the fact
that until an income of $800 was reached one-third of the
families were underfed. The proportion of the total food-
expenditure that was given for animal food increased, and that
expended for cereal food diminished. The cost of animal food
comprised 29 per cent. of the total food-bill of the families in
the six-hundred-dollar income-group, and 32 per cent. of those
in the one-thousand-dollar group. Cereals dropped correspondingly from 21 to 17 per cent. The expenditure for alcoholic
drinks increased, taking into account only those families that
reported this item, from the average of $27.25, or 4.2 per cent.

of the total expenditures in the six-hundred-dollar group, to $59.96, or 5.2 per cent., in the eleven-hundred-dollar group.

Clothing comes last of the three to a constant or a diminishing proportion of the expenditures. In the New York families under consideration the percentage expenditure rises slightly with each increase of $100 in income until the eleven-hundred-dollar group is reached, and thereafter remains constant at about 15 per cent.

The expenditures for other purposes than these three primary necessities are kept under until these wants are met. By the time something like an equilibrium between these three has been reached, say at $800 for our New York families, the expenditure for recreation, social obligations, care of the health, and all other purposes save fuel and light, claims a larger proportion of the income. The proportion is 1 per cent. higher at $700 than at $600, but at $800 it rises from 14 to 16 per cent. of the total expenditure, and continues to increase without sign of stopping. That is, the culture-wants are beginning to claim their own, which, under the necessity of keeping the wolf from the door, they could not be permitted to have.

A striking example of this tendency of subsistence-wants to claim the lion's share of all increasing income is found in Engel's comparison of the Belgian returns of 1853 with those of a similar investigation made in 1891. At the latter period, although the average income had nearly doubled, the expenditure for food comprised 65.7 per cent. of the total in 1891 as compared with 64.9 per cent. in 1853. In fact, food, clothing, rent, and fuel and light consumed 96 per cent. of the income in 1891 and only 94 per cent. in 1853.

The same general conclusion as to the relative intensity of the several classes of wants may be drawn from another method of handling the New York returns. A minimum standard, as exact as could be determined, was applied to the expenditures for food, clothing, and housing, and the number of families counted in each income-group who came short of the standard. For food, the minimum was set at an expenditure at the rate of 22 cents per man per day, as calculated after the manner made familiar by Professor W. O. Atwater in the Bulletins of the Department of Agriculture. This figure was reached, after an analysis of one hundred of the family reports, by Dr. Frank P. Underhill of Yale University, a competent expert. Professor Atwater's estimate on the basis of data gathered in New York City a few years previous, when a lower scale of prices prevailed, was from 23 to 25 cents. For housing the minimum was fixed at one and one-half persons per room, i. e. not more than six persons to four rooms. For clothing the minimum was set at an allowance of $100 for the assumed family of five persons; expenditures for washing being included in this sum.

For our present purpose the accuracy of these estimates of a minimum requirement for physical efficiency does not concern us, but only the variations in the departures from them that appear in the several income-groups. Measured by these standards, of the families with incomes between $400 and $500 all are underfed, 88 per cent. are underclad, 63 per cent. are overcrowded. That is, the want of shelter is being satisfied at the expense of food and clothing. In the next income-group ($500-$600), the underfed are 65 per cent., the underclothed, as before, 88 per cent., the overcrowded, 71 per cent. In paying more attention to the need for food, less attention is paid to shelter. A higher rental is paid, but more persons are crowded into the accommodations offered. In the next income-group ($600-700) the underfed have fallen to 33 per cent., the underclad to 63 per cent., the overcrowded to 57 per cent. For every income-group thereafter, the overcrowded families preponderate over both the other classes. Even in the $1,100 income-group 21 per cent. are overcrowded, but none underfed and only 6 per cent. underclad. These figures, taken as a whole, imply that the most urgent need at the minimum income is for shelter, out-clamoring not hunger perhaps, but at least the want of adequate food. With a larger income a pause can be set to the desire for better housing, while more attention is given to the providing of food. With an income still larger, of nine hundred dollars and above, the deficiencies in diet are supplied, and at ten hundred dollars the minimum allowance for clothing has been attained by practically all the families. Not even at this point, however, does the desire for adequate housing, at the price which must be paid for it, suffice to persuade more than three-fourths of the families to go without enough of other things to secure it.

Another alternative to expansion of expenditures, for whatever purpose, as income increases, is saving. Saving becomes easier, as income increases. But the point where savings begin is not necessarily the point where a standard even of physical efficiency is attained. There are families that save at the expense not only of comfort, but even of health, and there are families that no increase of income would induce to save. Of the underfed families just alluded to, one-half reported a surplus of income over expenditure of at least $25; 65 per cent. of the families reckoned as underclothed, and 44 per cent. of the overcrowded likewise reported such a surplus. When this is compared with the percentage of all families that reported a surplus, namely 36.5, it seems fair to infer that the desire to save repressed expenditures to meet actual physical necessities.

On the other hand, by no means all families on a larger income preferred saving to spending. Not until $1,300 is reached is there a constant increase in the number of families that report a surplus of income over expenditures. This indicates that there are Micawbers on large incomes as there are misers on small incomes, but also that the social influences of New York City, at least, encourage adding to the good things included in standards of living quite as much as they encourage saving. The proportion of savers among the Russian and Italian families was found to be much higher than among families of more thoroughly Americanized stock.

On the whole the conclusions drawn from the New York investigation substantiate the restatement of Engel's "laws" given by Stephan Bauer in his article "Konsumtionsbudget" in Conrad's *Handwörterbuch*, as follows:

With increase of income:

1. The proportion spent for food, especially for vegetable food, falls.
2. The proportion saved constantly increases.

3. The proportion spent for housing, fuel, light, falls until a certain income is reached, then remains constant or increases.

4. The proportion spent for animal food, drink, clothing, culture, and recreation rises until a certain income is reached, then remains constant or falls.

II. Source of Income.—The real standard of life enjoyed by a family is profoundly influenced by the sources from which its income is derived. To explain, let me make a classification, on the basis primarily of amount of income, of the relation of income to family life. Let us consider five classes:

1. The income is so small that the family cannot be maintained, but is broken up. Our charitable societies are only too familiar with cases of this kind. The father is incapacitated by accident or disease, or the supplementary earnings of other members of the family are cut off—from whatever cause, the income is diminished to a point where it is so far below the needs of the case that unless liberal relief is given the family must be broken up and the children provided for outside of the home.

2. The income is inadequate to the maintenance of a normal standard, but the family is kept together, living on a plane below the requirements for the working efficiency of the parents and the healthful bringing up of the children. It is possible to maintain life for a long time on a diet of bread and tea. Human beings can exist although sleeping three or four in a room. Dr. Foreman's budgets of the Washington poor contained instances of regular underfeeding for one week in each month—the week in which the monthly rent had to be paid. The figures already cited regarding underfed and overcrowded families, even on incomes of $700 and $800 are evidence that cases of this class are only too frequent. The outcome in the long run is the early extinction of the family under the attacks of disease, or race deterioration, as in the case of the London "hooligan."

3. The income adequate in amount, but adequate because the wages of the father are supplemented by the earnings of his wife and children. Such a family may maintain a normal standard, providing the children are fairly of working age and are not overworked. But where the mother's employment takes her away

from the home and where the children are set to work too young, the real standard of living is lowered. The family income cannot be as wisely expended when the mother is away all day, and the addition of outside employment to the woman's domestic work makes a burden that often impairs her health. The earlier a child goes regularly to work, the more is cut off from his rightful inheritance of opportunity to improve upon his father's standard of living.

4. The income adequate in amount, but made adequate by taking in lodgers or boarders. This case is similar to the preceding, and the effect upon the solidarity of the family, economic considerations aside, is hardly less deplorable. The taking of lodgers not only introduces outsiders into the midst of the family, but it frequently means an impairment of a normal standard in the matter of housing. Recent investigations have brought out the facts regarding the crowding of many tenements with lodgers. The relative frequency of the practice is perhaps indicated by the fact that one-half of the families included in the investigation of the New York Conference Committee were taking lodgers. The proportion increased with the increase in amount paid for rent—23 per cent. of families paying from ten to fourteen dollars a month for rent took lodgers, but they were taken by 62 per cent. of the families paying over sixteen dollars a month. The results in overcrowding are shown in the fact that 70 per cent. of the families having lodgers were reported as below our arbitrary standard of housing accommodations.

5. Families with adequate income, derived from sources such that the well-being of the family is not impaired. These families are the only ones that can be said to have reached a decent standard of living. They are the only ones in which the children have a "white man's chance" for the future. They are, for the most part, families supported by the father alone, or by children who are far enough along to handle their own wages and pay their own board into the family treasury. The number of families where the father really supports the family is not so large, among the wage-earners of our American cities, as is popularly supposed. Especially in those occupations where men's wages are not over

two dollars a day they are the exception, not the rule.   Forty-eight of the laborers, teamsters, and garment workers included in the New York Committee's report, gave in a family income of from eight to ten hundred dollars; but in thirty-eight cases the father's earnings were supplemented from other sources.   In almost every compilation of working-men's budgets that has been published in this country, has appeared the same frequency of composite incomes among families reporting the higher amounts for total income.   Further, among the families with composite income the proportion of underfed and of families reporting deficit is greater than among the whole number of families.   This means, of course, that the family of a man with a six-hundred-dollar wage can maintain a standard that calls for an expenditure of eight hundred dollars only by endangering the integrity of the family life by taking lodgers or sending mother and children out to work.   In other words the standard of wages does not reach the standard of living.

The influence of income on standard of living, therefore, may be traced in reference both to amount and sources of income.   As the amount of income increases expenditures increase most rapidly along the line of the strongest desire, unsatisfied hitherto. This desire is likely to be the desire for better food, then for better clothing and shelter, until what may be called a saturation point for these essentials has been reached.   As this point is approached, expenditures for things not connected with immediate material subsistence claim a larger share of the income, and finally increase most rapidly of all.   A minimum point is fixed by the environment natural and social.   The education of the particular family, the custom of its social equals, are the forces that determine at what point above the subsistence minimum the income will be diverted from physical satisfaction to the meeting of higher wants.   The maintenance of a decent standard depends on the father's earning, in ordinary cases, enough to meet the wants of the family until the children are really fit to go to work.   When the father's earnings have to be supplemented by the earnings of others, or by taking lodgers, the standard of life is lowered and the integrity of the family is imperiled.

THE FAMILY IN A TYPICAL MILL TOWN

MARGARET F. BYINGTON
Member of the Staff of the Pittsburg Survey

The effect of our industrial system on family life is in most cities rendered indefinite by the pressure of complicating factors. In a small community, however, which is dependent on a single industry, the factors of the problem are simplified, and therefore the relation is clearer and the conclusions more obvious.

For this reason I venture to offer a very simple and concrete description of the type of family and the conditions of family life in a steel-mill town, believing that it may serve at least as an illustration for this afternoon's discussion. The facts offered are the result of a six months' investigation as to the cost of living in Homestead, and are, I believe, true in the main of the steel towns of the Pittsburg district.

When, in 1881, Klomans started to build a small steel mill, he located it in a little village seven miles from Pittsburg, appropriately enough called Homestead. The industrial development of the city had seemed too remote to affect it. But the mill became a part of the United States Steel Corporation and is now the largest steel plant in the world, while the village, which has grown with it, now has a population of about 25,000. Not only did the initial impulse of the town's growth come from the mill, but throughout the industry has, for two reasons, definitely determined Homestead's development—one, that, as there is no other considerable industry in the town, the men are dependent for occupation on the mill; the other, that, since the strike of 1892, when the power of the Amalgamated Association came to an end, the corporation has, by its decisions as to wage and hours of labor, determined practically without hindrance the conditions under which the men live. Because of these two factors we may consider that the social and economic institutions of Homestead are typical of those which a powerful organized industry is likely to develop, a statement limited by the fact that conditions would be very different in a community where the prevailing industry was of another type.

The conditions to be discussed are simplified by a marked homogeneity of type in the families of Homestead, in itself a result of the industrial situation. Marked distinctions of wealth are totally absent. Two groups do indeed exist with different standards and no common interests; the Slavs and the English-speaking workers; but this distinction is of race rather than of wealth. The Slavs are usually day laborers, while the majority of the English-speaking men are skilled or semi-skilled, but in spite of these differences both groups are wage-earners. Even the number of professional men is not as large as in a town farther from a city, while the owners of the mill—the stockholders—scattered throughout the country, knowing their property only as a source of dividends, have no part or interest in the town's development. As a result, this town of working-men has not the lack of mutual understanding resulting from great differences in wealth and standards, but neither has it the stimulus which comes from the presence and leadership of men of education with leisure. What the town offers is what the working-people have created for themselves under the conditions imposed by the industry.

From the standpoint of family development probably the most significant fact about the town is that it offers work for men only. Aside from the steel mill and one machine shop, the only work in the town is in providing for the needs of the workers, with but chance work for women. As Pittsburg is a 45 minutes' car ride distant the work it offers is not easily available. The wage in the mill, moreover, though by no means abundant, is fair and steady. The laborer earns at a minimum rate of 16½ cents an hour, $1.65 a day, while the semi-skilled or skilled workers earn from $2.00 to $4.00, and occasionally as high as $5.00 or $6.00 a day.

The work is in addition regular. From the panic of 1893 to that of 1907, I am told that the mill was not shut down for a single day. The day men, therefore, who are paid their full wage unless the mill actually closes, have a steady income the year round, except in periods of industrial depression. The tonnage men, who are paid according to output, do feel even a temporary cutting-down of orders, but as they are the ones who ordinarily receive the highest pay, the occasional lessening of their wage is not so disastrous.

As a result of these factors the town in general seems to have adopted the position that the women should stay at home, and, by good housekeeping, make the money go a long way, rather than go out to work and earn a little more. This is shown concretely in the incomes of those families whose budgets were secured for the investigation. Among the English-speaking people the husbands and sons contributed 92.8 per cent. among the native whites—practically the entire income, and 94.6 per cent. among the English-speaking Europeans. There was no income from the work of women unless one would so consider what was received from lodgers. This constituted 4.6 per cent. of the total income in the European group, and 2.7 per cent. among the native white.

We find, then, that as a result of the kind of work offered the town consists of a group of working-men's families; the man is the breadwinner. The effect of the industrial situation is further shown in the work of the children. The girls show little more tendency than their mothers to become wage-earners. In the thirty-eight English-speaking families there were fifteen girls over fourteen, not one of whom was at work. Four were in the high school, the remainder at home helping with the housework. While this is probably an extreme figure, as some girls in Homestead do go to work in stores or offices, it reveals a general feeling in the town that "the home is woman's sphere." While one may question whether from the standpoint of the present the additional income from the girl's wages would not add more to the comfort of the family than her help in the household, from my acquaintance with housekeepers of all sorts I am convinced that good home training is invaluable in preparing girls for their own homes later. The four champion housekeepers of my acquaintance were the daughters of Pennsylvania farmers. One of them, when I expressed my surprise at how much more she had accomplished than others with the same income, gave as the reason for her success, that girls who had been in stores or factories had no training in management and were quite helpless when they faced a housekeeper's problems.

The situation as far as the sons are concerned is somewhat different. Fifteen of the seventeen boys over fourteen were at work contributing among the whites 9.6 per cent., and among the English-speaking Europeans 18 per cent. of the total income. Though the other two boys were still in the high school, we find on the whole a marked absence of interest in academic or even in technical training for these sons. As the daughters, instead of learning trades, are at home becoming practical housekeepers under their mothers' direction, so the sons, following in their fathers' footsteps, are entering directly into the practical work of the mill to get there the training for future success. That the best-paid men in the mill, such as rollers and heaters, have secured their jobs through experience in the mill rather than through outside training has doubtless much to do with this attitude. Through the influence of the fathers, the boys sometimes get what are known as pencil jobs, or other places where the work is light and apparently more gentlemanly, but where the pay is seldom so high. Usually, however, they begin in the regular boy's work, as messenger-boys in the yards, or door-openers. Though these give no special training for the future, as the line of promotion is usually open a boy has a good chance of becoming at least a semi-skilled workman on fair pay. Promotion is sometimes unduly rapid, however, so that boys of 16 or 18 are earning men's wages, with little chance of further promotion. One woman who regretted that her son had not learned a trade, said that he was unwilling to go through a long apprenticeship when in the mill he could earn good pay at once. In spite of the fact that because of long hours and the danger from accident, women often wish their sons to take some other work, they usually do go into the mill. This means that as for some years they stay at home and contribute their share to the family income, they create a period of economic prosperity.

The family is at this time often able to make extra provision for the future, as, for instance, buying a house.

We find then that the industry has by its very nature helped to create a type of family life. But in those factors where it has a choice open to it such as wages and hours, has it by its decisions, made possible for these families a genuine home life, a carrying out of their ideals for themselves? For two facts must be considered in any study of standards of living, one the limitations or opportunities from without, which the family cannot affect, the other those family ideals, sometimes limited in themselves, sometimes hampered by outside forces, which are continually struggling toward realization. How far are Homestead's ideals realizable on the pay the mill offers?

It is impossible in the limits of this discussion to consider at all in detail the results of the budget investigation in Homestead. Figures are too complicated without elaborate explanations. A few facts however may be used in this general discussion.

To my mind, the fundamental fact brought out by the investigation was, that, the question of expenditure is always one of choices, of doing without some things in order to get others. This may seem axiomatic, but when applied to a wage of less than $12 a week it expresses pretty much the whole problem of life. Do we find that in order to carry out ideals of home life, such as having an attractive house, making due provision for the future, or buying a house, certain absolute essentials must be gone without? Any study of the budgets of families receiving less than $12 a week, or even those earning from $12 to $15 demonstrates very clearly that this is the case. As the unskilled men, who earn $10 and $12 a week, compose 58 per cent. of the employees, it is worth while to consider briefly the problem which this large percentage of Homestead's population is facing.

To indicate its extent I will give the average expenses of 40 families with an income of less than $12 a week. Of a total expenditure of $530 a year, $241 goes for food; $103 for rent; $50 for clothing; $18 for furniture; $25 for fuel; $11 for medical care, and $13 for tobacco and liquor. In addition an average of $38 was spent annually for insurance, leaving but $31 a year for amusements of all sorts, church expenses, savings, and the necessary sundries. Now obviously no one of these items is adequate, to say nothing of being superabundant. Rent, for example, at $2 a week provides only a two-room tenement, and that without water or toilet in the house. Food at $4.64 a week would mean for a family of five, only 20 cents a day, two cents a day less than Prof. Chittenden estimates as absolutely essential in New York. Fifty dollars for clothing is just one-half the sum Mr. Chapin gives as necessary. The tobacco and liquor item which is especially large among the Slavs, could, of course, be cut with profit, but in no other way can that pitiably small sum of $31 be increased. Yet from that sum savings must come if there are to be any.

The different nationalities meet this problem in varying ways according to their ideals. Among the native white families a comfortable home is an essential proof of respectability. Consequently we find that they spend for rent 21.2 per cent. as against 16.4 per cent. among the Slavs. On the other hand, the Slav spends 54.3 per cent. for food, while the native whites spend but 44.7 per cent. That is, the Slavic family will have enough food anyway, while the American demands a big enough house. Inadequate food or bad housing alike endanger physical efficiency, while with overcrowding any semblance of home life becomes impossible. In neither group is there any margin for amusements.

It is not a question of good management. The cleverest housekeeper I know was doing marvelously on $14 a week, and the following statement of her average expenditure for 8 weeks, shows how she did it: Food $7.05; clothing .57; household expenses .59; rent $2.50; insurance and lodge dues .65; church and charity .09; recreation and spending money .03; doctor $1.46; sundries .35. Though, as you may see, she was keeping the unessential elements of expenditure at their lowest point, her food-supply was still quite inadequate. I found by a rough estimate that it was deficient about 20 per cent. in both proteida and calories. The budget revealed a wise choice of foods aside from a possibly extravagant expenditure for fresh fruit and vegetables.

If a skilful woman of Pennsylvania Dutch stock cannot manage on this wage, what can be expected of the average housekeeper?

The necessity of facing these problems three times a day has its effect also on the overtaxed mother. One woman, who on an income of from $2 to $3 a day was providing for five children, had bought a small farm and was carrying heavy insurance. In order to accomplish this, she told me, she must not spend even five cents for a visit to the nickleodeon. When she described to me her hunts for bargains and her long hours of sewing to make her girls presentable, I did not wonder that she had the reputation of being a cranky person.

These two women were Americans, but by far the largest majority of the laborers are Slavs, and it is among them that we find the worst results of the low wage.

The mill has sent out a call for young vigorous men who will do its heavy work for a small wage. In answer to this has come a great number of Slavic immigrants. As is often true of a new group most of these men are either single or with families in the old country. Of the 3,602 Slavs in the mill, 1,099 or 30.5 per cent. were single men. This has had a disastrous effect on the family life of the Slavs, for these men usually board in families of their own nationality who live in the wretched courts in the Second Ward of Homestead. A study made of 21 of these courts revealed appalling conditions. Among the 239 families living there, the 102 who took lodgers had on an average four persons to a room. Fifty-one of these families—more than one-fifth—lived in one room. The two-room tenements were not infrequently occupied by a man, his wife, two children, and two or three boarders. Under these conditions any genuine family life becomes impossible.

The death-rate among the children is high, twice as high as in the other wards of Homestead. Moreover, training children under these conditions is difficult and a terrible knowledge of evil results from the close mingling of the children with this group of careless, drinking men.

Aside from the presence of these single men and a growth of population with which the number of houses has not kept pace, the overcrowding is due to the dominant ambition of the Slav to own a bit of property here or in the old country, or to have a bank account. As we have seen, strenuous economies are necessary if their desires are to be attained. That it is ambition rather than a permanently low standard which is responsible for the bad conditions is shown by the comfort and even good taste displayed by some who have succeeded in buying their own homes.

These people do need, however, to have impressed upon their minds the value of education. As there is no effective school enumeration, and the responsibility is divided between the public and parochial schools, it is easy enough, where the parents are indifferent, for the children to drift away from regular attendance. As the steel mill with its heavy work and enormous machinery cannot utilize the work of children there is almost no labor problem in Homestead, but usually as soon as the children are fourteen they start in to work.

Between ignorance and ambition these newcomers are failing to secure for themselves or their children a real home life, that would result either in the physical or moral efficiency of the next generation.

The mill which demands strong, cheap labor concerns itself but little whether that labor is provided with living conditions that will maintain its efficiency or secure the efficiency of the next generation. The housing situation is in the hands of men actuated only by a desire for the largest possible profit. More intelligent members of the community, on the other hand, though realizing the situation, do not take their responsibility for the aliens in their midst with sufficient seriousness to limit the power of these landlords. The Slavs, moreover, people used to the limitations of country life, are ignorant of the evil physical and moral effect of transferring the small rooms, the overcrowding, the insufficient sanitary provisions which may be endurable in country life with all outdoors about them, to these crowded courts under the shadow of the mill.

Summing up the results of indifference on one side and ignorance on the other, we find a high infant death-rate, a knowledge of evil among little children, intolerable sanitary conditions, a low standard of living, a failure of the community to assimilate this new race in its midst.

As we waited in one of the little railroad stations in Homestead, a Slavak came in and sat down next to a woman and her two-year-old child. He began making shy advances to the baby, and coaxing her in a voice of heart-breaking loneliness. But she would not come to him, and finally the two left the room. As they went he turned to the rest of the company, and in a tone of sadness, taking us all into his confidence said simply, "Me wife, me babe Hungar." But were they here it would mean death for one baby in three, it would mean hard work in a dirty, unsanitary house for the wife, it would mean sickness and much evil. With them away, it means for him isolation and loneliness and the abnormal life of the crowded lodging-house.

While this low wage, either among Slavs or Americans, is insufficient to maintain a standard of physical efficiency, the industry adds further that element of uncertainty for the future so destructive to ambitions and plans. Accidents are frequent. Even though they are not often fatal, one that lays a man up even for two weeks has a disastrous effect on a slender surplus. One family had saved $300 to buy a house, but when the man was injured by a weight falling on his feet, and was laid up for six weeks, $80 went from the surplus. Soon after, when last winter's hard times came, practically all the savings had to go for food. Now the family wonders whether, with all these possibilities of disaster, it will ever dare to put all its savings into a house.

In addition, cuts in wages are made periodically. As these most frequently affect the better-paid men, even they cannot start out on any plan involving any number of years without realizing that before the end of the time conditions may have changed so as to make its carrying out impossible.

By the 12-hour shift as well as by the low wage the mill is affecting the lives of these families. Though the long hours and hard work may seem to be hardships that only the man would feel, they do react on family life. Not only do his weariness and his irregular hours make him less inclined to enter into the family pleasures, but he also fails to change, through political or other action, the conditions under which they live. Because of this weariness-induced apathy, a man usually stays at home and smokes his pipe instead of troubling himself with outside affairs. This tendency is doubtless intensified by conditions within the industry. As since the strike of 1892 there have been no labor organizations in the town, the men do not meet to discuss the conditions under which they work, and accept passively whatever is offered. This same indifference seems to affect their attitude toward politics, so that instead of taking an active part they allow the wholesale liquor interests to dominate. Yet, through schools and through sanitation, the political situation does bear a close relation to family problems. In Homestead, for instance, the drinking water comes, only partly filtered, from a river which has already received the sewage of a number of towns and cities. The man continues to go three times a day for water from a neighbor's well and pay him 50 cents a month for the privilege instead of insisting that the borough provide a decent supply. There are no ordinances requiring landlords to place water or toilets in the houses, though the family are longing for the day when they can move to a house with these conveniences. An industrial situation which creates an attitude so passive that men accept, without protest, perfectly remediable evils that immediately affect the family, is a serious one.

These long hours have a further harm in their tendency to lessen the demand for amusement. Aside from roller-skating rinks and the five-cent variety shows known as nickleodeons, there is, outside of the home, no real chance for amusement save the ever present light and refreshment offered by the fifty or more saloons which Homestead licenses. The mothers, who realize that the rinks are a source of danger to the girls, and the saloons an ever-present menace to family happiness, make a heroic and often pathetic effort to keep the home attractive enough to offset these temptations. While the results are perhaps not undesirable when the mother succeeds, every woman is not a genius, and when she fails there is little wholesome amusement to compensate for her failure. The people do not want this provided for them by philanthropy. When speaking of the Carnegie

library, men often said to me "We didn't want him to build a
library for us, we would rather have had higher wages and spent
the money for ourselves." Aside from the money, and the
margin for amusements, as we have seen, is painfully small, they
need the leisure to plan and enjoy. The town offers to its in-
habitants the chance to work but it gives them little chance to
play. And yet play is essential if even physical efficiency is to be
maintained.

To sum up the situation then, we find that the mill by the
nature of the work offered helps to develop a normal family type,
but because of low wages, long hours, and opposition to industrial
organization, it has done much to hamper the family in carrying
out its ideals.

May I in conclusion state briefly what facts as to the relation
of family to industrial life were clarified in my own mind by this
investigation? In the first place, in a town dominated by one
industry the type of family is largely determined by the nature
of that industry. Theoretical discussions as to the normal family
have little effect, even the ideals of individual families must often
be modified to meet this situation. In a cotton-mill town, for
example, we are almost sure to find the women at work, while
in a steel town it is the man's place to earn and the woman's to
spend. This relation, obscured in commercial or large manufacturing centers, stands out clearly in Homestead with its one
industry.

In the second place, the industry limits the development of
the family life by the effect of long hours and overwork, and the
absence of the stimulus which trades unions might supply.
These react on the family, not only in the man's personal attitude toward them, but through his failure by political or other
united action, to improve the conditions under which they live.

The most obvious and fundamental relation of industry and
family is the economic one. Without the background of a sufficient wage, even such distinct domestic virtues as thrift become
not only impossible but harmful. If to buy a house means to
underfeed the children; if to have a bank account means to take
lodgers till there is no possibility of home life, we are certainly

foolish to laud the man who realizes these ambitions, and class as extravagant and thriftless those who do not. Our preaching must have a closer relation to the economic situation of the families.

In years gone by the family was the industrial unit, the work was done in the house, was close to the problem of the home, and the two developed together. The family ties were strong and the industrial conditions strengthened them. Now the situation is changed, and the industry is dominant. More and more the very nature of the family, its ideals, and its every-day existence are alike molded by the opportunities for work. If we are to keep any abstract ideals of what family life should be, and are to translate these into actualities, our primary query must be whether our industrial system makes them possible. Without the development of the personal virtues economic prosperity might be futile, but the converse is also true. In Homestead at least, I believe, there are more ideals than the industrial situation allows to become realities.

RESULTS OF THE PITTSBURGH SURVEY

EDWARD T. DEVINE
New York City, N. Y.

The Pittsburgh Survey represents one way of studying family life in an industrial and urban community. The method of personal observation by an individual investigator is obviously inadequate to such an undertaking. Life is too short, prejudices too ineradicable, individual qualifications too specialized, the personal equation too disturbing, to permit any single individual however gifted to see for himself the community as a whole, and to measure the influences and forces that shape the family destiny. The writer who boasts that he has known many cities, if by that he means that he has known them intimately by the method of first-hand observation, invites distrust. The Chicago stockyards district alone, or the lower East Side of New York, or the Pittsburgh steel district, affords a problem too complex and difficult for any single-handed observer and reporter of social conditions. Individual inquiry and personal interpretation have brought us a certain distance but they cannot take us much farther. Their limitations have suggested the plan which we have tried in the experiment the results of which you have asked us to lay before you. That plan is in a word to organize a staff to survey the community as a whole, a group working under common direction, and rapidly enough so that the results refer to a particular period and to relatively definite conditions which can be clearly described.

Whether in this first experiment we have succeeded is of course still to be determined, but this was the underlying idea of the Pittsburgh Survey. In attempting thus to reckon at once with the many factors of the life of a great industrial community, we may not have been able to go so deeply into most of them as, for example, special inquiries have gone into tuberculosis, child labor, housing, or the standard of living; although on the other hand we may have gone into others, such as the cost of typhoid, the effect of industrial accidents, the status of the steel workers, the boarding-boss system, and the place of women in modern industries, more deeply than has heretofore been attempted. In any case our main purpose has been to offer a structural exhibit of the community as a whole and not to make an exhaustive investigation of any one of its aspects. We have not dealt with the political mechanism, and we have not to any great extent dealt with vice, intemperance, or the institutions by which the community undertakes to control them. We have dealt in the main with the wage-earning population, first in its industrial relations, and second in its social relations to the community as a whole.

There are certain immediate, tangible results in Pittsburgh. An Associated Charities, an increased force of sanitary inspectors, a comprehensive housing census, a typhoid commission, and a permanent civic improvement commission are certainly very tangible and striking results, especially as they are in the nature of by-products to an investigation concerning which very little has as yet been published.

These developments, however, interesting and gratifying as they are from the point of view of social progress in the community, are probably not the results of the survey which are in your minds, as you forecast this discussion. I take it that what is of interest to the Economic Association and the Sociological Society, is rather the answer to the question: Have you really found out anything about Pittsburgh that we did not know perfectly well before? What are the results of your survey for students of society and of industry? The discoveries, then, which I have to report, are as follows, taking the adverse results first:

I. An altogether incredible amount of overwork by everybody, reaching its extreme in the twelve-hour shift for seven days in the week in the steel mills and the railway switchyards.

II. Low wages for the great majority of the laborers employed by the mills, not lower than in other large cities, but low compared with the prices—so low as to be inadequate to the maintenance of a normal American standard of living: wages adjusted to the single man, not to the responsible head of a family.

III. Still lower wages for women, who receive for example in one of the metal trades, in which the proportion of women is great enough to be menacing, one-half as much as unorganized men in the same shops and one-third as much as the men in the union.

IV. An absentee capitalism, with bad effects strikingly analogous to those of absentee landlordism, of which also Pittsburgh furnishes noteworthy examples.

V. A continuous inflow of immigrants with low standards, attracted by a wage which is high by the standards of southeastern Europe, and which yields a net pecuniary advantage because of abnormally low expenditures for food and shelter, and inadequate provision for sickness, accident, and death.

VI. The destruction of family life, not in any imaginary or mystical sense, but by the demands of the day's work, and by the very demonstrable and material method of typhoid fever and industrial accidents, both preventable, but costing last year in Pittsburgh considerably more than a thousand lives, and irretrievably shattering many homes.

VII. Archaic social institutions such as the aldermanic court, the ward school district, the family garbage disposal, and the unregenerate charitable institution, still surviving after the conditions to which they were adapted have disappeared.

VIII. The contrast—which does not become blurred by familiarity with detail, but on the contrary becomes more vivid as the outlines are filled in—the contrast between the prosperity on the one hand of the most prosperous of all the communities of our western civilization, with its vast natural resources, the generous fostering of government, the human energy, the technical development, the gigantic tonnage of the mines and mills, the enormous capital of which the bank balances afford an indication, and, on the other hand, the neglect of life, of health, of physical vigor, even of the industrial efficiency of the individual. Certainly no community before in America or Europe has ever had such a surplus, and never before has a great community applied what it had so meagerly to the rational purposes of human life. Not by gifts of libraries, galleries, technical schools, and parks, but by the cessation of toil one day in seven and sixteen hours in the twenty-four, by the increase of wages, by the sparing of lives, by the prevention of accidents, and by raising the standards of domestic life, should the surplus come back to the people of the community in which it is created.

As we turn the typewritten pages of these reports and as we get behind them to the cards of original memoranda on which they are based, and as we get behind them again to the deepest and most clearly defined impressions made in the year and a half on the minds of the members of the investigating staff, it is the first and the last of these results that we see more clearly than any others—the twelve-hour day, and social neglect. Sunday work and night work are but another expression, as it were, of the same principle of long hours of overwork, of which the typical and persistent expression is the twelve-hour shift. Nothing else explains so much in the industrial and social situation in the Pittsburgh district as the twelve-hour day—which is in fact for half the year, the twelve-hour night. Everything else is keyed up to it. Foremen and superintendents, and ultimately directors and financiers, are subject to its law. There are no doubt bankers and teachers and bricklayers in Pittsburgh who work less, but the general law of the region is desperate, unremitting toil— extending in some large industries to twelve hours, for six days one week, and eight days the next. There is no seventh day save as it is stolen from sleep. There are of course occupations, as in the blast furnaces, in which there are long waits between the spurts of brief, intense expenditure of energy, but the total effect of the day is as I have described.

For the effect, as well as for the causes of the twelve-hour day, and for a more exact statement of its extent, its limitations, and the exceptions, I must refer to the reports. We have attempted to trace the influence of the great contest of 1892, and of the incoming waves of immigration, to indicate the effect of the long day on the length of the working life, on industrial efficiency, on home life, on citizenship. When it has all been done, however, the unadorned fact that in our most highly developed industrial community, where the two greatest individual fortunes in history have been made, and where the foundations of the two most powerful business corporations have been laid, the mass of the workers in the master industry are driven as large numbers of laborers, whether slave or free, have scarcely before in human history been driven, is surely an extraordinary fact. I do not mean to suggest that the conditions of employment are less desirable than under a system of slavery. What I mean is merely that the inducement to a constantly increased output and a constant acceleration of pace is greater than has heretofore been devised. By a nice adjustment of piece wages and time wages, so that where the "boss" or "pusher," as he is known in the mills, controls, time wages prevail, and where the individual worker controls, piece wages prevail; by the resistless operation of organized control at one point, and the effort to recover earnings reduced by skilful cuts of piece wages at another; by the danger of accident, and the lure of the pay which seems high by old-country standards, the pace is kept, is accelerated, and again maintained. There is one result and there is no other like it.

All of these results of the survey, relating to overwork, low wages, immigration, destruction of families, archaic institutions, and indifference to adverse living conditions, appear to me worthy of your very careful consideration. They are presented without exaggeration or prejudice in the papers that have been written and in the fuller reports that are to follow. It is possible that yellow journalism would find here some justification. When Mr. Brisbane the other day gloried in the yellowness of his newspaper, chuckled over the unsuccessful attempts at imitation by other journals, compared his color effects with the Almighty's painting of a lurid sunset, and reached his climax by expressing regret that they had not yet been able to make a noise resembling thunder, I confess that having in mind the unpublished records of our Pittsburgh Survey, I had a momentary pang of regret that we were not in position to set them free by some such methods as those which Mr. Brisbane so unblushingly defends. The reading of a paper in a scientific society and the publication of a few special numbers of *Charities* seem inadequate. However, we must accept the limitations along with the great advantages of the media in which it has pleased Providence to permit us to work. I proceed to present other facts which I would not wish to classify as either adverse or favorable, and to give a brief and inadequate enumeration of the distinctly favorable indications.

Outside the mills, the wages of ordinary day laborers in the Pittsburgh district are from $1.50 to $1.75 for a ten-hour day. The municipality pays more: $1.75 to $2 for eight hours. In skilled trades, in seasonal trades, and in thoroughly unionized trades, compensation is higher. The level toward which wages tend is $9 to $10 for a sixty-hour week. Common laborers in the mines, because of their union, earn from 50 to 90 per cent. more by the hour than laborers of a similar grade outside. Motormen and conductors, under their union agreement, earn 25 per cent. more per hour than teamsters, although their occupation requires no more time in which to become proficient. In the building trades, which are seasonal and organized, the wages are $3.40 to $5.20 for eight hours; and in the metal trades, which are continuous and partly organized, wages are $2.75 to $4 a day of nine or ten hours. The destruction of unionism in the steel mills has had effects which are too far-reaching and important for brief summary here, but they are described by Mr. Fitch in the reports with thoroughness and a wealth of illustrative detail. In general I may say that the low wages of unskilled immigrant labor are higher than they were fifteen years ago, but that the wages of skilled labor formerly organized are lower.

Though it may seem extravagant, I am inclined to claim for the survey the discovery of the Slav as a human being, though I do not overlook the scientific studies of Dr. Steiner or the illuminating articles which we have previously published in *Charities* from Miss Balch on the Slavs in Europe and in America. I refer here, however, more especially to Mr. Koukol's study of his compatriots, his analysis of their character, their attitude toward America, and the effect on them of such conditions as those under which they live and work in Pittsburgh and the neighboring mill towns. Over one-half of the workers in the steel mills are Slavs, and in the total immigration Slavs are one of the three largest racial elements which we are now absorbing into our population. An anomalous feature of this whole situation is that our greatest industrial community should thus be dependent on the supply of able-bodied laborers from agricultural communities five thousand miles distant.

On the credit side of the account there are at least the following considerations:

I. The adverse conditions are, after all, conditions which naturally, or at least not infrequently, accompany progress. They are incidents of the production of wealth on a vast scale. They are remediable whenever the community thinks it worth while to remedy them. If the hardships and misery which we find in Pittsburgh were due to poverty of resources, to the unproductivity of toil, then the process of overcoming them might indeed be tedious and discouraging. Since they are due to haste in acquiring wealth, to inequity in distribution, to the inadequacy of the mechanism of municipal government, they can be overcome rapidly if the community so desires.

II. There are many indications that the community is awakening to these adverse conditions and that it is even now ready to deal with some of them. I have already cited instances of new movements in this direction, and the detailed reports cite many other favorable signs. The arrest of councilmen and bankers for bribery may for a time divert attention from the improvement of conditions to the prosecution of individual malefactors. But this interruption to fundamental social reform may serve to strengthen the determination of citizens who see what work is to be done, and that the city administration is courageously undertaking it, to defer the anticipated reversion to ordinary machine politics and its corrupt alliance with predatory business interests.

III. It is fair to point out as a favorable result of the inquiry that there is an increasing number, including the mayor and other city officials, officers of corporations, business men, social workers, and others, who are entirely ready to enter with others and with one another on the dispassionate search for causes and remedies, recognizing that the adverse conditions are there, recognizing that distinction lies not in ostrich-like refusal to see them, but in statesman-like willingness to gauge them and to understand them, and so far as it is possible to remove them. Pittsburgh is unique only in the extent to which tendencies observable everywhere have here actually, because of high industrial development, and great industrial activity, had the opportunity to give tangible proofs of their real character and inevitable goal.

IV. It will be made apparent also when the survey publishes its findings that in the period immediately preceding the undertaking there had been several noteworthy advances in Pittsburgh. A reform mayor had been elected. Greater Pittsburgh, with Allegheny as the principal accession, had been decreed, and incidentally in this process one of the most conspicuous of our national "fences" for thieves and other criminals had been thrown down. Plans had been made for a suitable civic celebration of the one hundred and fiftieth anniversary of the founding of the city. The administration, with the co-operation of smoke manufacturers, had entered upon a death grapple with the smoke nuisance. A big boulevard system had been created, and a five-and-a-half-million-dollar filtration plant had been installed.

The net result of the survey, so far as it throws light on the inquiry formulated on the programme, whether modern industry and city life are unfavorable to the family, is to suggest an affirmative answer. Very unfavorable, very disastrous consequences are clearly discernible. Whether they are inseparable from industrial life in the city is for the future to determine. Yellow journalism, one very crude but not altogether ineffective method of popular education as to certain of the unfavorable effects of modern industry, we reject as not consistent with our traditions. As a corrective, we shall do well to utilize in the classroom and in serious discussion such material as is furnished by the Pittsburgh Survey and by other similar inquiries. Assuming accuracy in the field and suitable editorial revision, it is within bounds to say that we shall soon know more about Pittsburgh than we have known about any other of our American industrial communities. That in itself is something, but our chief interest in that result will lie in the stimulus which happily it may give to the desire and the determination to learn as much or more by similar or by better methods about other communities.

ARE MODERN INDUSTRY AND CITY LIFE UNFAVOR-ABLE TO THE FAMILY?

PROFESSOR CHARLES RICHMOND HENDERSON
The University of Chicago

The essence of the question under discussion.—It is *not:* Is life in an industrial city more unfavorable to the family than it formerly was, i. e., are we advancing? Nor, Is life in an industrial city more unfavorable to sound family life than country residence? but rather, What are the facts about urban conditions which have a harmful tendency, and are these conditions necessarily inherent in urban organization of industry or are they capable of improvement by known means? If not by known means then at what points should we direct and concentrate our investigations? It is not necessary here to reiterate the proof that the cities are growing rapidly in all parts of the civilized world, nor to explain the movement cityward. This is already familiar to all. If any tendency is part of destiny and fate this seems to be such. Even when people are perfectly aware of the effect of urban ways on longevity, they seem to prefer the brief and merry, or at least exciting, career in cities to the cycle of far and drowsy Cathay.

"Modern industry" is almost equivalent to "city life," because the great industry, the factory system, builds cities around the chimneys of steam engines and electric plants. Cheap production of commodities by machinery requires some degree of proximity of operations. Our systems of transportation and trade work in the same direction. We may then, ignoring exceptional conditions, discuss directly the effects of urban residence on family life, and treat the mill, shop, and factory as special aspects of city life.

The dwelling, the street, the places of work and recreation are the outward and physical factors which directly affect the fortunes of urban workmen and their families.

The habits and conduct of the people under these outward

conditions are also causal factors, and all the influences react upon each other and reverberate in countless ways.

I. What are the facts in relation to the *physical well-being* of the family in cities? The social function of the normal family is to maintain the life of the community at its best by producing, rearing, and educating sound and vigorous offspring.

The statisticians have assembled for us the evidences of relatively high morbidity and mortality in cities, and it is not necessary to reproduce the tables; the general results are sufficient for our present purpose.[1]

Density of population is characteristic of cities and tends to increase morbidity and mortality. The death rate in cities is generally, though not always, higher than in the surrounding country. This is true of every state in the Union. The death rate is usually greater in the ratio of the size of the city, although the improvements in modern sanitary methods are telling with better effect on cities than on rural communities owing to the more prompt and the better administered application of science under municipal government.

The death rate of infants has hitherto been especially marked in cities owing to the defective supply of milk, and probably to the neglect of infants by mothers who work for a living away from home. The exhaustion of girls in factories and mills tends to increase the mortality of these infants after marriage.

The danger from infectious diseases is increased in crowded tenements. Tuberculosis and pneumonia are made more common and fatal by the fact that common halls and corridors carry the germs of these dreaded diseases into every apartment, so that a single patient quickly exposes numerous neighbors. When light and ventilation are defective these evils rage with all the more intense virulence.

The diseases caused by occupations affect the vigor of the family in various ways; directly by impairing the general health

---

[1] Mayo-Smith, *Statistics and Sociology*, pp. 128 ff. (deaths), pp. 154 ff. (sickness); Weber, *Growth of Cities*, chaps. vi, vii; Westergaard, *Morbidität und Mortalität*; Bailey, *Modern Social Conditions*, p. 243; Newsholme, *Vital Statistics*; these give the primary sources.

and poisoning the germ plasm, and indirectly by reducing the food supply and the comforts of clothing and dwelling.

In the absence of adequate and compulsory sickness and invalid insurance the cessation of income of the stricken husband and father means gradual starvation and the diseases which always prey on bodies imperfectly nourished. The people of the United States have not yet become awake to the misery which assails the domestic life from this cause; and we are behind all other civilized nations in providing insurance. We have, after stubborn resistance of the *laissez-faire* tribe, secured compulsory poor law and compulsory education. The next logical step is compulsory insurance in its whole range, on grounds of public health.

Not only injuries and diseases caused by occupation, but also the employment of women and children under unfavorable conditions is a factor in the destruction of sound family life; and, as a rule, these evils are more serious in urban than in rural industries. Exposure to the elements and the rapid increase of complicated machinery, sometimes driven by steam power, are facts of importance in agricultural occupations, and require more attention and investigation than they have hitherto received.

The dwelling has been the center of anxious interest in cities for a long time. The sweated industries, carried on in the same rooms where the family lives, are more difficult to control than the factory industries, and they are a perpetual menace to health. After the great work of De Forest and Veiller on the tenement-house problem little remains to be said in this connection; although local investigation must be made to arouse the conscience of the people and authorities of any particular community. We need another volume, based on scientific study, of the perils to health in country residences. It is amazing how little impression an investigation in Pittsburgh or New York makes in St. Louis or Chicago; it is so easy to parry a stroke by pleading a difference of situation.

The places of recreation and culture in cities are often crowded and almost always perilous to health and hence to the family. Theaters, dance halls, saloons, and even churches are not rarely means of infection.

How far are these evils due necessarily to industry and to urban life? and how far are they preventable, avoidable by known measures? Preventive medicine and public hygiene have already done more for cities than for the country and we seem to be at the beginning of a powerful and concerted movement to combat all these evils.[2]

II. Are the conditions of city life favorable or unfavorable to *fecundity?* The answer must be guarded and must take account of the elements of population, occupations, presence of immigrants, age groups, demands of fashionable society, etc.

"In Germany the birth-rate for the entire country is from 4 to 6 per cent. higher than for cities of 50,000 and over."[3]   In Hungary this is true. In Massachusetts the birth-rate was higher in towns. In Sweden the birth-rate of cities has gained upon and passed the rural birth-rate. The birth-rates of large cities, as London and Paris, are slowly falling.

The social position of the family has a decisive influence, the births being in inverse ratio to income.

"The most obvious explanation of a high birth-rate would be a large proportion of women in the child-bearing period. The cities have a larger percentage of such persons, hence for this reason, and not because of greater fecundity of city women, do the cities often have a high birth-rate."[4]   The cost of living is greater in cities than in the country, and the necessities of life must be paid for in cash. Income is more uncertain. Multitudes of unskilled workingmen are liable to discharge on an hour's notice; and this is true of clerks and salesmen. This uncertainty of income is an important factor in relation to the production of offspring.

Furthermore, the city child is not so early a producer as the child on the farm, whether boy or girl. Very early a rural child

[2] See Dr. Kober's paper on "Industrial Diseases" in *Bulletin No. 75*, Bureau of Labor, 1908.

[3] Bailey, *Modern Social Conditions*, p. 108.

[4] *Weber*, p. 331.

can be a real aid in kitchen or field. This can be modified by earlier trade training from the sixth grade up, as is now provided in some cities for half-day schools and shops.

The attractions of pleasure and comfort make a stronger appeal to the urban dweller than to the farmer. The difficulty of securing quiet and retirement during pregnancy in a tenement house or expensive apartment residence is a factor of no slight significance, especially when public sentiment among women makes maternity ridiculous.

III. Communistic urban habits tend to create and sustain communistic beliefs and sentiments; and these are distinctively unfavorable to the principles upon which the monogamic family is based. Paul Göhre describes his experience in a German industrial community, where men work all day in a common shop, eat their luncheon in crowds, seek their entertainments in throngs, travel in a mob, and, before marriage, satisfy their sexual appetites in a common brothel. The same phenomena may be observed in any large industrial town. If the type of family we have known and which is maintained in the country is desirable, then these forces must be regarded as disintegrating and perilous.

Are the evils of such communistic living avoidable? Are there socializing influences mixed up with the dangerous tendencies which may well be fostered?

IV. Certainly there are advantages in urban life which must favorably affect the domestic institution. There are wider and more rapid means of communication and of receiving impressions; although the rural telephone and trolley are making marvelous changes outside the cities. There are more mental stimuli in the thronged street than in the sleepy lanes, and along the quiet waters of pastures and meadows.

It is possible that the urban socialization of industries gives to the city woman the advantages of slavery without its cruelty, and thus creates a wider margin of leisure—the first condition of higher culture. Certainly, as all admit, our largest leisure class is made up of women from whom wealth and modern mechanical devices have taken away numerous household cares and labors.

V. Divorce is an effect of urban conditions and beliefs; it is an effect of evil and sometimes the milder evil selected out of many worse miseries. In the United States in about 95 per cent. of the cases the rate is higher in the counties in which large cities are situated than in the counties where the population is principally rural;[5] and this in spite of the fact that Catholics gather in cities.

Only of recent years has the prevalence of venereal diseases, and especially gonorrhea, been carefully studied. Even yet the public is not fully aware of the domestic misery caused by these diseases contracted by extra-marital intercourse by men and communicated to innocent wives and children. The records of divorce courts rarely mention the real ground on which good women apply for divorce, and the federal statistics, therefore, must be studied in the light of investigations on which judicial records throw little light.

Now, the social evil is distinctly an urban evil, and so far as it leads to divorce must be charged in great part to the conditions of urban life. The same is true of the use of narcotic poisons and alcohol to which so much domestic ruin can be traced. It is not creditable to many of the scientific men of America that they have underestimated the importance of this factor and some of them have so written that their sentences are used in advertisements of brewers and distillers to blind the eyes of the uneducated.

VI. Some writers have emphasized the value of city life as an agency of social selection; the strong and capable are given a career while the feeble in vitality and character go to ruin and are weeded out. But this kind of social selection is too costly; its lightning strokes kill many of the finest human beings along with the neglected; and not seldom the nursery of deadly germs, physical and moral, is in the homes and streets of the so-called unfit. Those who fall into the doom clutch at the fair and competent and drag them to ruin with themselves.

The incompetent must either be educated to fill a useful place and feel strong for productive labor, or be sent under guard to die at peace in celibate colonies. That is the only social selection

[5] Bailey, *op. cit.,* p. 206.

which is worthy of the name of rational; all the rest is wasteful accident, trusting to chance which plays with loaded dice.

None of the urban plagues which have been mentioned are in the realm of destiny or blind nature; all are products of human choice and conduct; and by human energy, guided by science, they can gradually be diminished or removed; but none will disappear without effort. Even laziness may sometimes be cured by medicine. In *Uncle Tom's Cabin* Mrs. Stowe put into the mouth of her Yankee woman visiting the South the descriptive words, "Oh heow shiftless!" Now comes Professor Stiles and tells us that "anaemia, malnutrition, marked indisposition for sustained exertion, and resultant social condition, usually described as 'shiftlessness,' which have characterized large numbers of the poorer class of rural whites in the South, are due to a widespread infection with the *Uncinaria americana,* or hookworm."[6]

It would be a rational ground for hilarity, to make even a Quaker or a Puritan laugh, if some of the worst demons of economic vice could be expelled from the system with a good dose of vermifuge. Who shall set a bound to science?

The form of the topic limits our discussion to description of present facts, and, rigidly interpreted, would not permit us to consider how far these actual evils are remediable nor by what means. Of course the greater and only final human interest lies in the methods of amelioration provided by the sciences of sanitation, public hygiene, and education.

But the detection and description of the adverse factors implies the possession of a standard and the consciousness of the wrong as wrong. This is in itself an important step on the way to betterment.

A multitude of people will, for good reasons, choose rural homes; another multitude will select urban homes; both may be aided to live a rational life with wholesome surroundings; both can, up to the measure of their capacity, live a complete human life; and already men in institutions of learning, on farms, in cities, and in administrative positions are seeking the ways to the best possible life for farmers and residents of cities.

[6] Dr. H. B. Young, *N. Y. Medical Journal,* November 28, 1908, p. 1028.

The literary and scientific man is tempted to regard the farmer as lacking in intellectual quality because the latter has not expressed his ideas in melodious phrases or buried them in laboratory memoirs.

If we look closely we can discover that farmers have really a vast fund of valuable knowledge—knowledge of vegetables, animals, wounds, diseases, remedies, technical processes, government, law, markets, prices, transportation. The farmer is an experimenter. All he learns he expresses, not in literary form, in articles in books, but in improved land, in selecting according to biological principles the best seeds and the best stock for breeding, in adapting his methods to climate and soil, in building up schools and churches, and in rearing healthy children.

We need not be too industrious in making out *differences* between rural and urban populations. The differences in homes, habits, and satisfactions on which comic cartoonists and some social philosophers lay emphasis either do not exist, except in imagination, or are merely superficial. The broad hat, rough boots, wild beard, and exposed suspenders of the caricatured "hayseed" have little meaning in respect to the essentials of human character. The city dweller judges by what he sees and he does not see much of the real farmer. Many of the railroad kings, whom our British ambassador praises as the ablest men of our nation, are the children of "clod-hoppers" and may retain a little of the ancestral trick of getting over rough ground to their destination. We need to be on our guard against hasty, unfair, and misleading generalizations, and the prejudices of our Brahmin caste. Many of our rich men, under expert medical advice, are living a rural life several months of each year for physical and mental health. They are wise who return periodically to the conditions of life which have thus far helped to maintain the vitality of our nation at the highest point. The aristocracy of England, and their imitators, are ambitious to own and occupy country seats. This will lengthen the life of this group—not always with eugenic consequences.

But what of the poor in our cities, whose crowded rooms are pestilential in winter and purgatorial in summer? Is the best we can do for these to send them to the country for a week, or give dying babes a charity ride in a floating hospital? Are even the small park and playground, the miniature reminder of real country, the horizon of our vision? We have already adopted in our building ordinances a minimum standard of cubic atmosphere and square feet of window space for actinic rays; but as yet we have not come in sight of a standard of outdoor space per man, woman and child. We are merely making unscientific guesses and leaving the real control of sky and grass room to individualism and commercial motives, that is, to the besotted and the blind. In many cases suburban manufacturing villages, built to escape the rule of trade-unions, soon develop unsanitary conditions of smoke, dust, unwholesome housing, and bad drainage and water supply, without securing any of the advantages of moral surroundings.

A more comprehensive system of social control is required in order to promote social selection economically and effectively. What direction must this control take?

1. It has been proposed that we try to educate the prosperous and healthy to produce more children. In the first *Report of the Committee on Eugenics* of the American Breeders' Association it was urged:

> It is a pressing problem to know what to do to increase the birth-rate of the superior stocks and keep proportionate at least the contribution of the inferior stocks. One of the most promising influences is the eugenic movement started in England by Galton and Pearson to make proper procreation a part of religion and ethics, rather than a matter of whim only. . . . . Our appeal should . . . . be directed to men of average ability to have families which will bring at least two children to maturity and parenthood and especially to men of superior ability to have larger families.

With this conclusion and with this appeal there can be no reasonable ground for controversy. Unquestionably something can be gained by persuading people to consider procreation from the point of view of racial interest and patriotism. The Roman Catholic church has certainly succeeded in Canada and the United States by urging its members to outpopulate the Protestants; whether always with eugenic results must be a matter for further investigation. At any rate the universal and persistent teaching and counsel in the confessional secures results; general freedom from divorce and from childless marriages. If this mighty religious influence could be made *scientific* and eugenic—and why not?—it would be an immense help toward improving our American stock.

But there is a limit to the willingness and the duty of persons of ability and health. If they should really try to run a race with the thriftless, the reckless, the dwarfs, the neurotic, the vicious, the criminal, the insane, the feeble-minded, what would be the outlook? Can we seriously urge this policy without further measures? The effort might be too costly, might even lead to the exhaustion and degeneration of a large number of conscientious and morally earnest mothers. Society has no right to ask of such persons unreasonable sacrifices in a hopeless competition with the unrestrained appetites of the unfit and undesirable.

2. There is a way by which society can secure a better stock in one or two generations, and that is by the use of legal powers which it already exercises without raising any ethical or constitutional questions. It is not necessary to reproduce in a brief report the mass of facts collected and presented with almost passionate earnestness by Dr. Rentoul.[7] We have at hand the celibate colonies of insane, feeble-minded, and epileptics. The policy of *segregation* nowhere raises doubt or general opposition. It is clearly and distinctly the right of a commonwealth, when called upon to support a large number of the obviously unfit, to deprive them of liberty and so prevent their propagation of defects and thus the perpetuation of their misery in their offspring.

But the policy of segregation has one disadvantage, which Dr. Rentoul has made prominent: the insane are discharged when cured, and yet become parents of degenerates; and the feeble-minded and epileptic cannot always be guarded so as to prevent propagation. Therefore the policy of painless asexualization is offered.

3. But no social policy of segregation or of asexualization can

[7] *Race Culture or Race Suicide.*

be complete or adequate without vigorous and comprehensive measures for arresting the forces which tend to poison the germ, the very source of life and inheritance. The aim of eugenics is not limited to selection of parents; it includes all the measures which promise to improve the quality of the parents or to prevent their degradation.

It is slow and uncertain work to persuade the capable to attempt to outpopulate the defective and abnormal; society in self-defense must seek to diminish the causes of degeneration.

Several able writers on eugenics have declared that we cannot look to improvement of conditions for improvement of the human race. Granting that better food and housing will not enable tuberculous and paralytic parents to produce healthy offspring, it remains true that impaired wages, nutrition, and wholesome conditions would prevent the beginning of a new series of degraded and exhausted persons.

It seems to be established, and admitted by Weismann, that the germ cells in their most intimate structure can be so affected by poisons and even by malnutrition as to transmit certain evil effects to offspring. Therefore it is not necessary to enter upon a discussion of the controverted topic of the inheritance of acquired characters. The sperm cells or the ovum or both may be so damaged in the parent or parents that the offspring will show the consequences. Forel writes:

By blastophthory (*Keimverderbnis*)[8] I understand . . . . the effects of all directly abnormal and disturbing influences which affect the protoplasm of the germ cells, whose inherited determinants in this way are injuriously altered. Blastophthory works in this way on germs not yet united by means of their bearers (*Träger*) and in that way effects a beginning of what we call inherited degeneration, of whatever kind it may be.

These evil results then pass on from this beginning to subsequent generations. Among the poisons which have the power to damage the germ cells Forel mentions especially alcohol. Idiots, insane, epileptics, dwarfs, psychopathic persons are the issue of alcoholized parents, parents who themselves may have been vigorous and sound in every part.

[8] *Blastophthory* (*Keimverderbnis*) ; cf. Aug. Forel, *Die sexuelle Frage*, p. 33.

This brings into consideration the facts relating to other poisons; as the toxic results of tuberculosis and other diseases, of lead poisoning, phosphorus poisoning, and nicotine in strong doses. The so-called industrial or professional diseases gain a new interest in this connection.

The contest with venereal diseases, both gonorrhea and syphilis, becomes significant for eugenics. It is well known that syphilis acquired by a parent sometimes destroys or cripples the offspring. Gonorrhea is a common cause of blindness; the inherited effects upon the constitution of the children require serious investigation. Dr. E. Kraepelin says:

> We know some of the important and widespread causes of insanity, the combating of which lies not only within the realm of the duties, but also of the powers of the state. The first of these is the abuse of alcohol. . . . . About one-third of the surviving children of dipsomaniac parents will become epileptics. According to Bourneville more than one-half of the idiotic children proved to have alcoholized parents.[9]

This author, with many others, emphasizes the frequent connection between even slight intoxication and the occasion of venereal diseases with all their sad retinue of suffering, especially to women.

Some educational advantage may be gained by laws requiring a medical certificate of health from a public physician as a condition of receiving a license to marry. This measure would cause many a young man to reflect before he brought upon himself a loathsome and highly infectious disease. But such a law would have little influence on unscrupulous persons who satisfy their appetites without regard to marriage laws. They must be reached by other means.

Competition with the inferior and the unfit is one of the influences which cause thoughtful and provident persons to limit their offspring. This was the conclusion of one of our greatest economists, President Francis A. Walker:

> Whatever were the causes which checked the growth of the native population, they were neither physiological nor climatic. They were mainly social and economic; and chief among them was the access of vast

[9] *Die psychiatrischen Aufgaben des Staates*, p. 2.

hordes of foreign immigrants, bringing with them a standard of living at which our own people revolted.[10]

Now, the excessive increase of any undesirable class will "give a shock to the principle of population" among persons of higher standards of life. Thousands of persons of the Society of Friends and others who would not or could not own slaves emigrated from the South before the Civil War to escape competition with slave labor and from the sense of social inferiority which went with manual labor. But now there is no way of escape; therefore the families of superior ability and higher standards grow smaller. To encourage persons of normal life and civilized standards to have more children some better guaranties must be given them by government that these children will not be driven to the wall by immigrants of a lower order. This is not an argument against immigration, but only against the immigration of persons who can never be induced to demand a civilized scale of life. A great deal is justly said of a "simple life;" but that should not mean a return to savage life.

Any discussion of the unfavorable effects of urban life on the family must give large room for these forces which tend directly or indirectly to enfeeble or prevent offspring. The vices which destroy, the unwholesome physical conditions, and the excessive competition in cities of the North with immigrants are all amenable to action by concerted volition; they are not results of inevitable forces outside the range of human choices.

[10] *Discussions in Economics and Statistics*, Vol. II, p. 426.

RURAL LIFE AND THE FAMILY

PRESIDENT KENYON L. BUTTERFIELD
Amherst, Mass.

This paper does not pretend to be a scientific statement of all of the reactions which environing conditions may bring to bear upon the family living in the open country. So far as I am aware, this whole matter has not been worked out by anyone with any degree of fulness. I wish that some of our sociologists would take up seriously the study of the effect of typical rural life, not only upon the rural family, but upon the rural individual, and determine the relationships between the rural environment and the rural mind. I am here merely setting down some observations which are the result of considerable association with the rural people in different parts of the country, and of some attempts to study the structure and influence of various rural social institutions.

Isolation is the chief social characteristic of rural life. But, so far as isolation is a physical fact, rather than a state of mind, the word must be used in a wholly relative sense. Isolation of country life varies all the way from the occasional hamlets and villages of the closely populated irrigation districts, to the genuine loneliness of the almost boundless stock ranges, with all gradations between. It is, however, the one great fact that stands out in any comparison between the social environment of a family living on the land, and a family living in the town or city.

This isolation is a separateness of the farming class from other classes. Consequently, a family belonging to this separated class must be influenced by the characteristics and the standards common to the class as a whole. It is also an isolation of families. A very small proportion of our American farm families live in hamlets or villages. The families of the farm are scattered; few farm homes are closely adjacent, at least from the point of view of the city man.

Of course it is to be observed that physical contact in the city means nothing, from the family point of view. Contiguity does not necessarily breed acquaintanceship. Probably the mere fact of farmhouses being twenty rods apart, or half a mile apart, is not so significant as the fact that separateness of the farming class and scattered farm homes produce a lack of social friction between individuals, between families, and between classes, that has a significant bearing on all those concerned.

What, now, are the chief influences of this isolated mode of living upon the life and characteristics of the family, considered as a unit? I list them as follows:

1. Family life in the country is tied to the industry of the country. This unquestionably makes for interest in the work of the farm. Of course, it may also result in hatred of farm work. It makes drudgery easy. It makes it difficult to get away from one's work. But this much is true, nevertheless, that the farm family may be considered an industrial, as well as a social, unit, whether the influences of this condition are good or bad, or both. It probably has both good and bad effects; but, on the social side, it certainly has a significant result which may become our second point:

2. There is a co-operative unity in the farm family that is rather striking. The whole family is engaged in work that is of common interest. The whole family often "turns to," when a task is to be carried out. When the holiday comes, the whole family takes part in it. Compared with the average city family, individual interests are subordinated. Each member of the family knows what is going on. Each is in touch with the plans of the head of the family, in general if not in detail. The mother's work is ever before the eyes of all the members of the family, including the boys and men. This co-operative unity must have a powerful effect upon the life of the family. Perhaps it has a tendency to give that life too much of an industrial character. There may be too much inclination to "talk shop." There may be too little opportunity for the cultivation of the heart life, or of the hearth life, of the family; but there is a certain solid-

arity in the farm family that makes for the permanency of the institution.

3. Speaking particularly now of the youth growing up in the farm family, it can hardly be gainsaid that family life in the open country is remarkably educative. First, by reason of the fact that both the boys and girls, from even tender years, learn to participate in real tasks. They do not merely play at doing things, they *do* them. They achieve real results. They take part in the world's work; and, secondly, by association with older heads in this work, by having a share in these real problems, by understanding at an early age the good or evil results that come from definite lines of action, there comes a certain maturity of mind, a certain sureness of touch, when a job is to be done, that must be a powerful means of development, particularly in an age when the achievement of tasks is the keynote of success.

4. I believe that, on the whole, the moral standards of the farm family, as a family, are kept on a very high plane; partly by the fact of farm interests already alluded to, and partly by the openness of life prevalent in country districts. There are in the country few hiding places for vice, and vice usually has enough modesty not to wish to stalk abroad. I do not mean to say that the moral influences of the country are only good; but I do say that, so far as the purity of the family as an institution is concerned, the country mode of living is conducive to a very high standard.

Thus far I have named those reactions of the environment upon the rural family which seem to be, on the whole, favorable. There is something to say on the other side.

1. Probably, on the whole, mediocre standards are encouraged. If you are brought up in the Ghetto of New York, and manage to get money enough together, you can move up on Fifth Avenue, if you want to. The average farmer doesn't move unless he moves to town, or to a new region. If low standards prevail in the community, a particular family is likely to find itself influenced by these lower standards. There is a tendency to level down, because of the law of moral gravitation, and because it takes a long time to elevate any community standard. The

average country communities are illustrating some of the disadvantages, as well as some of the advantages, of democracy. In
some farm communities, the presence of hired laborers in the
family circle has been distinctly deleterious to good social customs, if nothing else. In the country there is a tendency toward
a general neighborhood life on the social side. There is a probability that aspiration, for either personal or community ideals,
will get a set away from the farm, with the result that these
ideals are likely to lapse in the country.

2. A great deal of farm life is of such a character that it
makes it very hard for the mother of the family. Perhaps the
effects of isolation are more abiding in her case than in that of
any other member of the family. This is not to give currency to
the popular, but I think erroneous, notion that there is a larger
proportion of insanity among farm women than among other
classes; but it cannot be denied that the type of work in the farm
home in many communities, and few social opportunities, are
likely to give a narrowness that must have its result on the
general life of the family.

3. The health of the average individual of the country is all
that could be desired, at least during the earlier years; but it is
not unfair to say that the sanitary conditions, from the public
point of view, are not good in the average open country. This
must have considerable effect, in the long run, upon the health of
the family, and must have a bearing upon the development of
family life.

4. There is, on the whole, a serious lack of recreative life in
the open country, and this fact unquestionably has a strong influence upon the atmosphere of the average farm home. It tends
to give a certain hardness and bareness that are not proper soil
for the finer fruits of life.

5. The lack of steady income of the farmer's family is a
factor that has a great deal to do with the attitude of the members
of the family toward life, toward expenditures, toward culture
wants, and toward those classes of people that have salaries or
other steady income.

It should be noted that country life develops certain traits in the individual, which, without any special regard to the question of family life, must nevertheless influence the general spirit of the family. I refer particularly to the intense individualism of the country, and the lack of the co-operative spirit. There is neighborliness in the country; there is intense democracy; there is a high sense of individual responsibility; there is initiative; but this over-development of the individual results in anaemic social life, which in turn reacts powerfully upon the general life of the family.

To my mind, the advantages of the country, in respect to family life, far outweigh its disadvantages. This statement must, of course, be understood to have in mind the great mass of farm families, as compared with the great mass of urban families of somewhat similar industrial and social standards. I make no defense of many woe-begone rural communities that can be found in all sections of the country. But I do believe that, on the whole, the family life of the open country, whether judged with respect to its intrinsic worth, its effect on the growing children, its permanency as a social institution, or its usefulness as a factor in our national civilization, is worthy of high praise.

DISCUSSION

PAUL U. KELLOGG, NEW YORK CITY

There are four points which I should like to make. In such a discussion I am under no special obligation to relate them to each other.

In his annual address President Patten made a plea for the pushing out of the economist and his works into practical affairs. Three years ago in a talk which he gave to a group of visitors of a charitable society, he told them that dealing as they were with lop-sided families, families which had something ailing with them, they were bound to get lop-sided views of relief. They should study for every family they dealt with on a philanthropic basis, one normal family. This preachment strikes me as indicating a line of joint activity for the economist and the social worker—where the broad view of the one and the methods of the other could be brought together. The case records of charitable societies have long been storehouses of valuable social information. They have been analyzed on the basis of the causes which throw these families into positions of dependence.

In the Pittsburgh survey we have applied these methods of investigation and record-taking to normal families, which may not be thrown into dependence but are thrown into economic distress and lessened economic efficiency, by disease or accident. We have taken out as units for study not the cases applying for charitable relief, but certain geographical areas or periods of time. Comparing cities of corresponding size for the past five years, Pittsburgh has ranked first and highest in both typhoid fever and industrial casualties. These two are the prime expression on the one hand of civic neglect, and on the other, industrial hazard and ruthlessness. Our purpose was to measure the social effects on the people themselves. Here we had units more compelling than death statistics, or tax-costs.

This was illustrated in the economic study of typhoid fever by Mr. Frank E. Wing, associate director, who collected data for six wards for a year, showing the proportion of wage-earners among typhoid patients, the income before and since, the number of weeks sick, the loss in wages by patients and by those who are obliged to give up work to care for them, sickness expenditure for doctors, nurses, medicines, foods, funerals; and the less tangible but even more severe tax involved in lessened vitality, lessened earning power, and broken-up homes, which follow in the wake of typhoid. Of 1,029 cases in six wards reported in one year, 448 cases were found and studied. Of these 26 died. One hundred and eighty-seven wage-earners lost 1,901 weeks' work. Other wage-earners, not patients, lost 322 weeks—a total loss in wages of $28,899. The cost of 90 patients treated in hospitals at public or private expense was $4,165; of 338 patients cared for at home, $21,000 in doctors' bills, nurses, ice, foods, medicines; of 26 funerals, $3,186. The result was a total cost of $58,262 in less than half the cases of six wards in one year—wards in which both income and sickness expense were at a minimum. But there were other even more serious drains. A girl of twenty-two, who worked on stogies, was left in a very nervous condition, not so strong as before, and consequently could not attain her former speed. A blacksmith will probably never work at his trade with his former strength. A sixteen-year-old girl developed tuberculosis and was left in a weakened physical condition. A tailor cannot work as long hours as before and was reduced $1 a week in wages. A boy of eight was very nervous, would not sit still in school, and was rapidly becoming a truant.

Similarly in the case of industrial accidents. At this morning's session Miss Eastman has told you of the economic incidence as found by her analysis of the 500 industrial deaths in Allegheny in the course of the year studied, where half of those killed were under thirty years of age, where half were getting less than $15 per week, where half had families to support, and where, of these latter cases, less than half received any contribution whatever from the employer toward the income loss.

Dr. Patten has told us that the greatest need of the generation is the socialization of law. Here we were putting court decisions and the master-and-servant law to a pragmatic test, apart from any legal theories of liberty of contract and assumption of risk. How does the common law work out in practice? How does it cash in when it comes to the common welfare? Similar card systems have since been made use of in Wisconsin and Illinois.

My point is, then, that the family affords a responsive, delicate litmus for testing many of the economic facts of the present-day social order. Its usefulness as such is only as yet partly explored. The serious studies recently made of standards of living—not of dependent families, nor even of normal families under emergent stress, but just the everyday economic issues of life, are perhaps the purest examples of such scientific treatment. Such studies as Mr. Chapin has made illustrate the large body of social facts available from such sources.

My second point is that we are dealing in Pittsburgh with overloaded families. In agricultural and domestic industry great numbers of household operations were performed as by-products by the male workers. Thus the water supply for a man's kine and for his household were identical. Not only is this changed with the division of labor, but the household must be maintained amid city conditions where the single family unit cannot master many wants, and in industrial towns badly located for any purpose other than production. My point is illustrated by a dispute between the superintendent of the Pittsburgh Bureau of Health and the controller of the city, since deceased, a bluff, honest, old-fashioned saver of city funds. The superintendent of the Bureau of Health wanted a rubbish-removal system; the controller held that rubbish removal was a householder's private duty. "It is as if," said Dr. Edwards, "every householder in Pittsburgh used his ashes to build his front walks, lit his morning fires with old newspapers, and fed his swill to the pigs." Dumping-places are few and remote in Pittsburgh, and the results have been that every alley, gutter, and corner has festered with refuse; and the problem of keeping the city clean and well has been a hundred fold increased. Long, scientific, medical names on a death certificate, translated in common parlance, were nothing more than a filthy tin can plus a house fly.

Similarly, we find Pittsburgh for the last ten years knowing its typhoid problem was a water problem and yet depending for immunity upon bottled water at 15c per bottle; and we find 50,000 old individual privy vaults in the city proper. Time does not admit of the expansion of this idea, from these homely illustrations to some of the more debatable undertakings of the family analyzed yesterday by Mrs. Gilman. Miss Butler's studies of women in industry, for instance, go to show that in Pittsburgh the whole tone of wages in certain women-employing trades is fixed by the assumption that the girl is half supported at home. My point is that the sooner we disencumber the family of many tasks it is not equipped to handle under modern conditions, the quicker it will be in position to perform its real functions.

Homestead is an example, as Miss Byington has described it, of how the whole task of civilization is thrown back upon the home. Here is a town which is created by the greatest steel plant in the world; one of the master industries of the country, protected by our national tariff policies as few industries are protected, and studied at the close of one of the greatest periods of prosperity the country has known. What has that prosperity meant to the workers? Here, on the other hand, we have a town where time is measured since the strike when associated effort among men was crushed out, there has been no organization or civic life to meet the community problems. The mill, and the town because of the mill, have thrown the burden on the family life of the place. And in many things above the average, we find Homestead a town with gulched streets like a mining district and high death-rates, with, until a year ago, ungraded, unguarded railroad crossings, with rank water and no clean public recreation. It is a town where a majority of the workers are left no leisure by the mill to bear their share of the family responsibilities, and where, stated roughly, the families of 50 per cent. of the workers must choose between eating insufficient food or living in un-American homes, between giving children a normal life or owning a home.

It is a town which sums up the overloading of family life. Eliminating these encumbrances, the standard of living-studies should afford us clearer notions of just what functions we should expect of families, and the minimums which are demanded for their performance—minimums of comfort, as expressed in rentals and clothing, minimums of refreshment, as expressed in food and leisure, and minimums of reproduction, as expressed in terms of strong physical parenthood, household equipment for caring for the young, and child-training. On the test of these standards public opinion could base its judgments as to immigration, hours, wages, working-men's compensation in case of accident, and other influences that affect or jeopardize these standards.

My third point is that the household, existing against these odds, is made the goad for that damnable driving of men to which Mr. Devine has referred. The mill workers are for the most part tonnage men. They are paid on out-put. As Mr. Fitch states in his report, when the rate of pay is judiciously cut from time to time, this tonnage system of payment becomes the most effective scheme for inducing speed yet devised. Whatever a man's earnings may be, high or low, his family adjusts itself to that basis and that becomes his minimum of comfort. The man who has had six dollars a day and is reduced to four dollars has a harder time getting along on that than the man who never has been able to develop four-dollar tastes. The mere possibility of greater earnings than any yet enjoyed does not suffice to rouse men to the required degree. Only a reduction accomplishes that, for it makes it necessary to struggle to reach once again the old wage which was the minimum of comfort.

My last point has to do with the relation of the family to the dynamic character of the population of our industrial districts. In the Royal Museum of Munich is a group of models of mediaeval towns, carved out of wood. The spires and the markets, the city wall and gates, the houses, gardens, and out-buildings are shown with a fidelity that has outlived the centuries. There was entrenched the fixity of things. A man was his father's son. He was burgher, or freeman, or serf, as his father was burgher, or freeman, or serf. His looms and his spinning wheels and his vats were as his father had contrived them. He lived in the house of his fathers and it served him well. Pittsburgh is the antithesis of all this. It is all motion. The modern industrial community is not a tank, but a flow. Not the capacity but the currents of its life are important. Sixty per cent. of the working population of Homestead are unskilled laborers. The great majority of these are new-comers, foreign-born. In one of the plants of the Pittsburgh district, the employment agent hired 20,000 men in one year to keep up the pay-roll of 10,000. Unless the skilled worker keeps himself free to sell his labor in the highest market, he is economically at a disadvantage.

I should not want to claim for this idea of flow as the distinctive element in industrial community life, such a revolution of conceptions as Professor Clark wrought in defining the production of wealth in terms of a flow of utilities. But two things are to be noted. First, that it strengthens the demand that we relieve the family in an industrial community from many of the old household responsibilities. Sanitation cannot be left to Tom, Dick, and Harry if they are on the go. Local health authority must be developed with strength and scientific standards enough to maintain clear water, adequate sewerage, good drainage. Men must have leisure enough to back up this sort of administration with effective citizenship. The lodgings of the floating immigrant labor force cannot be left to boarding-bosses and petty landlords.

The second point is that civic conditions and social agencies must be adapted so that mobile family units shall not be at a disadvantage. Let me illustrate in the matter of shelter, by pointing to *the man who lives in a company house, who rents from a local landlord,* and to the man who buys his own house. The English co-operative housing movement by which a workman buys, not a building but stock in a housing company, is a movement to give the sense of ownership without clogging mobility.

Similarly the ordinary form of accident-relief association ties the workman up tight, while a rational form of working-men's compensation would give him emergency resources whatever his changes in employment and whatever the disrupting influences of industry upon the family.

The development of such schemes is not more communistic than the development of organized work in a mill is socialism. They may be defined as giving elements of stability to the family other than geographical. They should lessen the overburdening of the family. By that degree they should equip the workmen to the more readily withstand exploitation and advance his living standards.

SOME QUESTIONS CONCERNING THE HIGHER EDUCATION OF WOMEN

PROFESSOR D. COLLIN WELLS
Dartmouth College

This brief paper is intended to afford an opportunity for discussion and makes no claim to original investigation or new conclusions. Statistics upon the subject-matter are unsatisfactory and practically unattainable at the present time but such information as we have seems to be unquestioned and sufficiently suggestive for our careful consideration. We are to consider the modern education of women in as far as it is different, in amount and kind, from the education formerly afforded them. Until quite recently the educational privileges of women were not greater than those now afforded in the grammar grades of our best public schools. The training of women in high school, college, and professional schools is a late nineteenth-century notion and some of the new questions raised by it are our present concern.

Permit me to say at the start that, in my opinion, the whole movement is natural and inevitable. Political philosophers would say that it is a logical corollary from the principles of social democracy. Others that it is the outcome of the effort toward self-realization. It is the demand of native powers to be given a chance to develop freely. In it the insistence of the human personality upon the right to express itself has come to full consciousness. In it women protest that they are no longer to be regarded merely as mothers of men or as housekeepers to minister to the comforts of men but as autonomous persons with all the privileges appertaining to such. If motherhood and the activities of the home satisfy a woman of today she will be content with these, if they do not sufficiently express her personality enlightened justice will afford her appropriate educational opportunities equal to those of any man. To continue to exclude half of humanity from the cultivation and exercise of native talent would appear to involve economic wastes as well as an a-priori assumption of the inferiority of woman.

This hospitality toward woman's aspirations does not exclude the admission that there are essential psychic differences between the two sexes. In the cultivation of her talents she is still expressing a woman's self, not a man's. Her spiritual satisfactions need not be identical with those of men but this is a matter for her to decide and each woman, in a free community, may be safely trusted to feel her way toward her own decisions. Parenthetically be it observed that this logically involves allowing such women to vote as care to exercise the suffrage. Our principle is far from meaning that the education of women ,should be identical with that of men. It may be and it may not be—experience alone can decide. Two considerations make us pause here. The first is that our experiment in giving women the same education as men is too recent to allow us to draw a satisfactory conclusion in this matter. In the end, if she wants an identical education and it suits her, she will deserve it and continue to get it. Just here it may be proper to express the opinion that there is no more wholesome place for girls of sound health and considerable intellectual capacity, during the trying period from eighteen to twenty-two years of age, than at a well-regulated college. They are there better off, physically and morally, as well as intellectually, than at home in so-called society. The second consideration that makes us thoughtful as to the details and methods of education for women is that these must be adjusted somewhat to the fact that a woman is after all a woman. For her, educational methods should be related to wifehood and motherhood, whatever else they may strive to accomplish.

In the majority of cases a woman must be a domestic economist and understand the management of a household, if not quite in Aristotle's sense of the term. Naturally, also, she may be expected to find her deepest joys in motherhood. In this she differs from man only in conditions set by the accidents of a physical process. His nature is equally incomplete and unsatisfied without parenthood and the home. If it appears, in too many cases, not to be so it is because of a spiritual atrophy due to the vices of an aging civilization and furnishes a warning rather than a principle of conduct for women to adopt. It should, however, be remembered that fatherhood may be momentary while motherhood must be continuous. This inevitably permits him to devote a large part of his energies to external affairs, as it confines a woman considerably to her home. Only in appearance does this lessen the participation of the father in the nurture of children. His personal influence is just as constantly and imperatively needed for their wholesome development as is the mother's, only it is of a different kind. May not the loss of personal contact with the father in the artificial urban life of civilized communities be a more common source of moral weakness than we suspect? My argument, you see, tends toward an equality in the sacred obligations of parenthood and condemns both husband and wife for the neglect of this fundamental duty. At the same time the father can be much of the time away from home and remain a good father while the woman cannot be and remain a good mother; unless we become disciples of Plato and substitute the public nursery for the home, in contemplating which case we can only exclaim with him "Good Heavens, what skill will then be required of our rulers!"

Let us now go a bit deeper into the question, in expressing the obvious opinion that it is for the advantage of mankind that superior women should become mothers. This is for reasons both of nature and nurture. As for nature, there is greater probability that the offspring of superior women will also be superior. This is fortunately not a certainty. If it were we should abolish all human incentives and much of morality. Intellectual ability is not a dominant Mendelian character that breeds true to parental type. What Galton calls "filial regression" prevents it. The "pull of the race" which keeps us sane, keeps us somewhere around the average. But, in the words of Karl Pearson,

Exceptional fathers produce exceptional sons at a rate three to six times as great as non-exceptional—the superior stock produces above the average at over twice the rate of the inferior stock. Pairs of exceptional parents produce exceptional sons at a rate more than ten times as great as pairs of non-exceptional parents.[1]

Obviously the greater the number of children there are to such parents, e. g., when both are college graduates, the greater the likely proportion of ability in a community for social selection to work upon. Reid has expressed this as follows:

> We cannot improve races of plants and animals by improving the conditions under which they exist. Such a course benefits the individual but results in racial degeneration. The race can be improved only by restricting parentage to the finest individuals.[2]

Certainly we cannot expect to improve it by limiting the parentage of the superior individuals. As for nurture. The environment of the superior woman's children should be more favorable than the average. She is able to apply intelligence as well as character to that most delicate of all tasks, the proper training of children. She can wisely cultivate natural interests and unconsciously control as the spontaneous affection of childhood ripens into the respect of maturer years. Women must be intelligent to win that respect from their well-educated children, particularly from their sons. In this matter of nurture a mother's ability and training may be thwarted by an evil inheritance in the child. It is very untrue to facts to suppose that even an ideal environment can make anything of anybody. Reid grossly exaggerates in saying:

> According to the experience he has, an average baby may become a fool or a wise man, a yokel or a statesman, a savage or a civilized man, a saint or a thief.[3]

After all we cannot escape the meshes of heredity—talent is born and not made, and the better nurture of the one child of a superior woman will not offset the certain loss resulting from the restriction in the number of chances of a happy inheritance.

Now it is just this restriction in favorable chances and limitation of the better stock that the higher education of women appears to involve. This in several ways. To begin with, it seems to mean for college girls a lowering of the expected mar-

[1] *Phil. Trans.*, CXCV, 38.
[2] *Soc. Papers*, III, 10.
[3] *Soc. Papers.*

riage-rate. Probably not half of the graduates of women's colleges ever marry whereas nearly 90 per cent. of the women in the general population marry. At Bryn Mawr the marriage-rate for classes at least ten years out of college is apparently about 37 per cent. At Smith College about 45 per cent. of the women of the ten classes from 1879 to 1888 have married and the published statistics of Professor Thorndike are to the same conclusion. It is of course true that the marriage-rate of the social classes from which the college girls come is much lower than that of the general population. How much lower we do not know. The statistics already published upon this point are far from conclusive and it is certainly true that in our democratic society college girls come from all classes and those who are poor are more likely to contemplate earning their own living in single blessedness than are the rich. Are there not considerations both of sexual selection and of duty to the community which should make the marriage-rate of these brighter college-educated girls higher than the average in their social class?

In the next place the modern education of women involves a postponement of marriage at least two years for girls who stop upon the completion of the high-school course and much longer for college graduates. The former is probably desirable, the latter may be, but raises economic and psychological obstacles to marriage and certainly lowers the birth-rate. The birth-rate among college women is about half the normal. With the above-mentioned classes at Smith College there are about two children to each mother while in the general population there are upwards of four. With half marrying and less than two children to a marriage the college women are not replacing themselves. This is exactly the condition that prevails among the graduates of Harvard and Yale. Should this be so? Should not the trained woman take a higher view of her obligations to the race? As J. Arthur Thompson says:

Is there not need for getting rid of a prudery of selfishness which keeps some of the fitter types from recognizing that they have another contribution to make to the race besides their work.[4]

[4] *Heredity*, 536.

It is also, as Shallmayer has shown, a mistake to suppose that a lower birth-rate is entirely made good by a correspondingly lower death-rate. What is the result? As Lapouge says:

> If one group has a birth-rate of three and the other four the proportion between the two becomes in a generation 3:4. At the third generation 9:16. At the fourth the favored group forms 70 per 100, the other 30. This requires only a century.

The lowered birth-rate of the educated may in part be purposed and in part incident to nervous activity upon the assumption that individuation and fecundity are antagonistic. As Saleeby expresses it:

> In view of the antagonism between individuation and genesis, which Spencer discovered, the very best, being engaged in making the utmost of their individual lives, have less energy to spare for reproduction—that is to say for the racial life. One cannot write a system of philosophy and successfully bring up a large family.[5]

A parable may illustrate, in a homely fashion, this inverse relation of quality and fertility. My garden recently produced a marvellous squash. It was a dream of a squash, such as falls to the lot of few to taste. A command went to the kitchen that every seed must be saved. To which the reply was that there were no seeds. "Impossible! No one ever heard of a squash without seeds;" but investigation discovered only a small seed cavity, in which were a few minute atrophied seeds and among them a single developed one, malformed and almost certain not to produce its kind—but the squash was delectable!

So much for the biology of quality! Socially and psychologically the lowered birth-rate may be sufficiently explained by the incompatibility between motherhood and the gratification of the multifarious tastes and interests of a broadened life. As Munsterberg expresses it:

> From whatever side we look at it, the self-assertion of woman exalts her at the expense of the family—perfects the individual but injures society, makes the American women perhaps the finest flower of civilization, but awakens at the same time serious fears for the propagation of the American race.[6]

[5] *Soc. Papers*, 232.
[6] *The Americans*, 583.

Or as Tönnies says:

The rise of intellectual qualities also involves, under given conditions, a further decay of moral feeling, nay of sympathetic affections generally. Intelligence promotes egotism and pleasure-seeking, very much in contradiction to the interest of the race.[7]

To speak plainly, children have become, to many women, a nuisance, or at least unwelcome beings of an alien domestic world which years of intellectual training have unfitted the college woman to like or understand. Their environment has awakened their interests and then these imperious interests dominate their lives. Various as are the causes of this low birth-rate the effect is a comparative sterilization of presumably superior stocks. This does not appear to be a matter of much present moment but is sure to become alarming with the growth of the college habit among girls. In the United States, in 1905, there were 391,000 girls in public high schools, 43,000 women normal students, and 45,000 women in higher institutions. This latter number was only 10,761 in 1890, an increase of 400 per cent. in fifteen years while population certainly did not increase 40 per cent. The student of history condemns the celibacy of the Catholic priesthood from the selectionist standpoint—what will he have to say of the celibacy of tens of thousands of the most capable women of the country?

Now there certainly is a racial obligation, the obligation of motherhood and, let me add, an equal obligation of fatherhood. It may be admitted that if this obligation is incompatible with higher duties it ceases to be binding; but it should be borne in mind that this incompatibility is sometimes of woman's own making, sometimes pure selfishness, sometimes merely notional, and seldom of fact. The standard of social values is set by ourselves in the long run and possibly we may come again to value the more domestic virtues and the quality of self-sacrifice. You may object that a great woman teacher of hundreds of children may be doing more for mankind than by having children of her own; which is quite true, but is not a Kantian principle capable of very wide application. The fundamental obligation is, after

[7] Soc. Papers, I, 41.

all, at home and nature avenges its neglect upon individuals and people. In another way J. Arthur Thompson expresses this when he says:

> Is there any truth in the inference that failure in reproductive power is an expression of Nature's verdict against dis-social isolation of privileged classes, against every self-contradictory denial of the solidarity of the social organism? [8]

We can by no means abolish the grim facts of inheritance and selection from human society. Do not misunderstand me. My sympathies are heartily with the higher education of women but some of its present biological effects are certainly questionable. The hopeful feature of it all is that these are in part unnecessary and can be avoided by a more enlightened moral code.

From the higher education of women we have a right to anticipate two happy outcomes. Primarily it is likely, through sexual selection, to elevate men's notions of what character and conduct is becoming in them if they are to win educated women as wives. The real trouble, at the present time, is with the education of men. Their coarseness and vulgarity, even when college-men, makes them unfit husbands of college women; they offend them. If there were more men of spiritual insight and moral elevation more college women would wish to marry. What else than celibacy can you expect when a college girl returns to a small community which all the college men, such as they are, have left for the city? She must go too, or remain single. In this there is often real tragedy. Helen Bosanquet had this in mind when she wrote of American women:

> Her disinclination to marriage is often intensified by the fact that she feels herself mentally superior to the man whose education has stopped short with his entry into practical life while she has continued her studies in school and college.

There is, however, the persistent danger that the college girl's own qualification of intellectuality may become uncomfortable to men. A wise man in a recent number of the *London Spectator* wrote:

> Intellectual airs are disliked by both sexes. Dr. Johnson, while generously defending the able woman in whatever direction her ability may

[8] *Heredity,* 536.

lie, admitted that instructive and argumentative women are truly insufferable. "Supposing," said he, "a wife to be of a studious and argumentative turn, it would be very troublesome, for instance, if a woman should continually dwell upon the subject of the Arian heresy!"[9]

In the second place the increasing number of educated women in social and public life may supply that spirituality and ideality in which our modern world is so deficient. There are many dangers here, however. Among them is the danger that public life will become excessively emotional and even hysterical, in crises, and the greater danger that women themselves will be corrupted in competing with men for positions of material advantage. If women's interests become materialized women will surely be degraded to the base level of all material competitions. Her strength has always been in her detachment. Is it not our conclusion that women should have the highest possible education —not that she may struggle with men but rather that she may the better rule humanity by those qualities and in that sphere in which she is most nearly divine?

[9] *Spectator,* November 2, 1907.

HOW DOES THE ACCESS OF WOMEN TO INDUS-
TRIAL OCCUPATIONS REACT ON THE FAMILY?

PROFESSOR U. G. WEATHERLY
Indiana University

Although economists have discarded the classical distinction between productive and unproductive labor, it is not uncommon still to hear work that results in the creation of no tangible wealth referred to as unproductive. In the census schedules housewives not otherwise employed are classed as n. g., "not gainful." So persistent is this fallacy that Professor Smart has thought it worth while to enumerate some of those forms of income which escape assessment and which are not measurable in money, and to point out the ways in which they actually augment the social income. Among these he reckons as "the greatest unpaid service of all" the work of women in the household. With an enthusiasm unusual in an economist he urges that this service does not merely save the cost of servants' wages, but that it produces results which wage-paid labor could not possibly achieve.[1]

Recent studies in biology indicates that race efficiency evolves in proportion to the differentiation between the sexes. Among the lowest orders of men, as also among the peasantry of European states, male and female are strikingly similar in physique and dress, and the character of their labor does not materially differ. Even though it has been true since the crudest stages of culture that some distinction in labor functions was observed, industry itself in the earliest periods was so simple in character as to leave little room for separation. In the patriarchal family group there arose a more definite division of labor by which certain functions were set aside as women's work. The primitive agricultural family group, of which pioneer American households are a survival, assigned to the wife's care those arts which were necessarily centered about the house, poultry-raising, gardening,

[1] *The Distribution of Income,* 70.

weaving, soap-making. This differentiation is to be explained, in general, on the theory of diverse capacities based on fundamental sex difference. Professor Thomas believes that the greater motor activity of the male and the natural fixity and conservatism of the female account for the whole history of the division of labor on sex lines. "With respect to labor," says Aristotle's *Economics,* "the one sex is by nature capable of attending to domestic duties, but weak in duties out of doors; the other is ill-adapted to works where repose is necessary, but able to perform those which demand exercise." While productive processes remained simple this differentiation of functions generally involved nothing more than setting off to each sex definite parts of the same task. To the roaming, active male the share was the procuring of such materials for consumption as could be gotten only through aggressive effort afield. To the female fell work of a more sedentary character, chiefly that which was immediately connected with consumption. Of very high antiquity, therefore, is the habit, much exploited by recent humorists, of referring to the male head of the family as the "producer" or the "provider." Aristotle again, who certainly was not a humorist, declares that "man is adapted to provide things abroad, while woman's work is to preserve things at home."

Two coincident changes have, within the past two centuries, profoundly affected the economic relations of the family. One is the concentration and specialization of industry following the industrial revolution, and the other is the shift from a predominantly rural and agricultural to a predominantly urban type of life. As the most conservative of social units, the family has but slowly adjusted itself to these changes. The home-production economy has been gradually supplanted by the money economy. Instead of being made in the home, nearly all consumption goods in the city, and an increasing portion of them in the country, are produced in specialized industries and purchased with money.

In pointing out the extent and consequences of these changes Miss Heather-Bigg says:

People who assert glibly that wives in the past had enough to do looking after their homes seldom realize what looking after the house meant one hundred and fifty years ago. It meant chopping wood, fetching water, baking bread, spinning flax, weaving, knitting, pickling, curing, churning, preserving, washing. But now water is laid on into the house, bread is bought at the baker's, it is cheaper to buy garments than to make them, wood and coal are brought round to the door in carts, and jam and pickles, butter and bacon are all to be had from the general shop. So that now, for dwellers in big cities at any rate, "looking after the house" means only cleaning, cooking, washing, mending; care of children being the same in both cases. Even washing is ceasing to be the essentially domestic occupation it used to be, many women finding it more profitable to work at some trade in their homes and to give their washing out to a poorer neighbor to be done in municipal wash-houses or in the places set apart for washing in the model buildings.[2]

Historically this is only the latest of a series of industrial transformations which have affected female labor. Very early in this series women relinquished agriculture to man, as she is now surrendering to the factory those handicrafts which she then retained as her peculiar care. She would now cease to be economically functional were there not open to her some alternative sphere of activity. She might, where means permit, give herself up to the cultivation of her finer personal and social graces, and, frankly accepting the position of a parasite, become wholly dependent on man for material support. By means of specialized domestic service, housekeepers, nurses, governesses, she might even be freed from the burdens of home management. Among portions of the so-called upper classes this is the actual situation. Or she might, by a more intensive devotion to purely domestic and maternal duties, find in these full play for her powers, even though the training of children has been partially socialized through such agencies as the school and the Sunday school. With the typical bourgeois family this is a not uncommon solution of the problem. In justification of it may be urged the unquestioned fact that home-making and the careful nuture of children are functions so vital that they are worth whatever they cost to society. Another alternative is woman's entrance into the new productive processes as a wage-worker, contributing to the family income her proper share in money earned in work

[2] *Economic Journal*, IV, 57.

at home for the market or in the workshop for the market. In this class the question is not whether women shall work, for they have always worked. It is rather a question of the conditions under which their wealth-creation shall proceed. Specifically it is a question not of work but of wage-earning.

Insofar as it reacts on the structure of the family, two phases of the problem are to be clearly distinguished. One has to do with the class who work because they must, the other is connected with the status of those who work or who might work because they choose to be occupied rather than idle. Accepting as valid the logical deductions from census figures, the increase of female bread-winners in the United States is one of the most striking phenomena of recent decades. Growth in the numbers of gainfully employed females has outstripped the increase both of male workers and of total female population. In 1900 one out of five of all females over ten years of age were in gainful pursuits, and between 1870 and 1900 the number more than doubled.[3] In Massachusetts 22 out of every 100 females were employed in 1870, as against 27 out of every 100 in 1900, and, while in the same period male workers increased 95 per cent., employed females increased 156 per cent. In the country as a whole the increase of employed women between 1890 and 1900 was 33 per cent., that of males 23 per cent. Although this growth has accompanied the rapid development of the great industries in general, it is worthy of note that it has been most pronounced in those occupations which particularly appeal to the more intelligent and ambitious. The proportion in the textile trades has not kept pace with that which is employed in clerical and mercantile branches. In domestic and personal service also, once the leading field of female wage-earning, the increase in the last decade was only 38 per cent., while that in trade and transportation was 120 per cent.

Of unmarried women of native American stock a smaller proportion are employed than among the children of the foreign-born. They undoubtedly contribute relatively less than do the foreign-born directly to the general family treasury, and are

[3] Special Census Report, *Statistics of Women at Work*, 191 ff.

therefore the less to be reckoned as a factor in the economy of the family. Their earnings go either toward their own necessary support or toward providing for themselves comforts or luxuries not otherwise obtainable. Frequently, too, their wages provide the outfit for their own marriage or for future housekeeping. As an industrial class they are exceptionally weak, because the hope or definite expectation of marriage interferes with effective wage-bargaining. Of them it is particularly true that "the permanency of women in industry is as a class and not as an individual."

Numerically the young unmarried predominate overwhelmingly. In 1900, 85 per cent. of the female workers were single, and 44 per cent., were between sixteen and twenty-four years of age. How far employment has operated to lower the marriage-rate, to increase divorce, or to advance the age of marriage cannot, of course, be clearly determined, owing to the presence of other causes for these phenomena. The average age of marriage in Massachusetts increased from 23.4 in 1872 to 24.6 in 1901, and the rate declined from 23.4 per 1,000 in 1851 to 17.3 per 1,000 in 1901.[4] In Massachusetts as in England the marriage-rate is generally found to be lower in districts where much female labor is employed. But on the other hand it is probably true that wage-earning, by developing a sense of pride and independence, saves women from the single alternative of marriage or dependence. It is also to be noted that young women employed in the skilled trades under good conditions are the less disposed to surrender their independence to men who are likely to be willing to live in idleness, supported by the wages of working wives, just as married women capable of earning a living are under similar conditions more ready to resort to the divorce courts.

Equally weak and subject to exploitation is the class of married women whose elusive position in industry makes organization impossible. The very fact that a married woman must seek employment is construed as a confession of economic stress.

[4] *Report of the Bureau of Labor Statistics*, 1902, 247, 248. For the age of marriage in relation to industry in Europe, see Bailey, *Modern Social Conditions*, 152–62.

Furthermore, members of this class find it difficult to escape the suspicion that their labor is only incidental, home and family remaining the fundamental considerations. A noticeable proportion of those classed as bread-winners do not leave the home at all to do their work, and the fact that they do not visibly belong to the industrial army weakens the front that they might otherwise present in the struggle for a living wage. In bargaining with women workers the average employer assumes that he may safely ignore their necessary cost of living, because in general this cost is lower than that of men, and in the case of married women or widows it is calculated that the wages received are merely supplementary to the husband's income or to charitable relief.

Postponement of marriage may be in itself a less serious evil than the fact that employment in highly specialized factory or mercantile work weakens the taste and capacity for domestic management, where it does not breed a positive dislike for it. Employment in domestic service in good families, formerly almost the sole opportunity for female wage-earning, furnished an apprenticeship in housekeeping that stands in marked contrast to the work of girls today in textile mills, offices, or department stores. The study of conditions in Birmingham by Cadbury, Matheson, and Shann shows to what an extent slack conditions in the homes of employed women react on the unsteadiness and delinquency of husbands. The proportion of sober and steady men is nearly twice as great in families where the wives do not work as in homes presided over by employed women.[5] While it cannot, of course, be assumed that all delinquent husbands have been demoralized by abnormal home conditions, the conviction of such causal relation is the natural and logical one.

The family, not the state, must in the end determine the quality of population as it undeniably determines the quantity. It is in relation to childhood that the disorganizing effects of female labor are most clearly discernible. Sir John Simon showed fifty years ago that in certain English districts where women were largely employed outside the home infant mortality was from two to three times as great as in the standard districts.[6]

[5] *Women's Work and Wages,* chap. viii.   [6] Newman, *Infant Mortality,* 92.

Whenever from any cause industry ceases in a district, as it did during the siege of Paris or during the periodical cotton famines in England, the death-rate of infants declines, while the general death-rate increases, because mothers are then compelled to nurse their children. Manufacturing towns show a variation in infant death-rates so closely correlated with the number of employed married women as to leave little doubt about the cause and effect relation.[7] English and Continental medical authorities are agreed as to the disastrous results of the employment of mothers outside the home soon after confinement, and regulative legislation has been passed in all the progressive European states.[8] Cared for by older children or by friends, fed on unwholesome nourishment, dosed with narcotics, receiving only the fag-end of the mother's strength, children who outlive such an infancy have surely proved their fitness to survive. Day nurseries or philanthropies like the French Society for Nursing Mothers may minimize these evils for the relatively small numbers for whom their services are available, but at best they are only make-shifts, and are poor substitutes for the close individual care upon which alone childhood can thrive.

Acceptance of the "lump of labor" theory involves the recognition of a sort of Gresham's law of labor, according to which cheap female labor would drive men out of industry. This fallacy is partially responsible for the attitude of labor organizations toward the employment of women. But that there is much real supplanting of men by women may well be doubted. Mrs. Webb believes that if it exists at all in England it is only "to an infinitesimal extent."[9] The apparent transformation is attributable rather to necessary readjustment than to substitution. The transfer of so large a proportion of work from home to factory

[7] Compare the figures for Dundee, where large numbers of married women are employed, with those of Paisley, where female workers predominate but where few married women are employed. Newman, *Infant Mortality*, 116, 117,

[8] A summary of European legislation on this subject is given in Oliver, *Dangerous Trades*, 53, 54.

[9] *Problems of Modern Industry*, 101. Carroll D. Wright holds that in the United States women have largely displaced child-labor rather than that of men (*Report of the Industrial Commission*, VII, 74).

has objectified woman's share in the total output without materially increasing it. But even if it could be proved that she is a successful rival to man in getting labor away from him, woman remains an inferior bargainer for wages. Some of this inferiority is only apparent, explainable on the ground of smaller productivity, but there are numerous instances of smaller wages for equivalent work. This condition of women workers is due to a certain amateurishness inseparable from the sense of their impermanence, and to the absence of the technique of an industrial class. Mrs. Webb asserts that the real foe of the working woman is not the skilled male artisan, but the half-hearted female amateur who "blacklegs both the workshop and the home."[10] Examples are not lacking to prove that in districts where female and child-labor abounds the wages of men are lower than in similar trades elsewhere. Additional labor, with the consequent derangement of the home, thus brings, under these conditions, no amelioration of the standard of living, since the combined family income will little surpass that which the man alone must receive were he the sole bread-winner. Alleviation of this situation does not necessarily demand the abstention of women from industry, but it calls for such organization and intelligent application as shall enforce a wage that will really augment the family income.

So real and so patent have been the evils incident to the employment of those women who work because they must that attention has been deflected from the unwholesome idleness of those who are not compelled to seek occupation. The pathological aspects of idleness are perhaps less dramatic because more recondite. In his *Subjection of Women* Mill deplores the dull and hopeless life of women devoid of occupational interest. The void created by shifting the incidence of industry from home to workshop has, for certain classes of women, not been filled by any compensating life-interest. Under existing conditions ma-

---

[10] *Problems of Modern Industry*, 107. Mrs. Willett has demonstrated that in those branches of the clothing industry where women workers are organized their wages approach those of men (*Women in the Clothing Trade*, chap. iv).

ternity does not in itself constitute a vocation for all womankind. When mere number of population has ceased to be the final desideratum, when the family name and the perpetuation of particular stocks is no longer a fetish, the mere bearing and rearing of offspring need not monopolize the energy of one-half the human race. No other achievement of civilization can compare with that which substitutes an economical method of reproduction for the wasteful process of savagery. The prolongation of infancy and the elaboration of child-care that accompany advancing culture may reabsorb part of the energy thus released, but not all.

The problem of a supplementary occupational interest arising from this release, like that arising from the revolution in the industrial order, has called forth three types of solution and experiment. One wholly absolves women from the narrow slavery of sex and opens to her all the social activities of the male, full share. Another recognizes her emancipation from the oriental thralldom to reproductive functions, but seeks to so exalt the maternal and domestic functions as to make of them a social service worthy to be accepted, even under the new conditions of child-rearing, as woman's sufficient contribution to the state. A third accepts motherhood as a necessary service which, however, is to be supplemented by participation in specific production outside the home.

One of the tragedies of contemporary society is the woman who, through lack of an adequate occupational interest, is chronically sickly and inefficient. Her unused abilities ferment and decay. A source of personal discomfort to herself, this lack of self-realization is a loss to society by just so much as her latent talents fail of profitable employment or are turned to unwholesome ends. A prominent physician of Boston recently voiced the verdict of the medical profession when he declared that one-half of all the nervous people (chiefly women) who come to him are suffering for want of an outlet. "They have," he continues, "been going at half-pressure, on half steam, with a fund of energy lying dormant."[11] Much of the marital unrest of the

[11] Dr. Richard C. Cabot, quoted in the *American Magazine*, December, 1908, 204.

period is traceable to this absence of serious occupational interest among married women of the prosperous classes. Social disquietude, unwholesome forms of recreation, nervous break-down that results from overexertion in specious and profitless forms of activity, are the natural corollaries of an unrealized instinct of workmanship. Moreover, the deadening of latent powers in the unmarried through the absence of that individualization which can be realized only in the discipline of occupation is to be reckoned among the causes of the unfitness for service which characterizes so large a portion of young women.

Western civilization has imperfectly outgrown the ideal of the seclusion of women inherited from the older Orient. Missing the stimulus of a free career open to her talents, woman enters in only a half-hearted way into such trades and professions as will tolerate her presence. Yet there are certain branches of activity which are peculiarly adapted to women, and into which they have already entered in numbers.[12] When the process of industrial readjustment shall have more clearly shaped itself, it is likely that some occupations will again be definitely set aside for women and conditions therein adjusted to their peculiar needs. Without predicating the ultimate regimentation of industrial society, it is possible to conceive of a socially regulated division of labor which, while allowing a specialization of domestic service chiefly in the hands of women, shall also provide for outside occupations suitable to their capacities. This would employ in the home the whole time of some women and part of the time of others. It would remove from the home into specialized work-places much of the labor that is still retained in the household. Child-bearing would be accredited as a part of woman's work for society, demanding the fullest exemptions and safeguards. These might in some cases justify pensions for motherhood. They might require that society go farther than Jevons insisted thirty years ago, when he advocated "the ulti-

[12] Mrs. Willett has noted the trend toward a division of labor along sex lines in certain branches of the clothing industry in New York City (*Women in the Clothing Trade*, chap. iii). Women were found to preponderate in fifteen occupations in Massachusetts in 1885 (*Report of the Statistics of Labor, 1889*, 557).

mate complete exclusion of mothers of children under three years of age from factories and workshops.[13]

Vital as is the consideration that workers should, as Mill puts it, "relish their habitual pursuits," freedom of choice of occupation is of no less moment in maximizing social production. Both the ideas and the conditions that have been and are still dominant limit woman to a narrow range outside of domestic interests. In case she aspire to make a career for herself, she has to face social disapprobation on the one side and the surrender of whatever maternal instinct she may possess on the other. Child-bearing is not, under prevailing conditions, easily compatible with a "career," and yet it is both possible and desirable that a woman should, if she so desire, combine the two. The emancipation of woman, so far as it is related to the economic situation, does not necessarily involve the whole problem of women's rights as such. It need only recognize the right of the woman, whether wife or daughter, to make her contribution to the family resources in whatever manner may best suit her tastes and aptitudes. It necessitates only such a remodeling of the family economy as shall substitute co-operation for dependence. Whether she use a churn at home or work in a dairy for wages, whether she do the family washing or find employment in a laundry, her participation in production is equally valid and her contribution to the social wealth equally real.

But, granting that such larger liberty of choice is desirable, there remains the ultimate fact that the preponderant mass of women will continue domestic in taste, and for them the home will still be the center of activity. The "three generations of unmarried women" which an English reformer demands in order to produce a class who shall be emancipated from antiquated traditions of the family and who shall develop an industrial solidarity will, for obvious reasons, hardly appear. It is the woman of domestic tastes who marries and endlessly transmits her characteristics. The sexless woman, the woman whose distinctive trait is an egoistic ambition for self-determination as an independent unit rather than in the family group, may appear

[13] Jevons, *Methods of Social Reform.*

more and more numerously in each generation but her class is not likely to become predominant. Her type is increasingly recruited through imitation as her position becomes more tolerable, but her characteristic trait is an acquired one, and in this department of society, at least, imitation must in the long run prove less potent than heredity.

That the reactions of woman's increased participation in industry have been so largely pathological is in some measure due to the one-sided emphasis which modern life places on mere crude production. Whatever changes in the structure of the family have accompanied the attempt to adjust domestic conditions to the new industrial order have been associated with productive activities, but this social readjustment has not, in Anglo-Saxon lands, kept pace with the economic transformation. Now the family is conservative because it is the natural unit not of production but of consumption, and consumption is not easily revolutionized. For the purpose of using its resources society is less effectively organized than for creating them, since it does not recognize the management of consumption as a validly accredited career. During the period when all energies were being monopolized in the production of larger supplies and of new varieties of goods by processes so exacting as to call into service all available forces, there has been no commensurate effort to perfect the faculty of turning such goods to the most useful ends.

Woman, then, more conservative than man is through her position as mother and home-maker, most intimately connected with the functions of consumption, a phase of economic activity inherently more conservative than production. There is as much call for elaboration in this field as there was two centuries ago in the machinery of production. It goes without saying that the family standard of living and the total of social wealth are as much open to improvement, on the material side, by thrifty application of resources as by augmentation of income. Although imperfectly appreciated and inadequately developed, the social values that lie in estheticized consumption are the flower of modern culture. The typical modern, and particularly the American, gulps his pleasures as he gulps his food. Even where a certain degree of prosperous leisure exists, either conspicuous waste or unintelligent use neutralizes most of its cultural advantages. Society can afford to set its sanction on the guidance of taste in the thrifty use of goods as an economic career.

DISCUSSION
THE SELF-SUPPORTING WOMAN AND THE FAMILY
LYDIA KINGSMILL COMMANDER, NEW YORK CITY, N. Y.

The self-supporting woman is today the woman who is best serving the larger interests of her family, because she is fulfilling her historic mission, in the spirit of her age.

Women have always worked, and always will work. They cannot do otherwise. Woman is the working human creature. To work is an inherent tendency of woman's nature; with man it is an acquired characteristic. Woman works from instinct; man from habit.

Among primitive peoples the pursuits of the sexes, their interests, and their views of the purposes of life, are sharply differentiated. Speaking generally, the man follows war, the woman work. The man is ruled by his passions. He desires freedom, food, and sexual satisfaction; hence he seeks to conquer his enemies, to slay the beasts, and to subdue woman. The mighty hunter, the triumphant hunter, the husband of many subservient wives—such are the heroes of the tribe.

To the primitive woman the family is the supreme consideration. Her life is given to bearing children, and to laboring for their nurture. To this end she originated and followed various industries. She makes pottery, weaves, sews, gathers berries, roots, and grain, and ultimately tames the milder animals to her use. So closely is she identified with all forms of labor that to work is a distinctive mark of femininity. No primitive man who works, no matter what his excuse, commands respect. Because he works he is despised—he is a "squaw-man."

To persuade the primitive, free-roaming, fighting male to turn from war to work was a tremendous task, slowly accomplished through the long centuries. He was first induced to labor by his interest in the female. To win her favor he helped her in her chosen work of providing for her family. Soon he became interested in the children who consumed the fruits of his toil. Finally he began to enjoy the home comfort which resulted from their joint labors. Thus the woman, by attaching the man to the family group, doubled her working capacity, and gave to her children a new parent. In short, she made two parents grow where one grew before.

Inevitably, the families nurtured by both parents survived in greater strength and numbers than those left to the care of the mother alone. So were perpetuated and increased in man the feminine trait, industry, and the feminine interest, the love of the family.

Thus, because it was better for the family, the woman's ideal has prevailed over the man's. He has accepted her view-point. He could never make her fight; but she has made him work. This was her larger service to the family.

In his new capacity, as producer instead of a destroyer, man accepted first those out-of-door tasks, most akin to his natural pursuits. He cared for the flocks and herds, and in time adopted the various branches of agriculture. Much later he began to prepare raw materials for use, performing such ultra-feminine tasks as grinding corn, dyeing yarn, and weaving cloth.

Among civilized nations only traces of the original man now remain. We have left the hunter and trapper, who vanishes before the on-coming settler; and the professional soldier, for the tramp of whose departing feet many already eagerly listen. All other men are workers—they are "squaw-men." They have come to the woman's view-point—they believe, and live their belief that life is for labor. This change of heart has been complete and genuine. The modern man of toil accepts his new vocation, not protestingly, but with the enthusiasm of a recent convert. Not content with sharing woman's tasks, he has actually re-christened her ancient industries "man's work," and seeks to hold them as a sex monopoly.

But, though woman has taught men what to do, she has not yet shown him how to do it. True to his earlier instincts, man has transformed industry into war. He has taken the work out of the home, and built great factories and workshops; but he attacks cotton, wool, and flax as he formerly attacked his enemies. He lines up an army and huris it at the labor, without the least regard how his soldiers emerge from the fray. They come from the battle-field maimed and crushed and bleeding: the dead and dying strew the field. But the fight goes on. The leader is a "captain of industry," dominated by the lust of commercial conquest. To build higher, to produce more, to travel faster, to become richer than his competitors—these are his master-motives.

Man works as he fights—to win, to overcome his adversaries; and he cares more for the victory than he does for the safety and happiness of his industrial army. He has made the business battlefields as bloody as were ever the fields of war. There are in a single year, in the United States alone, 94,000 people killed and injured on the railways; and 232,000 more in the factories. In the last four years we have killed more people in industry—80,000 more—than all the soldiers slain in the Civil War, the Gray and the Blue combined.

With amazing energy man has developed industry far beyond the point where woman had brought it. He has done what woman possibly never could have done—invented vast power machinery and organized an immense and intricate system of production and distribution. But in his haste and excitement he has lost the vital part of the woman's point of view. He has forgotten what industry is for. He has been so intent upon his dividends or his pay-envelope that he has sacrificed himself and his family— he is sacrificing the whole nation—to carry on this industrial warfare. He is sapping the energies of the race, and by overstrain unfitting men and women for the best parenthood.

All manner of social ills spring from this masculine mistake of transforming industry into war. Many of these evils are attributed to the presence of women on the business battle-field. We are told, and truly, that the arduous labors of shop, mill, and factory drain the vital forces of women and unfit them for good maternity. But it is equally true that the over-taxed, under-nourished working-man, of whom we have millions, is incapable of transmitting to offspring the sound, strong body and abounding health which is the birthright of every child.

Because women suffer so cruelly in this industrial warfare they are frequently told that they should return to their homes. This is an utterly impossible proposition, and one which suggests the reversal of the whole process of social evolution. Women are not going out of industry; they are being irresistibly drawn and driven into it, by tremendous social forces. This tendency is indicated in the followng ways:

1. Self-supporting women are constantly increasing in numbers.

2. Their period of work, before marriage, is lengthening.

3. More of them remain at work after marriage; or, after a period of domestic life, return to work.

4. Their remuneration is increasing and they are securing more of the higher positions—those requiring long training and large compensation.

5. More women follow life-professions, even at the sacrifice of marriage, when necessary.

6. There are more skilled workers among women. Girls eagerly attend school or classes offering them industrial training.

7. Women workers are organizing, taking themselves seriously as a permanent part of the industrial world, and endeavoring to improve their conditions.

8. Society is, more and more, accepting the self-supporting woman as a permanent factor in industry, an essential part of the industrial organism. It is discussing her problems and making efforts to adapt conditions to her needs.

Meanwhile, the home activities are being continually narrowed, while the woman is being developed and enlarged. The housewife of the past, who had a meager knowledge of the three R's and whose outside interests were limited to her own town or village, found ample scope in the varied activities of the old workshop-home. But the educated woman of today, who is kept in daily touch with the whole world, finds too slender an outlet for her energies in the attenuated activities of modern housekeeping. Her mind registers a world-stimulus that demands more than a five-room flat for expression. Hence, the single woman, the childless wife, the widow, the divorced woman, the wife of the invalid or the unfortunate, and even the mother whose children no longer require her constant care, increasingly swell the ranks of the self-supporting women. Usually, it is only under the strongest pressure of necessity that the mothers of young children perform labor that takes them from the home, but even they are frequently met in the industrial world.

These women have become wage-workers, not only to earn a living, but to raise the standard of comfort in their families. The latest figures show that nearly 10 per cent. of women workers are the sole support of a family, while 30 per cent. more assist a parent or other relative to maintain a home. Even those who support only themselves, by relieving the family income of the burden of their maintenance, raise the standard of living for the rest.

Sometimes, it is true, the first effect of women working is to lower the wages of men, so that the family income is not increased. But this condition is not a necessary accompaniment of woman's labor. It can be overcome by intelligence and organization. The "iron law of wages" is an exploded theory in a country where New York bricklayers get seventy cents an hour and the cigar-pickers of Tampa, Fla., make $40 a week. These are but two of many trades in which the workers have, by intelligent organization, raised themselves financially, not only above "the level of subsistence," but beyond a mere "living wage," and into the comfortable middle class. Poorly organized workers, whether men or women, will always have low wages,.

On the whole the woman worker does raise the standard of living, for herself and her family. We are often told, contemptuously, that she works for "finery." But what does that mean? It means that she is working to bring herself to the American level, in a country whose women are famous, the world over, for their good clothes. If the working-woman is wrong in this, then the whole United States is wrong. She is simply trying to attain the standards of her age and race.

Nor does she, commonly, desert her family and climb alone. She tries to bring them up with her. Of working-women 80 per cent live at home; and they buy rugs and curtains and pianos, as well as feathers and bracelets and furs. Pathetic, even though ofteñ amusing, are the efforts of the young woman, who, through contact with the world has gained some new knowledge or culture, to impart it to her less enlightened parents. For instance, a New York tenement-reared girl, whose mother took in washing to make her a school teacher, is now carefully training the mother to read the *Outlook* instead of the Sunday papers.

Another teacher is the eldest of the six children of a common laborer, who drinks heavily. From the day that she began to teach she has been the self-appointed guardian or foster-mother of her five brothers and sisters. Through her efforts and her earnings they have all been educated. The three girls are now teachers, one brother is a physician and the other a civil engineer.

She has never married. In the census she is simply written down as a self-supporting, single woman, aged forty-two—one more to be mourned over, or condemned as unfaithful to her woman's duty of raising a family. But has she not, in the highest sense of the term, raised a family, by lifting into the ranks of the intelligent and educated, five sisters and brothers who might otherwise have remained permanently upon the life level of their drunken laborer father?

The self-supporting woman, however, usually marries. And in part her desire to dress well and to rise socially is due to her ambition to marry well, and thus insure to herself and her children a higher level of existence. The well-dressed girl, with refined friends, can meet and marry a higher type of man than the shabby girl, of unrefined associations. And how can a woman better serve her prospective family, than by marrying a man who will help her up, instead of one who will drag her down?

Thus, in various ways, the self-supporting woman is a direct factor in raising the economic and the social status of her family. That she gives this service at too great a health-cost to herself, is her misfortune and the misfortune of the race. It is not her fault; it is the result of the present organization of industry, which measures prosperity by profits, regardless of the welfare of the workers.

Women have been forced to work, by necessity and by their instinct of industry; but they are laboring under conditions which they have not created, and which they do not approve. They are doing their work in man's way, in the midst of the strenuous conflict which is his idea of business. Women suffer, not because they work, but because they work as men work, under conditions that men have created for themselves.

Where men live, act, or work together, and without women, they are always harsh, often brutal, and sometimes actually savage. The immigrant men who come here live like barbarians, so long as their wives are not with them. But once the women come the whole race moves upward, seeking constantly higher levels.

Let a group of American men, who have been well-behaved members of some quiet, law-abiding eastern community, go to a western frontier town; presently most of them will be carrying knives and revolvers, while half a dozen will have turned into fighting desperados.

So man-managed industry, though it is an improvement on warfare, is still destructive of life. Man the soldier destroys life and property. Man the worker produces property and therefrom preserves it: but he still holds life lightly, as a cheap and plentiful thing. Man, left to the guidance of his own instincts, will always be lavish of human life; for it does not cost him anything.

So long as industry remains warfare, it is not true industry. It is a sort of hybrid activity, a cross between war and labor, a semi-savage game, unworthy of a developed, humane people. It is as illogical and absurd as "civilized warfare;" and its chief value lies in the fact that it is leading up to something better.

Industry must be civilized—in the interests of woman and of the family. And only the presence of women in industry can civilize it. So long as the woman could live, work, and rear her children in the home, it was perhaps sufficient for her to civilize and humanize the home. But that is not enough today. She must live, work, and rear her children in the outside world as well as in the home. Therefore we must have a civilization that will reach from the heart of the home to the nation's outmost rim.

Men and women are working together, and more and more they will work together. But the conditions under which they work cannot continue to be determined by man's endurance; they will have to be altered to meet woman's need. She, not he, is the sex supremely important to the welfare of the race. "If she be small, weak-natured, miserable, how shall men grow." Wherever men and women live and act together, the conditions of life must be brought to her level, or the race will suffer; and industry must obey this law.

Already our six million working-women have had a humanizing effect upon many of the trades and professions. A direct result of the employment of women has been the whole movement for welfare work—the comfortable rest and lunch rooms, the girls' clubs, the summer vacation homes, the welfare secretary, and the numberless other comforts and helps provided by so many ·up-to-date factories, shops, and stores. The principal purpose of the Consumers' League is to improve the labor conditions of women—the same motive that animates the workers themselves in their trade organizations and in the Woman's Trade Union League. As working-women increase in skill and numbers, and therefore in influence, they will do still more to modify conditions, and to make the factory like the old-time home—a place of safe, cheerful, and companionable labor.

The great, present-day task of woman is thus to remake the industrial world, to change the basis of industry from war to co-operation, to put people before property, and life before labor. She must teach man that industry is but a means to an end; and that healthy, happy, noble-minded men and women are of more importance than sky-scrapers, factories, and steel rails. In this work, the self-supporting woman of today is the advance guard. She is working not for herself only and for her immediate relatives, but for the nation. She is giving a great social service to the race. And thus she is fulfilling, in a new, large sense, the historic mission of her sex—the nurturing and uplifting of the family.

HIGHER EDUCATION OF WOMEN AND THE FAMILY

Mrs. Elsie Clews Parsons, New York City, N. Y.

Whatever the virtues of the proprietary family, it does not encourage initiative, least of all feminine initiative. For its own safe-guarding, Manu's dictum is wholly to the point. "By a girl, by a young woman, or even by an aged one, nothing must be done independently, even in her own house"[1] In the mediaeval proprietary family just as in the Hindu there was no place for the innovating woman. In mediaeval and even later days she could be herself only on a throne or in a nunnery or brothel. Elizabeth of England, Elizabeth or Katherine of Russia, and many a less famous princess ignored the institutional family. Like the royal ladies of the African west coast, they made over domestic law in their own favor—substituting polyandry for the prevailing Christian type of polygyny. Other noble ladies in whose souls stirred the power of leadership but for whom no throne, or at least no undivided throne was available, betook themselves to the cloister. Radegund, of France, for example, who was modern enough to keep her royal husband waiting at meals for her, so absorbed was she in "charity"—and I have no doubt that some cross sixth-century paraphrase of "charity begins at home" was thrown at her—Radegund bullied a bishop into consecrating her a deaconess and then founded a nunnery at Poitiers. Here she undoubtedly found it far more agreeable to hob-nob with the notables of her day, one of whom, the poet Fortunatus, called her "the light of his eyes," than to have staid at home subject to the marital temper and occupying the somewhat irksome status of fifth among King Clothacar's seven wives. Conspicuous among other family iconoclasts were Agnes, of Bohemia, who, as soon as her father died, broke her engagement to Fredrich II to found, with papal sanction, a nunnery and hospital at Prague; and Hedwig, of Silesia, another famous founder of hospitals, who after having presented Duke Heinrich with a proper number of progeny, made herself liable to a suit for the restitution of conjugal rights. For any ambitious woman of humble birth who wanted to see the world, to correspond with scholars, to become an artist in caligraphy, embroidery, and miniature painting, to compile history and legendry, to write Latin dramas or materia medicas, the cloister was the only open door. If she were too utterly wayward to brook cloistral, as well as familial, discipline, she became an attaché of another institution, whose ways many a nunnery copied and whose inmates were licensed to take part in public processions, to entertain visiting notables and to contribute to the treasury of state and church.

All these queens, nuns, and *femmes de joie* were the celibate or grass-widow pioneers of woman's rights, the ancestresses of the modern emanci-

[1] V, 147.

pated woman. Nor did this genealogy escape popular notice. It is little wonder then that college education for women, one of the first steps of the woman's movement of the nineteenth century, was at first denounced as incompatible with family life.

Besides, it was. The first college women, like their mediaeval forebears, turned their backs on the family, but they were not so much traitors as outcasts. The proprietary family, or what was left of it, had stigmatized them as evitable spinsters, but whether, as one controversialist put it, it was the woman who would not marry who went to college rather than the woman who went to college who would not marry,[2] or whether the social ostracism or at least suspicion which the pioneer college woman was under itself disqualified her for marriage, must always be an open question. Where she was no longer on the defensive her matrimonial eligibility certainly increased. For example in a study of the marriage-rate of 1078 members of the A. C. A. in 1890 it was shown that of graduates over forty years old 83.3 per cent. of the graduates of western and coeducational colleges were married as against 41.7 per cent. of the graduates of eastern and separate colleges.[3] This difference was, of course, due in part to the numerical inferiority and consequent superiority in the strategies of courtship of women at large in the west, but we may also surmise that it was also due to the fact that coeducational colleges are twenty years older than separate colleges and that they accustom the potential husband to the college girl and perhaps vice versa. We may assume that this mutual toleration raises the marriage-rate 6.1 per cent. for the coeducated college girl above the separately educated from a comparison made in 1895 between the marriage-rates of both types of eastern college graduates—the influence of locality being removed.[4]

In all discussion of the unseemly marriage-rates of college women we must also remember that until quite recently it has been difficult to speak with much conclusiveness on the statistics of college women. Their record was too short-lived. For example, out of 705 members of the A. C. A. in 1885, 196 were married and 509 unmarried, giving a marriage-rate of 27.8 per cent., but then only forty-six were over forty years old.[5] Of the 1805 members of the A. C. A. in 1895, 28.2 per cent. were married, but of the members who were past forty, 54.5 per cent. were married.[6] This

[2] *Nation,* I, 330.

[3] *The Overland Monthly,* XV (1890), 444.

[4] Shinn, "The Marriage-Rate of College Women" in *Century Magazine,* XXVIII (1895), New Ser., 947.

[5] Howes, *Health Statistics of Women College Graduates,* Boston, 1885, pp. 25, 28. We must remember in using these figures that a greater proportion of married than of unmarried members of the A. C. A. withdraw from it.

[6] Shinn, *op. cit.,* 946.

higher rate is exceeded or approximately by still more recent figures. In 1903 the marriage-rate of graduates of the first ten years of Vassar 1866–76) was 55.41 per cent.; of Smith (1878–88), 42.70 per cent.; of Wellesley (1878–88), 46.55 per cent.[7]

With every allowance, however, the original college girl does not seem to have married at the same rate as her non-college-bred contemporaries— assuming that the superfluous or unmarried woman at large is to be calculated at 20 per cent.

During the last few decades several changes have come over the family which render it much more gracious to the higher education of women. The age of marriage is considerably later than it was. Our grandmothers married in their teens, our mothers in their early twenties, and we between twenty-four and twenty-six.[8] As the average of graduation from college is twenty-two, or even lower,[9] we did not have to choose between marriage and college from the point of view at least of life's time schedule.

Then in endless ways girls at large are far freer than they were. Not many mothers could any longer be found who, like Hilary's, would consider a daughter's proposal to work for a man indecent or caution her to always carry a parcel and an umbrella as a safeguard. The object of the nineteenth century's bloodless revolt of the daughters was the assimilation of their lives with those of their brothers, and a college education was naturally down on their programme.

Now the point of view toward the college education of boys has itself undergone a change which has reacted upon popular ideas on the education of girls. As late as the middle of the nineteenth century the college was conceived of as primarily a training place for service in church and state. Two-thirds of its graduates were priests or lawyers.[10] When the churchman began to yield to the business man, and the college became merely a continuation school for the undifferentiated boy, a college education became much more conceivable for the undifferentiated girl.

How closely the college girl has come to approximate in recent years to the type of her home-staying contemporary is seen in the careful study made by Professor Mary Roberts Smith in 1900 of 343 college-bred married women and of their 313 non-college-bred married sisters, cousins, and

---

[7] Hall & Smith, "Marriage and Fecundity of College Men and Women," in *Pedagogical Seminary,* X (1903), 301–5.

[8] In England in 1891 the average age of marrying spinsters was 24.8. In Massachusetts for the twenty-year period, 1875–95, the average age was 25.4 (Smith, 8).

[9] Howes, *op. cit.,* 16; Shinn, *op. cit.,* 246; over 22 for Vassar, Abbott, "A Generation of College Women" in *Forum* XX (1895–96), 378, 379.

[10] *Yale Review,* VII (1898–99), 341–45.

friends. The average age at marriage for the college woman was 26.3, for her kinswomen and friends 24.3.[11]

The most interesting point in this study is, I think, the comparison of the reproductive capacity of the two classes of women. The college woman had borne 1.65 children,[12] the non-college woman 1.875. The non-college woman had borne therefore an absolutely larger number of children than the college woman, but in proportion to the number of years of married life the college woman had borne 9 per cent. more children than the non-college women.[13]

And so we see that originally an exile, the college girl has been taken back into the bosom of a penitent family. In earlier days she may have been one of the many factors in the degeneration of the proprietary family. Has she any influence on its present day relics? She marries, bears children or is unable or refuses to bear them much like the non-college-bred woman. Some slight differences between her and the latter there may be. She marries a year or so later. Her marriage-rate is still no doubt comparatively low. She seems to add to the demand for college-bred and profession-following husbands.[14] Divorce statistics might show that she is a comparatively successful wife. Her children may be even a little sturdier or better cared for than those of non-college-bred mothers.[15]

But in all these ways is the college woman anything but a particularly emphatic expression of a changing family type? That she is actively accelerating the change in the only way that is at present open I fail to see. Her economic status is just the same as that of the non-collegiate wife. Her daily round of occupations is very much like that of every other housewife.

[11] Even this high average is somewhat misleading. It is brought down by a certain number of very early marriages among the non-college women.

[12] For early college classes this rate is, of course, higher. In 1903 the rate per married graduate of the first ten classes of Vassar (1866–76) was 2.03; of Smith (1878–88) 1.99; of Wellesley (1878–88) 1.81 (Hall & Smith, *op. cit.,* 301–5). In 1902 the birth-rate per married graduate of the six Harvard classes from 1872 to 1877 was 1.99 children (*Harvard Graduates Magazine,* XI (1902–3), 356).

[13] Statistics of College and Non-College Women" in *Publications of the American Statistical Association,* VII (1900–1), 24.

[14] In Professor Smith's study it appeared that three-fourths of the college women married college men, while only one-half of the non-college women married college men. Of the husbands of the college women 65 per cent. were professional men, as against 37 per cent. of those of the non-college women (18).

[15] Of the children of Professor Smith's college-bred mothers 96.3 per cent. had satisfactory health as against 95.4 per cent. of those of the non-college-bred mothers (15).

Her household may be run a little more systematically, but it is run in the traditional way. She too is the vicarious consumer of her husband's wealth, in Professor Verblen's lively terms, the foremost illustration of his power for conspicuous waste.

We have, of course, been considering only the undifferentiated college-bred woman, the woman who may work, who in large numbers does work, a few years after graduation and before marriage, but who at marriage becomes the conventional housewife, who leaves blank space in *question-naires* calling for her occupation. What of the relation of the college-trained professional woman to the family? In some ways she is in much the same position that the mere college girl once held. She is a family outcast. Her added period of professional training makes a later marriage more likely, although not more necessary. She can get her three or four years' training and apprenticeship before marrying and yet marry at the alumna's average marrying age. If, however, she practices that "art of detachment" which Dr. Osler so relentlessly insists upon for success in his profession at least, she may not marry until two or three years later. Then I surmise that in nine cases out of ten she comes to a parting of the ways, matrimony on the one hand, her profession on the other. Prejudice against married women in schools, in colleges, in government service, in almost any kind of work in fact, her suitor's traditions, the exigencies of his own work, her own traditions or her moral or intellectual faithfulness, one or another insists on a sharp cut answer as to whether she will

> run with Artemis
> Or yield the breast to Aphrodite.

Unfortunately we have no statistical information about her answer.[16] Nor have we of her answers to the even more interesting questions which confront her if she finds a way to combine matrimony and work. What is the birth-rate in *her* family? What incompatibilities has she found between maternity and professional work? Have they been great enough to force her to undergo either?

Had time allowed I should have liked to have as my contribution to this discussion the outcome of the following three queries made with considerable detail of course to the professional and ex-professional married women of the country. Did you give up your profession at marriage—if so, why? During childbearing and rearing—if so, why? How are you solving the problem of combining marriage and maternity with your profession?

[16] Professor Thwing has pointed out that of 633 distinguished women figuring in Appleton's *Cyclopedia of American Biography,* a publication dated 1886–9, one-half are married (*North American Review,* CLXI (1895), 549, 550); but then we do not know how many of these women took to a career after marriage or merely as a substitute for marriage.

My returns would have been an index to the rate of progress or, according to one's point of view, deterioration, in our contemporaneous family type. The emasculated form of the proprietary family which now prevails is in my opinion bound to persist until the economic status of the wife is altered, until she becomes independent through her own productive labor, whether or not her reproductive work is, as some would have it, state paid. Until she is economically independent she is bound to more or less approximate the harem type. Nor will she until then share equally with their father, either in law or custom, in the control of her children. Moreover, this economic independence must be won by the women of the higher cultural classes before the character of the family can be thereby affected. The hard-driven tenement house-wife who supports her good-for-nothing or unemployed husband, the farmer's wife who works harder than even her hardworking husband, or the factory hand's wife who supplements his wages, are in spite of their labor thoroughly unemancipated women. Because in many ways a more primitive type of woman they are perhaps even more subject to marital mastery than their leisure-class sisters. As Gabriel Jarde has pointed out to us, it is only the people at the top of the scale who have enough social prestige to negotiate radical social changes.

It is then on the fight of the professional woman to get back into the family that the future of the family will depend. But in the present temper of the community and under existing economic conditions it is likely to be a losing fight. Under our wasteful competitive system of production, the worker must adjust himself or herself to the standard economic day, or go to the wall. A whole day's work or no work are the alternatives. People who are capable of a good half or even two-thirds of a day's work are either worn out with over-exertion or forced into unmitigated unproductiveness—a sin against themselves, and an economic loss to society. Many men and almost all women suffer from this economic inelasticity. The working schedule of the potential or actual child-bearer must vary from time to time for the sake of both her productive and reproductive capacity. Women therefore should be peculiarly hospitable to any change in the productive system tending to eliminate competition either between men and women or between child-bearing and non-child-bearing women.

Mrs. Isabel C. Barrows

It was half past ten when Mrs. Isabel C. Barrows was called on for her word in the discussion. Owing to the lateness of the hour she took but seven minutes, in which brief time she rapidly considered the family itself, in order to see what would be the reaction upon it of outside industries, and of the higher education. The country family was a closer unit, she believed, than the city family. Any discordant element in it usually found a way to reach urban life. Those who were left worked as a whole for the betterment of the circumstances of the family, and though conditions were often hard yet a fine race of boys and girls was brought up under these influences, even when there was much outdoor work for all. Higher education coming into such a family was also to its advantage.

The city family that had to find outside work for each member was more likely to be a house divided against itself. The effect on the younger members was to lessen their respect for their parents. The effect on the mother, to be looked on as an underpaid wage-earner, a drudge, was also bad, quite aside from the fact that she had to neglect her duties as the head of the house and the mother of the children. No work could be good for any mother in a home unless it increased the respect of husband and children for her. She was justified in letting someone else do her domestic work when she could earn large enough wages to have it better done than she could do it. It may be true that there is a larger birth-rate among working-people who have not troubled themselves about higher, or indeed lower, education, but the birth-rate was of small consequence as compared with the *death*-rate, or the *life*-rate. The number of children dying in such families is appalling. On the contrary though the college woman may have fewer children she takes wiser care of them and the number of deaths in proportion to the births, so far as figures have been ascertained, is highly in favor of the educated woman. It may also be true that she has wider interests, and perhaps employment, that take her much from home, but with her larger earnings she replaces herself in the home so that that does not suffer.

In this country there is another home that one finds much less frequently in Europe, and that is a home made up of two women, usually professional women, but sometimes working-girls, who carry on all the functions of housekeeping, making charming centers for a wide and helpful influence in the community. They not infrequently adopt one or two children, so the mother-love in the heart has an opportunity for expansion and the child grows up in an atmosphere of industry, purity, and self-help, as well as with the spirit to help others.

It may be true, and it is sad, that the number of childless homes is increasing in this country, but Mrs. Barrows did not believe it was true of the majority of American mothers that they were unwilling to bear the joys and sorrows of motherhood. Even if true among the rich and gay, it is not true in the great number of modest homes, where the daily bread is not a source of wearing anxiety. There is much more danger to fear, judging from the painfully accurate paper of Dr. Morrow, that the fault lies not with the overwork nor the overeducation of women, but with the vices of men and the false standard of morals which requires purity of life of women and not of men.

Concluding Remarks of Professor Wells

However divergent our opinions appear to be I am sure that we all are united in a common aspiration for what is good and helpful to the world in which we live. May I plead for seriousness in the discussions of these questions and emphasize the fact that certain biological conclusions are now well established and cannot safely be ignored in the life of any people?

[We regret that the paper on "The Statistics of Divorce," by Dr. Joseph A. Hill, of the Census Office, which here followed, was not received for publication.—Editor.]

IS THE FREER GRANTING OF DIVORCE AN EVIL?

PROFESSOR GEORGE ELLIOTT HOWARD
The University of Nebraska

Increasingly for nearly four centuries the meaning of the freer granting of divorce has challenged the attention of thoughtful men. The moralist, the theologian, and the statesman have each shared generously in the discussion. Now the sociologist takes his turn. Emphatically this morning we have set ourselves a world-problem. It behooves us to use strategy in the attack. Possibly we may contribute most to the solution of the general problem by confining the discussion mainly to the part—by no means a small part—which the American people have in it.

The movement of divorce in the United States during the twenty years, 1887–1906, is now fully disclosed in the great report of the Director of the Census. That report is surprisingly satisfactory to the scientific student, when he considers the shamefully imperfect or totally lacking registration of vital statistics in most of the states and territories; and that the facts presented had to be gathered mainly from the manuscript decrees of some 2,800 divorce courts: which decrees, of course, were not framed to suit the sociologist. These carefully planned tables and luminous interpretations have provided the student of American society with a rich mine for exploitation during many years to come.

The admirable summary just presented by Dr. Hill renders any formal analysis of the report in this paper unnecessary. From that summary it seems reasonably clear that in our country there is a "freer granting of divorce." We need not beg our premise. Divorce is about three times as frequent as it used to be. This is the salient fact. In Europe, too, while the *number* of divorces is relatively small, generally the *rate* is rising. Clearly we are face to face with a phenomenon, huge, portentous. What is its meaning? How should it be interpreted? Assuredly it signifies somewhere the action of antisocial forces, vast and perilous. Doubtless here we have to do with an evil which seriously threatens the social order, which menaces human happiness; an evil to overcome which challenges our deepest thought, our ripest wisdom, our most persistent courage and endeavor. Is divorce the evil or the symptom? the cause or the effect? the disease or the medicine?

If we appeal to the decision of occidental thought since the Reformation, the answer is perfectly clear. From Luther and Bullinger to Milton and Beza, from Humboldt and Condorcet to the statesmen who have shaped the codes and molded the juridical theories of the twentieth century, always and everywhere the prevailing dictum is that divorce is prescribed as a remedy for a social malady. This is the justification of the divorce policy of the western world. Nay, this theory was acted upon with characteristic thoroughness by the Puritans of old New England. Logically, they instituted civil divorce as the counterpart of civil marriage. The documents of the colonial era, especially an exhaustive examination of the extant manuscript records of the ancient Massachusetts courts for nearly a century and a half, prove conclusively that in form and substance the American type of liberal divorce law and procedure was developed in Puritan days, long before the birth of our federal Union. Is this time-honored theory of divorce false? Is divorce, except perchance on the one "scriptural" ground, immoral, and therefore the fountainhead of the malady which afflicts us? It may be so; for often the sanction of centuries of traditional belief has but perpetuated a dangerous error. That which *is,* of course, is not necessarily a proof of that which *ought* to be.

Let us attack the problem by searching for the basic causes of the divorce movement.

I. IMPERFECT LEGISLATION AND FAULTY JUDICIAL PROCEDURE
ARE NOT A PRINCIPAL CAUSE OF THE DIVORCE
MOVEMENT

1. A certain, though not a large, percentage of the divorces granted, it must be confessed, is due to bad law and to lax

administration. In other words, if divorce be looked upon as a remedy, the disease which it seeks to cure may actually be spread through the mal-application of that remedy by our legislatures and by our courts. At first glance, this assumption appears to be inconsistent with the facts. A careful examination of the entire legislation of the last two decades reveals a decided improvement in American divorce laws. Gradually more stringent provisions for notice to the defendant have been made, longer terms of previous residence for the plaintiff are required, more satisfactory conditions of remarriage after the decree are prescribed, while some of the worst "omnibus" clauses in the lists of statutory causes have been repealed. Nevertheless, during the period the divorce rate has gained a threefold velocity. This result tends to prove, if proof be needed, that the real grounds of divorce are far beyond the influence of the statute-maker, and to sustain the well-known dictum of Bertillon that laws extending the number of accepted causes of divorce or relaxing the procedure in divorce suits have little influence "upon the increase in the number of decrees." It may indeed be impossible to measure exactly the effects of lax or stringent legislation. Still the reformer need not despair. Without the reforms accomplished the rate might have been higher. From all the evidence available, it seems almost certain that there is a margin, very important though narrow, within which the statute-maker may exert a morally beneficent, even a restraining, influence. He may render the legal environment favorable to the operation of the true remedy. Emphatically there are *good* divorce laws as well as *bad* divorce laws. From its very nature a bad law may become a dead letter, thus tending to destroy the popular reverence for law itself. It may even encourage domestic discord by offering opportunity for evasion, collusion, or lax interpretation. On the other hand, good laws may check hasty impulse and force individuals to take proper time for reflection. For this reason, the adoption of the decree *nisi* should be encouraged; while the sanction by the states of the remarkably sane recommendations of the Washington-Philadelphia divorce congress of 1906 would greatly contribute to the creation of the healthful legal environment, just mentioned. Eventually, this might aid us in getting at the root of the matter: the fundamental causes of divorce which are planted deeply in the imperfections of the social system —notably in false sentiments regarding marriage and the family; and which, as presently will appear, can only be removed through more rational principles and methods of education.

2. Regarding the effects of law and procedure in several points the report of Director North is enlightening. It is significant that only 15.4 per cent. of the divorces granted in the twenty years (1887–1906) were contested; and "probably in many of these cases," we are told, "the contesting was hardly more than a formality, perhaps not extending beyond the filing of an answer, which often has the effect of expediting the process of obtaining the divorce." The percentage of contested cases is slowly rising; and, except where the cause is adultery, the wife more than the husband is likely to resist the granting of a decree. Divorces on the ground of cruelty are most frequently and those on the ground of desertion least frequently contested. When notice is personally served, 20.4 per cent. of the cases are contested; while only 3.2 per cent. are resisted when notice is by publication. Usually the latter form of notice is "confined to those cases in which the residence and address of the libellee are either unknown or are outside the state in which the suit is brought," implying, "therefore, an existing separation either of considerable duration or of considerable distance or both." Now what is the meaning of these figures? Do they not in actual practice reveal an astonishing leaning toward a freer granting of divorce than that implied even in the enumerated statutory grounds, however ample the list may be? In effect though not in theory, do not these figures disclose a tendency toward dissolution of wedlock by mutual consent or even at the demand of either spouse?

3. On the other hand, the tables here presented confirm the conclusion based on the statistics compiled by Colonel Wright twenty years ago, that interstate migration for divorce has not much contributed to raise the average rate. For a particular state or town the judicial traffic with a divorce colony may be a serious matter; but contrary to the popular notion, on the divorce

movement as a whole the influence of clandestine divorce of this sort is almost negligible. Of the 820,264 divorces during the two decades granted to couples known to have been married in the United States, 21.5 per cent. were married outside the state in which the decree was rendered. But, of course, this does not mean that one couple out of five whose marriage was thus dissolved migrated for the purpose of obtaining divorce. "On the contrary," says Dr. Hill in the *Government Bulletin*, "it is probable that that motive was present in a comparatively small proportion of the total number of cases, and that to a large extent the migration was merely an incident of the general movement of population, which takes place for economic and other reasons, unconnected with the question of divorce." In fact, according to the census of 1890, 21.5 per cent. and by that of 1900, 21 per cent. of the native population were living outside the state or territory in which they were born. Making all due allowance for this striking coincidence of proportions, and considering that the average duration of marriage before divorce is ten years, it seems clear that Mr. Dike's judgment based on the statistics of the first report must still stand: "The establishment of uniform laws," he declared in 1889, "is not the central point" of the divorce problem.

4. Some light is thrown by this investigation on another objection to the modern divorce policy. In effect does not the very existence of liberal divorce laws constitute an incentive to unstable or other bad marriages? Are not risky, temporary, or immoral unions consciously formed in full view of their easy dissolution? The statistics, though inconclusive, afford little or no ground for an affirmative answer. The average duration of divorced marriages is ten years; while 60 per cent. of the total number of such marriages last less than ten years, and 28.5 per cent. of them less than five years. During the first year of married life are granted 2.1 per cent. of all divorces, or 18,876. The number rapidly increases until in the fifth year the maximum of 73,913 divorces or 8.2 per cent. is reached. "From this point on the number steadily diminishes year by year; but it does not fall below the number granted in the first year of married life

until the eighteenth year is reached." There are nearly twice as many divorces in the twelfth year of the wedded life as in the first. Now, when we consider that probably there are more people in the first than in the eighteenth year of married life, and that, as will soon appear, we have more cogent reasons to explain the laxity of the marriage bond during the early period, we are scarcely warranted in assuming that liberal divorce laws in themselves are perceptibly weakening the nuptial tie.

5. On the other hand, if people do not get married in order to be divorced; do they get divorced in order again to be married? Popular opinion answers this question decidedly in the affirmative. Yet in this instance, too, the popular judgment is doubtless wrong. Although only foreign evidence is available to test the point, it is not probable that restrictions upon the re-marriage of divorced persons in any large measure influence the divorce rate. Prussian and Swiss statistics, now too old to be very satisfactory, show that divorced men re-wed during the first three years at about the same rate as do widowers; while divorced women remarry somewhat more rapidly than widows.

II. THE MODERN DIVORCE MOVEMENT IS AN INCIDENT OF A TRANSITION PROCESS IN SOCIAL EVOLUTION; AND HENCE IT IS DUE PRIMARILY TO SOCIAL MIS-SELECTION AND THE CLASH OF IDEALS

1. As a general result of the foregoing discussion it may perhaps be admitted that, however harmful are the effects of bad law and administration, we must dig deeper to reach the secret of our problem. Of a truth, to the serious student of social evolution the accelerated divorce movement appears clearly as an incident in the mighty process of spiritual liberation which is radically changing the relative positions of man and woman in the family and in society. Through a swift process of individualization for the sake of socialization the corporate unity of the patriarchal family has been broken up or even completely destroyed. More and more wife and child have been released from the sway of the house-father and placed directly under the larger social control. The new solidarity of the state is being won

at the expense of the old solidarity of the family. The family bond is no longer coercion but persuasion. The tie which holds the members of the family together is ceasing to be juridical and becoming spiritual. More and more the family is dominated by the sociogenetic or cultural forces and less and less by the so-called "natural" or phylogenetic desires. Essentially the family-society is becoming a psychic fact. Beyond question the individualization for the sake of socialization is producing a loftier ideal of the marital union and a juster view of the relative functions of the sexes in the world's work. Immediately, from the very nature of the process it has inured most to the advantage of the woman. In the family, it is releasing her from *manu viri* and making her an even member of the connubial partnership; in the larger society, it is accomplishing her political, economic, and intellectual independence. In a word, it is producing a revolution which means nothing less than the socialization of one-half of human kind.

Now, this process of individualization, of liberation, is not yet complete. Indeed, its swiftest progress, its most visible results, belong to the last fifty years. Emphatically we are at the height of the transition from the old régime to the new. Therefore, it is not strange that there should be frequent mis-selection, many maladjustments of newly sanctioned social relations. The old forces of social control have been weakened faster than the new forces have been developed. The old legal patriarchal bonds have not yet been adequately replaced by spiritual ties. There is frequent and disastrous clash of ideals. The new and loftier conception of equal rights and duties has rendered the husband and wife, and naturally the wife more often than the husband, sensitive to encroachment, and therefore the reaction is frequent and sometimes violent. In the present experimental stage, the finer and more delicately adjusted social mechanism is easily put out of order. The evil lurks, not in the ideals, but in the mistakes of the social builder.

2. In the light of these facts, let us now examine the problem of divorce.

First of all, it is significant that liberty of divorce has a peculiar interest for woman. The wife more frequently than the husband is seeking in divorce an escape from marital ills. During the two decades (1887–1906) in the whole country over 66 per cent. of all decrees were granted on the wife's petition. Among the principal causes only for adultery was the number granted to the husband (59.1 per cent.) greater than the number granted to the wife; and in this case, were social justice attained, who can doubt that the ratio would be reversed? In large measure, directly or indirectly, this anomaly is due to the vicious dual standard of morality by which society still measures the sexual sins of man and woman, to the woman's disadvantage. The divorce movement, it is safe to say—and we shall gain more light on the subject presently—is in large part an expression of woman's growing independence.

3. Again, the process of liberation whose character has just been explained enables us to understand the underlying motive of the state in sanctioning an ever-extending list of legal causes of divorce. In the main, making all due allowance for mistakes, does not each new ground in effect give expression to a new ideal of moral fitness, of social justice, of conjugal rights? As civilization advances, the more searching is the diagnosis of social disease and the more special or differentiated the remedy. It is not necessarily a merit, and it may be a grave social wrong, to reduce the legal causes for a degree to the one "scriptural" ground. Adultery is not the only way of being unfaithful to the nuptial vow; not the only mode of betraying child or spouse or society. For example, the most enlightened judgment of the age heartily approves of the policy of some states in extending the causes so as to include intoxication from the habitual use of strong drinks or narcotics as being equally destructive of connubial happiness and family welfare. Decidedly it is not a virtue in a divorce law, as often appears to be assumed, to restrict the application of the remedy, regardless of the sufferings of the social body. Indeed, considering the needs of each particular society, the promotion of happiness is the only safe criterion to guide the law-maker in either widening or narrowing the door of escape from bad marriages.

4. A glance at the tables showing the relative number of decrees on each principal ground granted to the husband or to the wife, respectively, reveals the deep interest which the woman has in the divorce remedy. In 83 per cent. of all decrees granted for cruelty, in 90.6 per cent. of those granted for drunkenness, and 100 per cent. of those granted for neglect to provide, the husband was the offender and the wife the plaintiff. That the sources of the divorce movement are bad social conditions which may be remedied is illustrated by the sinister fact that directly or indirectly 184,568 divorces, or nearly 20 per cent. of the entire number reported for the two decades, were granted for intemperance; and in nine-tenths of these cases the culprit was the man. Surely the situation calls loudly, not for less divorce, but for less liquor and fewer saloons.

The extent to which divorce is due to desertion challenges our most serious attention. The number of decrees on this ground reaches the astounding total of 367,502 or nearly 38.9 per cent. of the entire number on all grounds for the two decades. Moreover, of the whole number of decrees granted to the husband for all causes, 49.4 per cent. (156,283) or nearly half were for desertion; while 33.6 per cent. (211,219) or one-third of all those granted to the wife were for the same cause. Here too, the woman is the chief sufferer and the chief beneficiary. The causes of the phenomenon of desertion are doubtless complex; but in a remarkable way it is a signal proof of a transition phase in American society. In large measure, is it not due to our vast sociological frontier, urban as well as rural? The marital renegade is lured by the ease with which under the existing conditions of social control he may hide himself on the range, in the lumber camp, in the mines, and amid the seething purlieus and slums of our great cities. Now for the abandoned family desertion often involves the bread-and-butter problem which the aggrieved spouse must have full liberty to solve. What is the remedy? Assuredly not the restriction of divorce, but the proper punishment of the deserter and the civilization of the sociological frontier.

5. There remains for consideration one more source of the divorce movement, and that the most prolific source of all. In no other way, perhaps, has mis-selection, the failure to develop methods of social control adequate to the new psychic character of the family been so harmful as in dealing with marriage. No one who in full detail has carefully studied American matrimonial legislation can doubt for an instant that, faulty as are our divorce laws, our marriage laws are far worse. There is scarcely a conceivable blunder left uncommitted; while our apathy, our carelessness and levity, regarding the safeguards of the marriage institution are well-nigh incredible. We are far more careful in breeding cattle or fruit trees than in breeding men and women. Let me repeat what I have more than once written: the great fountain head of divorce is bad marriage laws and bad marriages. The center of the dual problem of reforming and protecting the family is marriage and not divorce. One "Gretna Green" for clandestine marriages, like that at St. Joseph, Mich., is the source of more harm to society than are a dozen "divorce colonies" like that at Sioux Falls, S. D. Indeed, the "marriage resort" is the fruitful mother of the divorce colony. There is crying need of a higher ideal of the marriage relation; of more careful "artificial selection" in wedlock. While bad legislation and a low standard of social ethics continue to throw recklessly wide the door which opens to marriage, there must of necessity be a broad way out.

To the sixteenth-century reformer divorce is the medicine for the disease of marriage. Emphatically it remains so today. The wise reformer must deal with causes and not with effects. He will recognize that in a general but very real sense the divorced man or woman is a sufferer from bad social conditions. He will not waste his energy in unjustly punishing divorced people although some of them may deserve punishment. Rather he will strive to lessen the social wrongs of which the divorced man or woman is the victim. Let ecclesiastical synods, if they would serve society, concern themselves more with restraining the original marriages of the unfit. Let them reflect on the social wickedness of joining in wedlock the innocent girl with the rich or titled rake; of uniting in the nuptial bond those who are tainted by inherited or acquired tendencies to disease and crime.

Therefore, to the question today put to me: "Is the freer granting of divorce an evil?" I answer: While social disease increasingly menaces the health and happiness of the family—and this in part because the family ideal is rising—a more liberal application of relief is just and righteous. It is not without significance that the highest divorce rate is found in two of the most enlightened and democratic nations in the world—Switzerland and the United States. Yet divorce is merely a healing medicine for marital ills. It is needful to apply the radical or preventive remedy. That remedy is proper social control; but adequate social control can be achieved only through the thorough socialization of education. We are in sore need of a rational system of education broad enough to embrace the whole complex problem of sex, marriage, and the family. That is the noblest and the hardest task which now confronts the American people.

DISCUSSION

DR. SAMUEL W. DIKE, AUBURNDALE, MASS.

The paper of Professor Howard, it is enough to say, is worthy of the author of the monumental *History of Matrimonial Institutions* and admirably brings the subject before us. Let me first make some random remarks suggested by his statement of facts.

I should say that divorce is both the evil and the symptom, both the cause and the effect, both the disease and the remedy or relief. Nor let us forget that divorce implies the confession of the helplessness of the case. That is, so far as the family in question is concerned, it is not a case for remedial treatment but for surgery. From one point of view every application for divorce presents the question: Is the case hopeless except as we use the knife and sever the bond? Have the parties themselves, their friends, and society used every possible means for recovery, and are we taking the judicial knife as the last resort?

Let us beware, too, of taking certain percentages in the statistics at their face value. For example, that women are petitioners in 67 per cent. of the cases does not so much indicate that women are the chief sufferers to that extent as that it points to the probability that it is often more convenient for the wife to bring the suit. Desertion, cruelty, drunkenness, and non-support are made to cover a multitude of other marital sins. The technical grounds chosen for a divorce are often those most easily worked with little regard to their reality. Mutual consent as the real cause is probably increasing, perhaps rapidly. The large percentage of uncontested cases shows this. While women are more frequently the sufferers than men I think it probable that among certain classes the demand for dress and other luxuries, social ambitions, and sometimes aversion to mother-hood, as well as the selfishness and excessive sexual demands on the part of men, have much to do with divorce.

That easy divorce is something of an incentive to hasty and incon-siderate marriage is clear from positive private testimony rather than from any statistics on the point. One of our states, Connecticut, furnishes from its registration reports confirmation of Professor Howard's opinion that divorces as a rule do not issue in a speedy remarriage and that many divorced persons do not marry again. The number of divorced persons married in Connecticut for several years is about 40 per cent. of the num-ber divorced in the same time. And the fact brought out in the government report that on the average six years elapses between separation and the application for divorce and three years more between the application and the divorce points very clearly to the probability that the desire for another marriage is not present at the time of the seeking of divorce in a large majority of the cases as has been hitherto supposed. Then the restrictions many states are now making on the remarriage of divorced persons does not seem to affect the divorce-rate very much. What Professor Howard says of the limited extent of migration for divorce is quite true. An exami-nation of the statistics of the Dakotas by counties shows that the illicit divorce business in those states was confined to three or four counties and that the state as a whole was not very far from normal.

To my mind one of the most serious evils of our divorce business is suggested by the fact that in the last twenty years the percentage of divorces that occurred after twenty-one years of married life was 10.2 per cent. of the entire number of those divorced in the last twenty years and, what is more significant still, has risen to 10.2 per cent. from 7.8 per cent. in the preceding twenty-year period, an increase of 40 per cent. in twenty years. It is true that in one aspect of the case this is less of an evil than divorce earlier in married life. But I think careful reflection will discover a grave evil in it.

But now let us pass to some considerations which the second part of Professor Howard's paper suggests. His main proposition is that "the modern divorce movement is an incident of a transition process in social evolution; and hence it is due primarily to social mis-selection and the clash of ideals." Now while I think him substantially correct in this I would, for one, put the case a little differently. The word "transition" implies too much of suddenness and I think that "mis-selection" and the phrase "clash of ideals" do not quite cover the ground. I would state it in somewhat less of the terminology of scientific sociology. Perhaps I may use the generalization of Sir Henry S. Maine in his Ancient Law, when in looking over the drift of western society for more than two thousand years he said that modern society had been marked by a movement from the family to the individual and from status to contract, the two movements having gone on together. In other words, contract, which underlies most business law, has taken the place of status in our treatment of most social relations, and along with it and as its cause too, has gone the substitution of the individual as the unit of social thought for the family. The growth of the larger combinations has been very largely at the expense of the family notwithstanding their reinforcement of it in many ways.

The divorce movement is probably the most momentous of the evil consequences of this fundamental social change. The movement for the larger political rights of woman and for her greater industrial opportunities has gone along with it. And, as Maine also pointed out elsewhere, the movement in behalf of woman is not so much a movement in the interests of sex as it is a movement in the interests of property. It is the influence of property compelling woman to find an easier place under its industrial yoke that is forcing women into the ranks of the industries. The growth of property tends first to separate out individuals, both men and women, from all lesser corporate forms, like the family and the small business corporation, and, secondly, to combine them in the largest possible unities. Anarchy and socialism are the extremes of the outcome. The family, the primary social group, is between the upper and nether millstone of this process. Of course the great spiritual appeal of Christianity and of society to the individual during the centuries has had its part in the movement.

As a consequence of this profound social movement we have on the one hand the growth in much that is healthful for the individual and the development of the useful corporate institutions of modern society. But on the other hand we have an intense individualism with all its disintegrating forces. Egoism and selfishness do their destructive work in this soil. The family loses its organic character in the eyes of many and becomes a mere *modus vivendi*, dependent on the simple contract of business for its formation and easily dissolved by agreement of the parties who made it. This is the theory of the social contract, which we discarded in our Civil War, applied to the most fundamental of all social institutions. And here lies the political mischief of our lax divorce system.

But it has other than mere political evils. The 72,000 divorces annually, involving twice as many persons as husbands and wives, and about as many more children, and almost as directly as many more relatives are poisoning society quite as disastrously in other ways. For among the divorced reverence for each other, regard for the rights of others, love, sacrifice, and service as the nourishment of the sources of character are often entirely gone or sadly weakened. Industrial ambitions are lessened, frugal habits discouraged and the intellectual and moral training of a happy home that depends on a wholesome, honest facing of burdens, is weakened. In short the very warp into which is woven that religious, intelligent, industrious, and patriotic domestic life which makes the fabric of the nation is enfeebled at the place where of all others it should be strongest. The relief to the suffering individual is purchased at fearful cost to the social value of the individual, which after all is absolutely essential to his own perfection. The real problem is that of the family, whether we consider divorce, unchastity, lack of offspring, or the more subtle, yet I think more dangerous of its ills—those which come through the disuse of the family in the transfer of its legitimate functions to church, school, and other substitutes for the home.

The direct influence of lax laws in producing the great increase of divorce in the last forty years is relatively small. On the whole the lax measures added to the statutes of our states in the last forty years have been few and comparatively unimportant. And the tendency of legislation the last twenty years has been decidedly in the direction of greater stringency. The systems that we now have are largely a legacy from colonial days and the early settlements of the West. The remedies must be sought chiefly, though by no means wholly, in other directions. The instructions of the church and the school, better industrial conditions and an improved social sentiment must be our chief reliance for reform. We need what may be called the socialization of the individual through his better adjustment to society as a whole and that must come about through his better adjustment to the family and the other corporate institutions of society.

If divorce is due "to mis-selection and the clash of ideals," a form of statement that seems to me somewhat inadequate, nevertheless I do not think the correction of ideals or better selections necessarily the immediate cure of the evil or the chief means of meeting the difficulty. While undoubtedly better selections should be made and higher ideals held, yet there is more need of recognizing the value of loyalty to relations already existing, both for the good of society and the perfection of individual character. The moral cowardliness that runs away from a situation because it is hard is not a good thing out of which to make the men and women whom society needs. The ideal of a lifelong union in which hardships are used for the discipline of life should be the goal before us—that and not the feeble adjustment of laws and institutions to human weaknesses and whims should be our aim, toward whose attainment we should move as fast as we can. We should remember that in social evolution mutations are far more possible than in the lower ranges of life. For here and in proportion as we rise in the scale of being, the human will comes in as a mighty factor for changing the trend of movement. Human society has no business to succumb to drifting tendencies in its evolution. For it is called upon to resist tendencies and to shape them toward the highest ends.

The first stage in modern society found the husband and wife merged in one and that one, as Blackstone put it, the husband. The second stage has made them two individuals only with all the perils of individualism. May we not now have come to a third stage in which we are to find, not simply two individuals living in contractual relations, but two persons finding their relations to each other not only as individuals but as members of the family, which is something more than the sum of the parts composing it? To bring this about do we not need something more than a selfishly individualistic struggle for the narrow ideals of self? Must not the forces from within be directed and inspired to an evolution that finds its highest incentives from without? And may not what we need from the church be, not dogmas on divorce, but inspiration toward the highest ideals and real leadership in that direction?

THE MARRING OF THE MARRIAGE BOND

RABBI KRAUSKOPF, D.D., Philadelphia, Pa.

We are told that divorces are increasing three times as fast as our population; that during the past twenty years the marital bonds of nearly two millions of husbands and wives were legally severed; that, taking the United States as a whole, no less than one marriage in twelve has terminated by divorce; that in some states the proportion is as high as one to seven; that the number of divorces in our country is larger than that of all the European countries combined.

This report, though no surprise to those who have observed the trend of things in late years, has startled the nation, and has kept the prophets of ill quite busy since its publication. Some of these are practically counting the days when marriage will be no more. Basing their estimate on the present rate of divorce, they claim that in the year 1920 every marriage entered into will ultimately be severed by the law. Trial marriage, advocated a few years ago as a novelty, according to their view, has become a reality. When men and women plight their troth before a preacher or magistrate it is no more for a union that shall last "until death do them part" but until such time as the one shall cease to care for the other. But a step, they assert, separates trial marriage from that free love which is being advocated in some of our latter-day novels and plays, and large is the number of those who have already passed from one to the other. Man's modern conception of marriage, according to them, is largely that of the poultry yard. Men and women, having been polygamous and polyandric in the remote past, are fast reverting to the primitive and bestial type out of which thousands of years of civilization have labored hard to lift them. So great has become the corroding influence of prosperity on marital morality that, when the passions bid, there religion and law forbid in vain.

While the facts and figures contained in the latest census report are saddening, I fail to find in them a reason for utter disheartenment, or for such predictions of calamities as foretold by our prophets of ill.

At times I am rather inclined to find in those figures a hope of brighter days coming, of a nobler conjugal life and a larger domestic happiness than have yet obtained in human society. When I analyze the causes of unhappy marriages, when I note by whom, for the most part, divorces are sought, to whom they are granted, and for what cause, when I find that two-thirds of the divorces are granted to wronged women, that wives find it more and more insufferable to continue yoked to husbands who have disgraced their manhood, who have violated the sanctity of womanhood, who have polluted the purity of the marital tie—when these facts I note, I see the coming day when marriage will have a far different meaning from what it has now, when entrance into it will constitute a coveted privilege, not a convenience or speculation or diversion, when purity not purse will constitute the absolutely necessary prerequisite, when all the honor that is now demanded of women will be demanded of man, when a lack of it in man will constitute as much of a bar to marriage, or to continuance in it, as a lack of it now constitutes a bar for woman.

That there are more divorces in our country than there are in Europe we freely grant, but we do not prepare to grant that the fewer European divorces are a sign of a larger morality than is found among us, or of a higher regard for the sacredness of marriage, or of a greater respect for womanhood.

The less number of divorces in European countries is due principally to the fact that in a large number of them the church, as well as the law, forbids divorce. A wife in those countries may suffer the agonies of hell, her husband may neglect her, starve her, abuse her, outrage her, dishonor her, he may be a drunkard, an idiot, a brute, a criminal, he may consort illicitly with a dozen-other women, there is no help for her, she is yoked to him for life, she can escape from him only through the gateway of the grave. Although half a dozen matchmakers may have labored assiduously to effect the match, and although parents and notaries may have haggled long over the dower settlement, religion and law proceed in these countries on the theory that the match was made in heaven, and what God has joined, no man may sunder.

And in many of those European countries where divorce is permitted, woman has been so long accustomed to masculine tyranny, to being lorded over, to being regarded as belonging to a lower order of beings, to possessing few if any rights, to being wholly dependent on man, to being treated as a household drudge, as a man's sport, as a mere child-bearer and child-raiser, that no matter how great the injustice she suffers, no matter how great the indignity heaped upon her, she regards it her duty to lick the hand that strikes her, to honor the man that dishonors her, to submit to every whim of her lord and master, to bear her cross with patience and with resignation, for such is the lot of woman, such is the will of her Father in heaven.

Not so the American woman. Occupying a position of equality with man, she insists upon her equal rights. The honor and virtue demanded of her she demands of her husband. She does not believe in one standard of morality for the wife, and another kind for the husband. Responsible for the moral well-being of her children, she will have their father as well as their mother serve them as exemplars in virtue. What constitutes moral guilt in woman constitutes it no less in man. Her whole nature rebels against that injustice that forever expels from decent society the woman that is led astray, while it opens wide the best of homes and the best of marital chances to the moral leper, if his bankruptcy in morals is compensated by a plethora of wealth. She has not yet discovered, and never will, that difference in sex constitutes a warrant for different morals. To her the seventh commandment, as well as the other laws of similar import, are as binding upon the man as upon the woman. If her husband would keep her love and respect, he must, in turn, continue to give her all the love and respect to which her womanhood, her wifehood, her motherhood are entitled. It is well enough to teach the duty of blessing those that curse, loving those that hate, but woman, with all the divinity in her soul, is after all but human, and she cannot forever go on blessing where she is cursed, loving where she is hated. When much sinned against she has all she can do to keep herself from sinning; at times, alas, her struggle is hopeless and she succumbs.

The true American woman will not, cannot, condone moral depravity in her husband, in the father of her children. As pure as he wants her so pure does she want him, or not at all. Her nature revolts against continuing in holy wedlock, in its full meaning, with a man whose every thought is vice, whose every breath is pollution, whose body is a sink of corruption, a whited sepulcher. For the sake of the public she will suffer quietly, much, and long, but in the end, she will value her self-respect more than the public's gossip, and free herself from a presence that poisons her moral atmosphere, that debases her body, soul, and mind. Possessing the American spirit of independence, not afraid or ashamed to work, capable of self-direction, she will free herself from a bondage that is more painful to her than self-support and self-dependence can ever be. A thousand times rather will she brave alone the hardships of life, a thousand times rather will she battle alone single-handed for a livelihood for herself and her children, then continue in wedlock with a man whose troth at the marriage altar was a lie, whose professions of lasting love were but a hollow mockery, whose motive for marriage was but a bestial or mercenary one, who, notwithstanding sacred pledges given before God and man, continues after marriage the revels and debaucheries that marked his preparation for the holy state of matrimony.

But man is not the only transgressor against the sacredness of marriage. Woman, too, bears a large share of the responsibility for the present-day frequency of marital separations. We were told that two-thirds of our annual divorces were granted to wives. What of the one-third that is granted to husbands? What of the desecration of the marital tie by woman? Considering the nature of womanhood, its greater seclusion and protection, its larger and longer training in modesty and self-control, considering all this, is not the charge against woman as great as that against man?

The preparation which young women are given in all too many homes is but a training calculated to lead in the shortest time possible from the marriage altar to the divorce court. From the day the daughter enters young womanhood, the chief thought of such homes is man-catching. To that end, no expense is spared, no extravagance denied, no field barred, no artifice shunned, that shall enable the gorgeously decked-out huntress quickest to entrap her victim, and to bring him conquered to her feet.

With too many parents there seems to be little consciousness that, besides a body to hang clothes upon, and besides certain social accomplishments with which to charm, the marriageable daughter has also a mind, a heart, a soul, a pair of hands, that require training in the science and art of keeping the husband contented and happy within the home of her sovereignty, and keeping herself contented and happy with the prize she has won. There is no preparation for the needs and responsibilities of domestic life, of home-companionship, of economic housekeeping. There is no knowledge of the art of settling down contentedly and happily with the man to whom she is linked for life, no skill in harmonizing differences of tastes and temperaments, which unharmonized, often prove disastrous to early married life. There is no love implanted for the sacred joys of motherhood. There is no knowledge of the meaning of the word "helpmate." There is no conception of the difficulties involved in earning money, seeing how lavishly it is being expended upon her, seeing with what readiness her every demand for it is supplied.

There is probably no thought which occupies a young society woman more than the thought of being married; there is probably no thought which occupies her less than that of how to be happy when married, or how to make her husband happy.

Entering upon marriage with such a conception of its meaning, with such resolutions, it is not difficult to tell what its ending will be. When a young wife's hands and mind have nothing useful to do, they soon turn to the unuseful and ignoble. When a wife does not know the art of home-making, she soon opens for the husband the doors of other homes. When a wife has no love for her husband, when she refuses him her sympathy, encouragement, and companionship, a husband is very apt to seek these where he can find them. When a wife seeks to wield the authority of the husband, she soon loses the privileges of the wife. When a wife's time is so much occupied with society as to have little or no time for a husband, it is not long before he finds those who have plenty of time for him. When a wife, of her own free will, bars out of her life the blessing of maternity, and with it a peace of heaven, she is very apt to send her matrimonial bark adrift without anchorage, and to increase the danger of its foundering upon the rocks of discontent, dissension, and disunion. When a wife accustoms herself to seek her pleasures outside of her home, and without her husband, she not only points to her husband where he is to seek and find his pleasures, but also runs the danger of accustoming each other to seek apart pleasures that are forbidden. When a wife burdens her husband with extravagances beyond his ability to satisfy, she but hastens the day when he will endure neither the burden nor the wife. When, vampire-like, a wife saps a man of his manhood instead of inspiring his soul with strength and enthusiasm to fight his battles and win his victories as behooves a helpmate, she soon finds herself unable to live contentedly at the side of the wreckage of her making. When a wife feels that she cannot do without the extravagances which her husband will not or cannot grant, and if she has no resources of her own, she will endeavor to obtain them from others than her husband, and, not infrequently, at a cost for which settlement is made in the divorce-court.

It is not whether there shall be one way or another way or no way at all out of marriage that is of prime import to society, but that couples shall live so happily together that there shall be no need of any exit at all. The real remedy lies not in making divorce difficult or impossible, but in making entrance into marriage hard, in taking every precaution in advance that those who join in holy wedlock for life shall possess those absolutely necessary prerequisites that may render possible a healthy, happy, sacred marital union.

What better illustration of the truth of this than that which is afforded us by the history of the Jewish people?

Their code of law recognized the right of divorce from the very first, and granted it for offenses far less weighty than those for which divorces are issued in even so obliging a state as Dakota. And yet, notwithstanding this readiness of the law to dissolve marital unions even for slight offenses, divorces in Israel were exceedingly rare. And rare have they continued in Israel to this day, because the care that was exercised in olden days with regard to a proper entrance to marriage, with regard to a proper preparation for it, and a proper behavior while in it, is, for the most part, exercised to this day.

The chief care of society must therefore be the prevention of the rise of marital misery, so that divorce, rigorous or lenient, may become wholly unnecessary. The present large number of divorces will, I believe, effect, before long the needed cure. Where the church has failed the divorce court will succeed.

Alarmed at last by the large number of marital separations, parents will inquire into the cause, and but a little search will show them that they themselves bear a large part of the responsibiity. And the young woman, too, will recognize the seriousness of marriage, and will duly fit herself for it. She will recognize that it is largely the wife who makes or mars the home, that, however desirable a butterfly-life may be in maidenhood, it has no place in the wedded state.

Dr. J. P. Lichtenberger, Philadelphia, Pa.

I wish personally to express my appreciation of the admirable paper presented by Professor Howard. In the first half of the caption of the second division of his paper it seems to me he has given us not only the clue to the answer of the question under discussion but the basis for the right understanding of the whole divorce movement. My contribution to the discussion, therefore, will be little more than a confirmation of the conclusions to which he has so skilfully led us. His contention that the divorce movement is the product of causes inherent in our modern social situation is strengthened by a study of the correlation of the statistical curve of the increasing divorce-rate with those representing the growth of population, the movement in civil and ecclesiastical legislation and those describing such social phenemena as suicide and insanity. Population shows a relatively constant ratio, and, as Mr. Hill has pointed out, cannot account for the divorce-curve. Professor Howard stated, a fact easily confirmed, that civil legislation has tended slightly toward stringency, while a careful survey of the enactments of the churches comprising the Inter-Church Conference on Marriage and Divorce reveals a purposive and vigorous effort to meet the exigencies of an accelerated divorce-rate by restrictive measures on the part of the clergy and the church. If effective, or even greatly influential, the divorce-rate should have shown, in the second period, a diminution. As a matter of fact, there is no perceptible correlation between "the threefold velocity" which the divorce-rate has gained in the last twenty years and these movements. The case is different when we turn to those phenomena which are clearly the product of social causes. I quote from Morselli on suicide (p. 152): "The relation between the number of suicides and the general economical conditions is demonstrated by the continuous growth of the former in the century which beyond all others has witnessed the development of commercial relations, and the perfecting of the industrial arts by science. It seems almost as if the character of an epoch is reflected in that phenomenon of our social life, namely, the increase of psychological aberrations, nay, this reflection is such, that by the variable average alone, either of the mad or of suicides, or of criminals, the economical well-being of a year or of a country can be determined." The thoughtful investigator will not be at all surprised to find that the divorce rate bears a striking correlation to the phenomena here described, and Morselli, with equal propriety, might have included divorce among his indices of general prosperity. Unfortunately the waste products of an advancing civilization have often been mistaken for the signs of social deterioration and attention has been focused at the wrong point. Remedial measures have often hindered a process they were designed to help. We might as well seek to stop suicide by prohibitive legislation as divorce. The sane method, as Professor Howard has indicated, is constructive treatment of the causes rather than destructive treatment of results. Marriage, in the aspect we are discussing, is the legal sanction of the social custom of the family. It is dependent upon law neither for its institution nor for its perpetuation. We need to get rid of the fear that the family will disintegrate unless held together by law. The family always has and probably always will arise and disintegrate as the necessities of life require with scant regard for our laws on the subject.

It would be bold and presumptuous, within the limits of a ten-minute paper, to attempt to present a classification of the inherent causes which have produced "the mighty process of spiritual liberation" which Professor Howard assigns as the general cause of the freer granting of divorce. But since this spiritual process has material foundations it may not be amiss briefly to note them.

1. The roots of social causation lie deep in the soil of physical processes. Social institutions enjoy no exemption from the law of survival. A dynamic physical environment is destined to produce radical changes in the psychological and social processes. Therefore, in the new adjustment of the family, necessitated by the industrial revolution, are to be found, not only the causes of much domestic infelicity, but changed ideals regarding the family. Rising standards of living, pressure of the modern economic life upon the home, the passing of the economic function of the family and the economic emancipation of women are among the most important material facts which have produced changed ideas and ideals and serve as a partial basis on which to explain the movement toward spiritual liberation.

2. The struggle for social liberation in the United States has been particularly rapid since the Civil War. Individualism has thriven on our soil. Free from inherited traditions regarding the sacredness of institutions, inherent in a monarchical or despotic form of government, Americans assume toward them the same attitude as toward government itself. Institutions exist to promote "life, liberty, and the pursuit of happiness. When for any reason they become destructive of these ends, it is the right of the people to alter or abolish them and to organize new ones, laying their foundations on such principles and organizing their powers in such form

as to them shall seem most likely to effect their welfare and happiness." (Slightly paraphrased.) The popularization of law, increased popular learning, and the improved social status of women, conspire to render intolerable domestic conditions placidly endured under the régime of economic necessity and patriarchal authority.

3. These arguments seem to me implicit in Professor Howard's generalizations and I have merely called attention to them, but a third of no less vital and fundamental importance he has omitted. I refer to the transition in religious and ethical concepts which has taken place in the same period.

Since Darwin published his *Origin of Species* in 1859, the whole intellectual process has been transformed. The old static, dualistic view of the world has been replaced by the new scientific outlook with its evolution-concept and its stringent genetic method. What are the results in the sphere of religion and ethics? Two generations have witnessed the passing of the dogmatic age in Protestant theology. The heresy trials of the last few decades witness the throes of transition as clearly as strikes and riots do the struggle of readjustment in the industrial world. The time-honored landmarks of religious authority have been obliterated and the new basis has not yet been fully established. The case is not different in the sphere of ethics. With the changed point of view have come new ethical valuations. The stern morality of Puritanism, based on theoretical standards, is being replaced by a practical morality arising out of our changed social conditions. As a combined result, virtue no longer consists in literal obedience to arbitrary standards set by community or church but rather in conduct consistent with the demands of a growing personality. Whereas piety in marriage once consisted in loyalty to the institution, and any suffering which might arise was to be endured rather than to bring reproach upon an institution vested with peculiar divine sanction, today our revised ethical and religious ideas cause us to feel that marriage was made for man and not man for marriage, and that the moral value of marriage lies in the mutual happiness of those who enter into it. Popular moral sentiment, which more than ever regards the ideal marriage as the supreme method of realizing the perpetuity and education of the race, nevertheless recognizes worse evils than divorce and has come not only to approve but to encourage the breaking of the conventional marriage tie to the crushing of the human spirit.

A group of practical consequences are thus brought into view as the result of a rising and not a falling standard of ethics.

1. There is a growing intolerance of evils formerly endured. Assume that the moral status of marriage conditions remains the same and that moral perception is clarified. The result will be precisely the same as if the moral consciousness should remain undisturbed while immorality increased. Improved ethical standards or increased ethical culture may

therefore become as efficient disturbing causes as increased immorality. Until the time comes when moral conduct shall more nearly conform to improved moral ideals, the high divorce-rate will continue to be a vigorous protest against the discrepancy.

2. Practical ethics knows no distinction of sex and the "vicious dual standard of morality by which society still measures the sexual sins of men and women to the woman's disadvantage" is deemed ultimately to disappear.

3. Ideals compatible with the nature of the economic family of necessity are inadequate under improved ethical and religious standards. As the family ministers less to the necessities of life it ministers more to its amenities. A relation deficient in the higher ethical values, easily endured, if at all perceived, in the family whose coherence rested chiefly upon its economic advantage, may furnish the strongest motive for disintegration in the family based upon mutual happiness and helpfulness.

4. Perhaps the chief effect of the causes we are considering is manifest in the development of the new basis of sexual morality. As the function of the family undergoes the transition from that of practical expediency to the higher functions, uncongeniality and incompatibility become more serious matters. They are quite as capable of destroying the purpose of marriage as much graver difficulties under the old régime. Ethical values come to reside in those qualities of mutual attraction and preference which constitute the new basis of marriage. Aside from certain modifying limitations of social utility, sincere affection is coming to be recognized by society as the only normal and decent basis for marriage and parenthood. It is from this point of view that we begin to regard all marriages based upon economic or social advantage as a bargain in sex and a form of legalized prostitution. And furthermore, that coercion, whether on the part of church or state, which compels one person to live with another person of the opposite sex in repugnant conjugal relations, does violence to all the finer ethical instincts of the soul and thus comes to be regarded as a species of despotism incompatible with free institutions.

If these generalizations are approximately correct, then it is certainly clear that the actual compelling forces in the sphere of religion and ethics are not ecclesiastical enactments and reactionary clerical resolutions which represent the conservative influences in the church, but those which reside in the nature of our modern social, intellectual, and religious life, and while less spectacular are nevertheless actually producing the practical results we are witnessing in the accelerated divorce-rate.

It is in these three groups of causes, namely, economic development, social progress, and religious and ethical readjustment, all of which have exerted their most potent influences in this country in the period covered by the two divorce reports, that we find the basis of the divorce movement.

Adhering then a little more mercilessly to the forces of social causation I do not wholly concur with the leader of the discussion in the strong emphasis placed upon "bad marriage laws and bad marriages." So far as hasty, ill-advised, and misfit marriages are concerned, the relatively small number of divorces (2 1-10 per cent. in the first year) in the early years of married life does not reveal an overwhelming number of those marriages which result in speedy termination. That the great majority of divorces occur after the fifth year, and half after ten years of married life seems to indicate that causes other than those due to bad marriages are exerting a constant and increasing pressure. As to biological misfits and mis-selection, like those due to social diseases, it is difficult to show why these should become increasingly dynamic in the last four decades, except that the changed environment furnishes the stimuli, which I think is the true explanation. I should say, then, as Professor Howard did of divorce laws, that there are good marriage laws and bad marriage laws, but I should incline strongly to the same conclusion in respect to their effects, viz., that the solution of our problem would not be at hand even if all marriage laws were good so long as the forces operate as they now do in which we have located the causes of the rising divorce-rate.

The increasing disruption of the family is a clearly recognized evil, but the necessary readjustment of the legal and social status of persons whose marriage relations have broken down, which we call divorce, is necessary and moral. Until the new family finds its equilibrium in the changed economic, social, and religious environment a high rate of divorce is inevitable, and is an index of progress rather than a sign of social disintegration.

HON. WALTER GEORGE SMITH, PHILADELPHIA, PA.

1. Professor Howard is quite correct in tracing the origin of divorce to the Reformation. It is a strong inference from the theory that marriage is a civil contract, that the state recognized it and also recognized its dissolution.

2. The professor is right also in his conclusion "that the real grounds of divorce are far beyond the influence of the statute maker, and to sustain the well-known dictum of Bertillon that laws extending the number of accepted causes of divorce or relaxing the procedure in divorce suits have little influence 'upon the increase in the number of decrees.'" And, of course, all must agree with him that reforms of the statute may exert a morally beneficent effect, though a narrow one, and such laws as the decree *nisi* and the other recommendations of the Divorce Congress of 1906 "would greatly contribute to the creation of the healthful legal environment."

3. Again the professor is absolutely right in saying that the fundamental causes of divorce "are planted deeply in the imperfections of the social system, notably in false sentiments regarding marriage and the family, and

which can only be removed through more rational principles and methods of education."

4. Again his inference is just that from the analysis of the figures of the report of Director North, though he puts in, in the form of a query, that "they . . . . in actual practice reveal an astonishing leaning toward a freer granting of divorce" and "disclose a tendency toward dissolution of wedlock by mutual consent or even at the demand of either spouse."

5. And again we can agree with him and with the Rev. Dr. Dike that "the establishment of uniform laws is not the central point of the divorce problem."

6. I confess I do not understand the professor's reasoning from the statistics that "there are nearly twice as many divorced in the twelfth year of the wedded life as in the first. Now, when we consider that probably there are more people in the first than in the eighteenth year of married life, and that we have more cogent reasons to explain the laxity of the marriage bond during the earlier period, we are scarcely warranted in assuming that liberal divorce laws in themselves are perceptibly weakening the nuptial tie."

7. While it is not fair to assume that a very large proportion of marriages are entered into with the deliberate intention of obtaining a divorce later, yet here is the qualification to distinguish between that which is explicit and that which is implicit. The community are being gradually educated (if they are not now fully educated) to a knowledge of the fact that with little trouble, little expense, and a little loss of social prestige (the last becoming more and more negligible) marriages can be terminated practically at the will of the parties. Surely this must have the effect of making them more careless in assuming the marriage relation.

8. Nor can I believe with the professor that the proportion of divorces obtained for the purpose of entering into new marital relations is not very significant, notwithstanding the inferences he deduces from the Prussian and Swiss statistics.

9. With the rest of the professor's paper I am compelled for the most part to disagree. Perhaps this disagreement arises to a certain extent from a lack of appreciation of the professor's terminology. When he speaks of "the mighty process of spiritual liberation which is radically changing the relative positions of man and woman in the family and in society," and points out with apparent satisfaction that "more and more wife and child have been released from the sway of the housefather and placed directly under the larger social control;" when he speaks of the new solidarity of the state as being won at the expense of the old solidarity of the family, and says that "beyond question the individualization for the sake of socialization is producing the loftier ideal of the marital union and a juster view of the relative functions of the sexes in the world's work," and adds that "immediately from the very nature of the process it has inured most to the advan-

tage of the woman," he is expressing satisfaction with a gradual social revolution that fills my mind with alarm, because it is based upon an absolute extinction of a fundamental religious principle; it is attempting to do what nature has not done in giving an equality of responsibility to man and to woman, and is setting up a deified state in the stead of the God upon whose laws, both natural and revealed, our civilization has been founded.

I deny that the granting of divorces from 1887 to 1906, where the applicants in 66 per cent. have been women, has resulted otherwise than in demoralizing the attitude of men and of women toward the married state.

Fortunately, there are certain fundamental principles of natural justice that all men share in common, and there are certain benevolent tendencies known as natural virtues which exist strongly in some natures where religion seems never to have held sway. These noble dispositions, generous impulses and compassionate feelings appear in all that Professor Howard has said. He sees the evils arising from immorality in all its phases upon the part of the husband, and the consequent suffering that ensues to the wife, and he thinks that by removing the husband from the position in which he has been placed by nature and permitting the wife to hold over him the constant threat of divorce the situation will be cured. This is the "perverted chivalry" of which Sidney Brooks wrote not long ago in endeavoring to find an explanation of the marvelous growth of divorce laws in the United States.

Of course, Professor Howard and men of his school are at the opposite pole from men who look upon the marriage relation as a sacrament, as a relation that rises so high above a civil contract that the state is guilty of usurpation in attempting to dissolve it. Marriage, it should be borne in mind, up to the time of the Reformation was looked upon as a status creating the family, and the family antedated the state, the state proceeding from the family. The attempt to individualize so as to give to man and woman the same sphere of action is going contrary to nature. It is not a question whether man is superior or inferior to woman. I suppose most of us are united in the belief that to woman is given the greater natural purity, the greater natural spirituality. Certainly those virtues that are peculiar to the feminine will not lack of recognition in any assembly of educated men, and surely it is the finest test of civilization that it gives to woman that peculiarly exalted position that is, in accordance with true chivalry, the position that is hers, not by the compulsion of any law, but by the recognition of her real high place in the ideal community. But the attempt to establish an equality that results in comradeship, that endeavors to ignore the relative strength, mental and physical, of the male and female, men who have studied the philosophy of history aright, even without a religious bias, must conclude is founded upon fallacy. I suppose the nearest approach to an equality of the sexes in the sense in which the term is understood by those who are advocating it in these modern days existed in the time of the Roman Empire under Augustus and his successors to the time of Constantine. Is it desirable to have a similar social condition in these modern days?

It is a pleasure to agree with Professor Howard when he says "the center of the dual problem of reforming and protecting the family is marriage and not divorce." All he says upon this subject meets with my hearty concurrence.

To sum up, in my judgment divorce is both a cause and an effect. I do not believe that any education of the character that Professor Howard suggests, no matter how widespread, can ever change nature, and the legislator who endeavors to change it will find his laws are a dead letter. For many centuries, and even down to our own time, divorce was so exceptional among the masses of the people, even among those who followed the teachings of Luther and his associates, that it was practically negligible.

The contention that Switzerland and the United States are the most enlightened and democratic nations of the world would, of course, not be contested in either of them. But what shall we say of England, of Ireland, not to speak of the Latin countries and Canada, where divorce is practically unknown?

It seems to me that the chasm between men of the new school of thought, who believe that the tendencies of human nature implanted by the Creator can be regulated otherwise than by religious sanction, and those who believe that the inevitable tendencies of our common nature can be controlled only by an appeal to religion cannot be bridged. Professor Howard has presented in scholarly form the best results of what is known as the scientific method of considering the divorce problem. I trust I do him no injustice when I say that he forgets the proposition, which is old as time. A recent writer has expressed it thus:

"For that there is a distinction between right and wrong; that orthodoxy and heresy are absolute realities and not mere prejudices; that there is such a thing as standing on one's feet and seeing the world aright, and such a thing as standing on one's head and mirror-reading the universe. . . . . We have talked of progress, of the relativity of knowledge, of science and empirical realities until we have come to the conclusion that absolute reality and absolute truth are sheer adumbrations, the survival of phantoms created by the human mind in its myth-making and fetish-worshiping stages. 'General theories are everywhere contemned; the doctrine of the rights of man is dismissed with the doctrine of the fall of man. Atheism itself is too theological for us today. Revolution is too much of a system, liberty too much of a restraint. We will have no generalizations. Everything matters except everything.' But why this fear of the infinite and the absolute? Are not the finite and the relative equally mysterious? . . . . And since the credentials they produce fail to satisfy him, he decides that these noisy latter-day prophets are nothing but common heretics—men who struggle vainly in a topsy-turvydom of their own creation. They are obsessed by what he calls 'the negative spirit,' the spirit that discovers weakness and failure, the spirit of disillusionment and dead ideals. 'The eye that can perceive what are the wrong things increases in an uncanny, and devouring clarity, while the eye which sees what things are right is growing mistier and mistier till it goes almost blind with doubt. . . . . To us light must be henceforth the dark thing, the thing of which we cannot speak. To us, as to Milton's devils in pandemonium, it is darkness that is visible.' And yet we talk of progress, and modernism has become almost a religion."

PROFESSOR E. A. ROSS, UNIVERSITY OF WISCONSIN

First, a word touching ecclesiastical pronouncements on this problem. Clergymen say they are in a position to state what is the will of God in the matter of divorce. We sociologists, less fortunate than they, know no way of settling the problem save by painstakingly ascertaining what divorce policy conduces *to the greatest welfare of the individuals concerned and of society, in the long run.* Now, either these two standards—the divine and the human—accord, or they do not. If God wills the happiness of his creatures, then we may rest in the assurance that the right interpreters of the divine will regarding divorce will, along their chosen route, reach, with an enviable swiftness and ease, the same practical conclusions as the sociologists, who make the effect of individual and social well-being the basis of judging an institution.

If, on the other hand, it be held that the divine decrees regarding divorce may clash with the welfare of the individual and of society in the long run, then those who undertake to declare the divine will *had better provide themselves with very solid and incontestable credentials* if they expect people to follow their guidance, even at the expense of individual and social happiness.

The champions of marriage as a sacrament twit us with standing for marriage as a mere civil contract. There are, to be sure, many shallow people who take the latter view; but I do not believe that the scientific students of society assimilate marriage with an ordinary contract. Their view is that marriage is *a socially approved status,* which a man and a woman voluntarily adopt, but which they may not renounce without the consent of society.

I am not of those who insist a grown man and a grown woman may assume any mutual relation they please. The welfare of the children—if there are any—and of society at large must certainly come into reckoning. At the same time, I fear our discussion has so far dwelt too exclusively on these factors. Surely the individual happiness of the mismated couple should count as at least *a factor* in the settlement of the problem. After all, divorce is not a monster going about breaking up happy homes.

No harmonious union was ever ended by divorce. The fact that in twenty years the proportion of divorces granted to couples who had been married twenty-one years or more, has increased from 8.3 per cent. to 10.6 per cent. was cited as if something ought to be done about it. I agree it is sad to see a man and woman give it up after the years have brought them to the time of life when new and satisfying ties are not easily formed. Still, is it not rather presumptuous for society to tell two middle-aged people, probably without young children, who, after twenty-one years of experience, agree they would be happier apart, that it knows better than they do what is best for them?

Excepting the small proportion of cases of hopeless incompatibility of temperament, a divorce testifies, no doubt, to some defect in efficiency or character in one or both of the spouses. Our divorces are, therefore, symptoms of a great evil, but it does not follow that the evil is any greater now than it was formerly nor that the evil can be lessened by narrowing the way of exit from marital unhappiness. Let those who are alarmed by growing divorce look further back. Let them center their efforts on lessening the proportion of unhappy marriages. There are open to them a number of promising policies which I shall commend to their consideration without comment.

1. Instruction of girls in domestic science, housekeeping, etc.

2. Systematic instruction of the youth of both sexes in the ethics and ideals of the marriage relation.

3. Safe-guards in custom, perhaps in law, against the marriage of pure women to men tainted with venereal disease.

4. Marriage only at place of residence of one of the parties.

5. Repudiation of the "common-law marriage."

6. A filing of declaration of intention to marry not less than (say) six weeks before the issuance of a marriage license. (Statistics show that the success of a marriage is in direct relation to the length of time the parties have been acquainted before marriage.)

7. Where the volume of business warrants it, the creation of special divorce tribunals on which women shall sit as well as men.

CONCLUDING REMARKS OF PROFESSOR HOWARD

In his address closing the discussion of the session, Dr. Howard said in substance: It is objected by Dr. Lichtenberger that too much importance is assigned to bad marriage laws as a cause of divorce; and that this is inconsistent with the position that divorce statutes, good or bad, have little influence on the divorce-rate. In reply, it is freely admitted that bad marriage law is not the chief source of divorce. Nevertheless, it will account for the dissolution of wedlock in far more instances than will a bad divorce law. For, in reality, clandestine marriage are very often due to this cause; and clandestine marriages are apt to terminate in divorce. Moreover, bad marriage laws may permit or fail to prevent the union of those who are unfit because of venereal disease, insanity, crime, or degeneracy. Thus there is a radical difference between a bad divorce law and a bad marriage law.

Professor Ross likewise believes that too much stress has been laid upon "bad marriage laws and bad marriages" as the center of the divorce problem; and he believes that we must go deeper in harmony with the second proposition of Dr. Howard's paper. But do not "bad marriages" really go to the heart of the problem? Marriages, not legally, but sociologically bad, are meant. They include frivolous, mercenary, ignorant, and physiologically vicious unions. They embrace all that would be forbidden by Francis Galton's science of Eugenics; all that might in part be prevented by a right system of education. Indeed, bad marriages are the cause of the clash of ideals referred to. At present men and more frequently women enter into wedlock ignorantly, or with a vague or low ideal of its true meaning. The higher ideal of right connubial life, of spiritual connubial lfe, often comes after the ceremony. It is *ex post facto;* and it is forced upon the aggrieved by suffering, cruelty, lack of compatibility, "prostitution within the marriage bond." An adequate system of social and sex education would tend to establish such ideals before the ceremony. "An ounce of prevention is worth a pound of cure."

Dr. Dike objected to the form of the second proposition, believing that Sir Henry Maine's dictum, that the movement of progressive societies has been from status to contract, is a more satisfactory expression of the evolutionary process under consideration. To this criticism it may be replied that Maine published his *Ancient Law* in 1861, many years before the birth of sociology as now understood. While it is true that since Roman days there has been a great advance from status to contract in the sphere of legal relations; it is not less true that in the present half-century there has been a vast progress from individualism to collectivism, from the person to the state. Were Maine now living, doubtless he would see the need of reshaping his dictum to express the new process of "individualization for the sake of socialization." Not individual contract but social control is the key to our problem.

Mr. Smith has brilliantly presented the sacramental conception of indissoluble wedlock. "I have a proper respect," declared Professor Howard, "for the courage and firmness with which the ancient church of Rome maintains her ideals, even her mediaeval ideals. In truth, from her unity, her centralization of authority, the Catholic Church today holds the point of vantage which sometime under a wise and progressive head may make her among religious organizations the leader in social achievement. But progress cannot be won by clinging to the authority of ancient ideals in social questions. We are assured that indissoluble monogamic marriage is according to both natural and divine law. But did natural law cease to work in old Jewish days? May it not be possible that natural law now guides social evolution? Moreover, is marriage any more "divine" than other social institutions? Was the only sacred wedlock created in the Garden of Eden by the God of Abraham, Isaac, and Jacob? Verily there are more gods than one, if we are to judge from the comparative history of matrimonial institutions. Many backward, even barbarous, peoples, who never heard of Javeh, are quite capable of teaching us useful lessons regarding divorce and marriage. Nay, in the days of Abraham, 2250 B. C., according to the Code of Hammurabi, the Babylonians, the teachers of Israel, had developed marriage and domestic institutions in many respects far more "modern" than those described in the sacred scriptures of the ancient Jews. Besides, as Rabbi Krauskopf has just shown, the God of Abraham, Isaac, and Jacob did not forbid divorce.

Truly, for the apostle of social righteousness, God did not close his revelation in olden times. Today, more clearly than in Judaea, he inspires the hearts and brains of devoted men and women to cleanse the slum, battle with social disease, and rescue women and children from sexual or industrial slavery. It is high time to cease the appeal to mere authority, and to accept marriage, the home, and the family as purely human social institutions to be freely dealt with by men according to human needs.

HOW FAR SHOULD MEMBERS OF THE FAMILY BE INDIVIDUALIZED?

PROFESSOR JAMES E. HAGERTY
Ohio State University

The changes in industrial and social organization in recent times have modified greatly the relationship between members of the family which existed in the patriarchal régime. The relations of the patriarch to the members of the household and the economic system which he controlled are too well known to need restatement here. The family was organized to perpetuate the family name and unity, and no rights of individual members were recognized which compromised this purpose. This ideal has been changed to one where social welfare is sought in the recognition of the rights of individual members of the family to the greatest possible latitude in the development of their capacities and powers. The power of the father and husband in the family has gradually weakened, while the rights and privileges of the wife and mother and the children have been strengthened. These changes are expressed both in statute law and in public opinion.

The rights and privileges of the wife have been most completely developed in America. A discussion of the sphere of woman has attained a dignity which prevails in no other country, and this is a clear indication of her status.

The marriage contract still in use requires the husband "to love, cherish, and protect." The wife is required "to love, honor, and obey." The husband must support, protect, and be responsible for his wife. The wife is required to render personal service to the husband, and to obey him. While in places the wife is legally bound to these obligations imposed upon her, public opinion does not support the claims of the husband to the wife in these respects. While she is expected to conform to the habits, tastes, and peculiarities of her husband, he has no redress if she refuses. However, he is the head of the home and the wishes of the wife must yield to his when their interests clash.

When unmarried, woman's right to earn her own support by going into industrial pursuits is generally conceded in the United States. When she earns her living, she is free from the obligations due a parent arising from economic dependence on him, and is thus, so far as economic reasons are concerned, under no requirement to marry. If woman owns property when married, she is permitted to hold this property and to have jurisdiction over it in nearly every instance. In some states she has the same rights of inheritance as the husband and the tendency of legislation is to put her upon the same plane as the husband in this regard. While the common law does not give the mother the right to the labor and services or earnings of a child until it is of age or marries the same as the husband, there is a tendency to grant her these rights especially if she is a widow. Her title to the earnings of her children in the latter case ought to be much more clear than that of a husband in any case except that of misfortune.

There is a tendency to consider the earnings of the husband as a joint product to which both husband and wife have an equal title. Where this principle has given rise to the allowance system the wife is free from the petty annoyances of begging funds from the husband to meet the expenses of the household. She then enjoys a regular income which may be used for her own personal expenditures as well as for the keeping of the house. The allowance system may be used however in a way not in conformity with the above theory. The husband may decide how much the wife is to have out of his earnings for certain purposes, and the wife may have nothing to say in regard to the matter. Upon the other hand, without the allowance system the total household and other expenses may be met in such a way as to emphasize the fact that the family earnings are a joint product. Whether the allowance or some other system is used the method employed in meeting expenditures should not embarrass the wife; it should result from a conference in which the husband and wife are equal factors in the decision.

Recent laws which give the wife the same rights in inheritance as the husband tend to support the theory that the family earnings are the joint product of husband and wife in which each should share equally. The slow development of this theory must be traced to other factors in the subordination of woman than those connected with her relative earning power. Man's sphere has been almost exclusively in the productive occupations which yield financial returns. Woman's work has been that of home-making and home-keeping and consequently she has been engaged in the so-called unproductive consumption for which there is no monetary return. But in home-keeping she renders a service to her family and society which gives her an economic value equal to that of her husband. The recognition of this principle, however late, means much for the complete emancipation of woman.

In the household, in the making of the home, woman renders her greatest social service and finds her highest function. Here she should be queen and priestess and no household arrangements should interfere with the development of her personality in its highest functioning.

The education and culture of woman is conceded in the United States, and it has been made possible for her to receive training equal to that received by man. Opportunities for the higher education of woman have not until recently been afforded on the continent of Europe outside of Switzerland, and the necessity for training comparable to that which man receives is even now denied. In the United States the right to an education has been put upon individualistic grounds, that is, the right to self development, to culture, and to happiness. This notion has arisen here as a part of our democracy.

The social advantages of the higher education of woman have not been properly emphasized in this country. Women as mothers are the educators of the children and on this account they should be well trained. As soon as we understand that the environment of infancy and early childhood is of more importance than later training we will appreciate the social importance of cultured mothers. Long ago in his great essay "What knowledge is of most worth?" Mr. Spencer gave due emphasis to the social need for well-trained mothers.

A recognition of an equal partnership of husband and wife in the marital contract is the present tendency. Public opinion is tending to support this view regardless of the wording of the marital contract, and laws in the statute-books of states discriminating against the wife are becoming dead letters. In no group does public opinion support the coercive authority of the husband except among the lower classes, and even here laws protect the wife against cruel and malicious treatment by the husband. Most people are willing to concede the advantages of the equal partnership of husband and wife, both upon the contracting parties and upon the children of the family. The education of woman qualifies her for this relationship. Where the husband and wife are upon the same level, where the woman is educated so that she is in fact the equal of her husband, this sort of marital relationship elevates the social and spiritual status of the family. Where this relationship exists parents can co-operate to good advantage in training and in developing their children.

The emancipation of woman has introduced certain social conditions the value of which is questionable. When woman is educated she marries later in life and is less inclined to marry. She uses better judgment in marrying and will not marry in a given case unless the alliance gives a very definite promise of happiness. She is very likely to make head interests a necessary supplement to heart interests. With the opportunities for women in industrial pursuits she is freed from the economic necessity of marrying. When she marries later in life, she has fewer children. If this reduction in numbers means an improvement in quality, the outcome is wholesome.

Biological problems, however, are introduced which as yet are unsolved. All we can do is to state them. It is claimed that the chances of having offspring diminish with the better education and the higher development of woman, and when she becomes a mother, the offspring are not as healthy and vigorous as are those of other classes.

CHILDREN

The social recognition of the rights of the child against the inordinate claims of the guardian are now well recognized in democratic countries. There was a time when a child could be punished for failing to pay the debts of a parent and for the misdeeds of a parent, so strong was the family bond and the family obligation. These restrictions have long since been removed.

Nearly everywhere the father is entitled to the labor and services or compensation for the labor of a child until it is of age. Many restrictions have been placed, however, upon the labor of a child. Child-labor laws forbid the employment of children under a certain age in specified employments. In rural communities, as a rule, the parent is rewarded by the fruits of the labor of children until they are of age. In cities, however, where as a rule the minor does not work for the parent, public opinion does not support the claim of the parent to the rewards of the toil of the minor unless the income of the latter is necessary to maintain the household. When he lives at home he will pay his board and the balance of his income will be used in defraying his personal expenditures.

The child-labor legislative movement began in England in the early part of the nineteenth century as a result of the abuses connected with the employment of pauper children in the factories. This movement which continued throughout the century consisted in placing greater and greater restrictions on the employment of children. In the United States a movement comparable to this has taken place. Most of the Northern states have child-labor laws. Through the aggressive policy of the National Child Labor Committee this movement has extended to the Southern states. In the Northern states the tendency now is to make the child-labor laws more uniform and to raise the minimum age at which children can be employed.

These laws are passed primarily to protect the child, to give him ample time to secure the rudiments of an education, to give his body a chance to grow to normal proportion, and to protect his morals while he is young from the contaminating influence of evil associates. The secondary purpose of this legislation is to safeguard the interests of society, as its security and advancement depend upon a well-trained moral citizenship free from physical degeneracy.

The child may be protected immediately from his own desires, or from the selfishness of his parents, or from the needs of the family of which he is a member. Social experience has taught us that in the absence of child-labor laws, the child would neither be educated nor be given the proper physical development. The opportunity to earn money has enticed many a child to a factory at an early age. Here lack of either a mental or industrial education and a narrow routine position have condemned many a child to a permanent mediocre position and a low standard of living. The selfishness of the parent may also start the child of tender years to labor with the above-named results. In these laws the state invades the home and protects the child from its own ignorance and its parents' shortsighted selfishness. The right to pass child-labor laws, and the necessity for them are now generally conceded.

Education is becoming less optional than formerly, as most of the states are passing compulsory educational laws requiring children to attend school until they are 13, 14, 15 years of age, or until they have finished certain branches of study. Experience has shown that many children will not be educated unless they are required to go to school. Even with a compulsory law the truant officer must be vigilant to enforce it.

Reports of the Commissioner of Education show that our achievements in general education are even yet very restricted. In the report of the Department of Education for 1900 it is stated that

over 50 per cent. of all public-school pupils were in the first and second grades and were less than nine years of age; 87.5 per cent. were in the first five grades and under twelve years of age.

In his report for 1908 the Commissioner says that

The mere ability to read and to write indicates a very slight remove from a crass ignorance, and a large proportion of our people are in danger of stopping at this point. The early withdrawal of pupils from school is a fact universally recognized, although up to this time there have been few systematic investigations as to the extent and the causes of the evil. It is, however, significant that they all indicate a marked decline in school attendance between the fourth and fifth school years or grades, and continued decrease thereafter.

Education is considered a social function and social right has taken priority over family rights. In democracy everything depends on the quality of the citizenship, for without an educated citizenship democracy must fail. A census of our prison population will show that the great majority of criminals are ignorant. One-third of the 1,600 convicts of the Ohio Penitentiary cannot read or write and the education of another third of these convicts is limited simply to the ability to read and write. As conditions here are typical of those prevailing in similar institutions, the shortsightedness of our past social policy in not making education obligatory will at once be obvious. A showing equally as bad could be made for ignorance as a cause of pauperism. The positive side of social action is of more significance to the state than the negative. It is more important to train good citizens because of the value of such citizens to themselves and the state than it is for the state to protect itself against the demoralizing influence of the anti-social criminal and dependent classes.

The state invades the home for another reason, and passes judgment on the method of governing the family. If parents abuse or maltreat their children, if they allow them to have evil associates, if the moral atmosphere surrounding the home is impure and demoralizing, the state steps in and takes the children from the parents. Here parental authority reaches its last ditch. It may be exercised if it is wholesome, and if the function rendered cannot be performed in a better way by the state, as the educational function. However, when parents are deprived of their children by the state, the latter are placed in another home. The best judgment of child-saving authorities today is that the normal home is the best possible environment for the growth and development of children. Institutional homes for children have been tried but are now considered by the best authorities as very inferior substitutes for home training.

One other way in which parental authority has been weakened in the United States remains to be mentioned. The right of parents to dispose of offspring in marriage is a survival of parental ownership. In Germany the right of parents to choose a husband for a daughter or a wife for a son is still conceded. In a number of continental countries practically similar parental rights exist. In the United States the consent of parents to marriage of children is necessary only in case of minors, but when minors marry without parental consent, the marriage is valid. Who will deny that better unions result when choice is left to the contracting parties rather than to parents? Parental dictation in these matters is so repugnant to our theories of individual rights that efforts to control usually result adversely.

The modern family is becoming democratic in many ways. Coercive power is giving way to control by persuasion. It is generally admitted that children are under better control when persuasive instead of coercive methods are used. When given privileges and responsibilities this method of control trains them for efficient citizens in a democracy.

Certain social and industrial forces have been at work which have weakened the solidarity of the home and have released its members from some family obligations. Formerly certain household industries were well developed. Some of these have been taken out of the home in relatively recent times. The kitchen is now the only productive factor in the home, and the preparation of many kinds of foods which were formerly produced in the kitchen, is now left to factories. Where the boarding-house and the family hotel are in use, even the kitchen has ceased to be a factor in home economics. Where the industries have been removed from the home, children have been released from certain obligations of household duties.

The home was once a place of worship, and family prayers in religious families were regular features. The religious education of the children, which formerly took place in the home, has now been assumed by the Sunday school in connection with the church. The prayer meeting has tended to take the family from the home to the church for religious worship, and the church, in a still wider way, has assumed most of the religious functions of the home.

In education the former home interests have been invaded to the greatest extent. With the development of the public school, and especially with compulsory education, children are sent from the home to be educated. With the appearance of the kindergarten, the home is turning over very small children to the school for purposes of education. The play-ground, the social settlement, and the socialized school are meeting in a much larger way the educational needs of children.

These institutions are breaking up the solidarity of the family, and are making the individual members less dependent upon each other, and upon parental authority. What is still worse, parents are in danger of delivering over to these outside agencies practically all cultural and educational training, thus weakening still further the bonds between parents and children. Where will this social tendency stop? Will it lead ultimately to the disintegration of the family as a social institution? However, with all encroachments upon it, the family is still, and, I believe, will remain the fundamental social institution.

The use of boarding-houses and the establishment of homes in flats and family hotels mark a still further departure in the destruction of family unity. The boarding-house and the family hotel are abnormal institutions in which to develop family integrity and strength. Their influence on the personality and training of the child is very questionable. In these institutions family unity and the welfare of children suffer without any apparent advantages.

Family solidarity is better maintained in the country than in the city. In the country, children usually remain at home until they are of age. Many of the outside agencies above described are not present to weaken the influence of the home. In urban communities, social conditions are so diversified that new developments must of necessity be sought. In the city it would seem that the hope of the children of the poor lies in the social settlement, the playground and the school. The condition of home life in the city, so far as the great masses are concerned, makes it impossible for the home to do the functions well of any of these agencies. Family solidarity must be maintained by both rich and poor alike, by an increased interest by parents in their children and in the training of the children. A very busy college man once told me that he had a schedule of one hour a day with his two boys which he always kept. "I want a chance at them" was his statement.

No definite solution to the question proposed is attempted here. All we can do is to state the present tendencies and to point out the good and bad features in the development of the modern family. Living in large numbers in cities is a comparatively recent phenomenon and adaptation to city living is one of the great problems of the present. In the changes taking place it is inevitable that the family must change.

Less attention to clubs and less interest in club life by parents, and more interest in their children should be a present-day demand. With the better education of both fathers and mothers, it will be easy for them to supplement the training of the school, the church, and the socialized agencies. The state may provide better educational facilities than can the family, but state education, with its system and methods, must be supplemented by individual education by the parent. The development of personality needs individual influence and training and no one can give these things better than the parent. Persuasion must displace coercive authority, and, upon the whole, we will have better-trained, more cultured, more responsible young men and young women.

ALBION W. SMALL, THE UNIVERSITY OF CHICAGO

Professor Hagerty's valuable paper deserves thorough discussion. It seems to me, however, that, in the brief time at my disposal, I can do a better service by applying my remarks to our whole programme.

As I review my own impressions from the discussions thus far, it seems to me that a stenographic report of everything that has been said would give the city editor of a yellow journal all the excuse such an imaginative gentleman usually requires in such cases for asserting that this Society regarded the American family as on trial, with the presumption rather strongly against it.

I have no right to speak for the Society, but my version will have at least as much claim to a hearing as the city editor's. My dictum is that the thing on trial is not the American family, but every condition which interferes with general realization of the American family in full fruit of its spirit.

At all events I want to go on record in protest against everything in our proceedings which would tend to justify substitution of the yellow journal version for mine.

I do not believe I am phenomenally unsophisticated. It has been a good many years since I have heard of anything new in the way of sexual irregularity, except accidental variations of number and place. When I was a boy of ten, the nearest building to the school I attended was a brothel. More or less vitiated instruction about the meaning of the institution was the one thing I remember from the experiences of the school yard, and the stamp of those recollections is much more distinct on my mind than anything I heard from the teachers.

I cannot pose as a reclaimed rake. I am obliged to admit that my knowledge of sexual vice is entirely third personal. Unless that is a disqualification, I have had fairly liberal means of reaching informed judgments about the rôle which irregular relations of the sexes plays in our American society. From that tenth year I do not remember a time, till I was twenty-five or thirty years old, when additions to my knowledge of the subject were not accumulating. Fortunately or unfortunately, I had such progressive instruction, from my own observation with that of others, that I can recall only one or two instances in which variations of sexual depravity overtook me with surprise. It has been more than twenty years since anything reported from official or unofficial social clinics has added, except in quantity, to what I was already perfectly familiar with in principle about abnormal relations between men and women. I do not believe, therefore, that I am expressing the reaction of a recluse in a fool's paradise.

I do not deny the existence, in certain groups, of the prevalence of the evils that have been alleged or hinted at in some of the papers in our programme; I do deny most emphatically that those evils constitute in any considerable degree an indictment against the American family as an institution.

In the first place, the invidious inferences that have been suggested, more than uttered, by some of the essayists, get their supposed sanction from that delightfully simple mode of reasoning popularly known as putting the cart before the horse. It amounts to this: Because the family is sinned against, therefore the family is the sinner.

To this easy flippancy I would reply, Nothing that has been put in evidence proves anything very important against the American family. It merely proves that a large fraction of our population is more or less unfit for membership of a social group of that advanced type.

In other words, as a rough general proposition, all the disturbed or destroyed families that we know anything about in the United States are effects of causes independent of the family type itself. Of course these disturbed or destroyed families become in turn aggravations of some of the evils from which they resulted, and breeders of other evils, but this is merely equivalent to saying that the family institution has not force enough to counterbalance all the demoralizing conditions of surrounding society, or to neutralize all the unsocial propensities of the undomesticated persons who compose it.

In the second place, most of the point to most of the smart flings at the family is gained by manipulations of the evidence that are either ignorant or disingenuous. What I mean by that is this: The American family is out of gear in two strata, in both of which pretty much everything else is out of gear. On the one hand is the stratum of the over-wealthed, over-leisured, over-stimulated, under-worked, under-controlled. Nothing in their conditions is normal. Nothing is right. Only miracles could save this stratum from rot. Its families necessarily show the taint, and what else could be expected? On the other hand is the stratum of the over-worked, under-fed, under-housed, under-clothed, under-hygiened, physically and morally, under-leisured, under-stimulated except by the elemental desires. Nothing in their lot is right. Nothing in their lot could be good enough to hold its own very securely against the swamping bad. The family suffers in the general evil. It is as absurd to accuse the family institution on that evidence as it would be to denounce the amosphere in general because the air this stratum has to breathe is foul.

If we deduct the collapsed families in these two strata, where they must be regarded more as effects than as causes, and confine ourselves to the families that are in relatively normal conditions, the great mass of families in the industrious middle stratum of our society, the family is not breaking down. It is probably working at least as well as any other organ in our social structure.

Not as proof, but as illustration, I may draw from my own experience. Five years excepted, I lived in the state of Maine until I was thirty-eight years old. The last eleven of those years I had to visit all parts of the state, and I had acquaintances, sometimes a considerable number, in nearly every town. During those thirty-eight years I knew by name only one family resident in the state that had been broken up by divorce. The state contained few people at that time rich enough to be outside the working class. It contained relatively few dependants who were not defectives. The great middle class contained here and there a divorcé, but so rarely that most of the people knew them only as the average New Yorker knows of Navajo Indians.

I do not mean to question the statistics of divorce. I mean first, that when we subtract the divorces that occur in the upper and lower non-social strata, and divide the number remaining by the number of families in the substantial middle stratum, the percentage of divorces is higher than it ought to be, but far below the rate which decryers of the family would have us infer; and I mean, second, that the actual divorces in that stratum constitute no such case against the family institution as the same decryers want us to believe.

In the third place, I want to point out the hysterical character of another line of innuendo against the family. Because Frenchmen are supposed to treat conjugal fidelity as a joke, because English tradition places the wife among the husband's assets, because normal family relations are impossible in abnormal conditions of irresponsible wealth or insuperable poverty, because John Smith occasionally finds himself married to the impossible Jane Jones instead of the possible Hannah Johnson, and because an occasional couple that could not live with anybody try to live with each other, therefore all the evils in all these conditions are counts against the normal American family! This sort of neurotics has not been silent in these sessions.

It is not an uncommon thing for railers against the family to talk as though "the position of woman" in the United States were not merely like that of the wife under the common law until recent decades, but substantially like that of the wife at Rome in the palmiest days of the *patria potestas*. On the other hand it is not uncommon for European visitors to speak out the impression that the American husband is simply the jaded beast of burden collecting the wherewithal for his wife and daughters to be physically, mentally, and morally dissipated. One of these exaggerations is as superficial as the other. The average animus of the American family is more nearly reflected by an incident that occurred at the University of Chicago the year of its foundation. Between the unreclaimed swamps and the temporary caravansaries crowding the available sites to shelter World's Fair visitors, the immigrant faculty families had a dismal outlook for abodes. Upon their gloomy contemplation of the prospect there suddenly dawned a vision of relief. It was in the shape of plans and specifications for a block of model houses. An architect and his wife, the latter furnishing the ideas and the arguments, the former the drawings, were the messengers of hope. The wife called a meeting of the professors, and showed how an available block near the University might be converted into lots for forty-five houses, with a club house in the center, to contain heating plant, laundry, servants' quarters, and restaurant, which the families could use at their pleasure, or the meals could be delivered by a miniature elevated electric railroad to each family which so preferred. There was a co-operative purchasing plan attached through which each family in the group could order supplies as liberally or frugally as it pleased, and pay for them at wholesale rates.

Every man at the meeting pronounced the scheme ideal; and I am unable to explain why they did not then and there put their signatures to contracts, and order building to begin next day—or at least the first forty-five of them to crowd their way to the front. For some unrecorded reason it was decided to go through the formality of showing the plans to the wives of these exultant professors, before actually breaking ground. These supposed silent partners in those families assembled next day. They examined the plans. They listened to the eloquence of their authors. They thought again of their homeless condition, and then they—decided with one voice that they would remain homeless all their days sooner than consign their children to the unknown evils of a common community back yard. That settled it. Many of those families have remained wanderers on the face of the earth till the present hour, simply because in the American family man proposes but woman still disposes.

Seriously, it is worse than silly to talk as though the American family were a radically faulty institution. There will be a certain ratio of friction and frustration and waste, in every possible human association, so long as human beings lag this side of perfection. With our human nature as it is, there is no conceivable form of association in which men and women could be more helpful to each other and better placed to do their best for society, than in the form frankly filled by the spirit of the typical American family.

JAMES A. FIELD, THE UNIVERSITY OF CHICAGO

The question which we have to discuss is a very large question, and a very vague one. I shall confine what I may say to an attempt to make it less indefinite by suggesting one or two distinctions—by pointing out not an answer but a more specific problem to be solved.

The original query which Professor Hagerty has considered in his paper—"How Far Should Members of the Family Be Individualized?"— includes within its scope at least two questions. If we assume the continued existence of the family substantially in its present form we may inquire how we should divide and adjust the functions of family life among the members of the family, and how far the members as individuals, and especially the man and the woman, should in their family relations be regarded as equal in responsibilities and rights and in all that they are to give and to gain. That is one of the questions, and that is the one which Professor Hagerty seems chiefly to have had in mind. The other, which challenges what was before assumed, is this: Is an increase of individualization consistent with the continued existence of present-day family life? Such an inquiry suggests Spencer's familiar antithesis of individuation and genesis. Briefly Professor Hagerty has alluded to this phase of the problem by mentioning the effect of the higher education of women upon marriage and the rearing of children—though it is by no means only through woman that the dictates of individual ambitions may disrupt the normal family group. But I believe this second form of the question is too important to be so casually passed by. It demands attention if we but consider the real purport of further individualization. For, to the ordinary person, the thought of individual development means more than equivalence of privilege within the family. The individualization we strive for is an ideal individualization which means freedom in every way to develop and to do. It means achievement and a successful career. Consequently we must seek to see what distinction can be drawn between the standard of individual success and the qualification for parenthood.

To command the esteem of others a person must first of all show affirmative characteristics. It is not enough to go through the world harmlessly. We admire the person who takes the active attitude toward his surroundings and does things—who makes a mark that compels us to recognize him as a center of energy which he can direct as he chooses. Such masterfulness is admired even if it is exercised to the detriment of others; but to command genuine approbation it must serve the general advantage. Success, then, is essentially measured by the reward, in good or in good repute, given for positive acts of service. It comes as a sort of equivalent, in exchange. And here, as in other cases of exchange, it is easy to look too narrowly at the return and to miss the significance of what is given. So, in the effort to attain success, as success is judged, persons are led to excessive specialization and intensity of effort. This amounts to a process of self-exploitation, which, though it is destructive to those who thus overwork, seems to be acceptable to society, since the continual renewal of the stock by reproduction and the spread of ideas by imitation permit unexhausted persons to take up the unfinished tasks where their predecessors were obliged to drop them. The pursuit of individual success, then, really often involves, as a response to the demands of others, the sacrifice of what may still be regarded as the normal individual life.

The qualification for parenthood, on the other hand, is pre-eminently the even balance of abilities. The life of the specialist is ill-suited to parenthood, whichever of the functions of the parent we may emphasize. As the source of hereditary traits in the child, the parent should, so far as we can venture to decide, be all-sided, not one-sided. For the training and rearing of children unimpaired physical health is requisite. For the education of children in the home extreme specialists are not desirable unless we assume that the innate aptitudes of the child fit him for a special career which closely corresponds to the equipment of both his parents, and that such a career will be appropriate to future conditions as to past. But this inquiry into the qualifications for parenthood, perplexed at best, need not be pushed far here. Whoever, by specialization, becomes a distortion of the normal biological type, may fairly be regarded as poorly equipped for the essentially biological function of maintaining the race.

In the light of the distinction that has been suggested we may predict either that our present view of the family relations must undergo extensive change or that the further progress of members of the family in individualization, as this is commonly understood, will sooner or later be limited by the necessity of maintaining the species. Assuming that the family is likely to retain essentially its present form, higher and higher specialization by individuals will take us toward the point at which the reproducing of the stock will cease and the generation which stands to benefit by the sacrifices of specialists will no longer exist to justify or encourage these sacrifices. Without being pessimistic or radical one may therefore suggest that if increasing individualization is not to become a cause for concern we should revise our standard of success until it is more in accord with the living of normal lives.

MRS. ANNA GARLIN SPENCER, NEW YORK CITY, N. Y.

The question before us is too large and complex to be adequately discussed in the time allotted. Certain points, however, deserve special mention. First, the modern, individualistic family, consisting of two persons only with their children, is still too new an experiment in social order for us to be certain about all its tendencies. The older civilizations were all built upon a family life in which the character and capacity of the two young parents were reinforced and disciplined by a collective or patriarchal family connection. If one husband could not care for the wife and children the men of the larger family circle must. If one mother was not equal to the demands of child-life, as then understood, the rest of the women of the family were enlisted. Now for the first time, so far as we know, a young man and a young woman are left to make their own marriage choices, and on the character and intelligence of these two young people is placed the heavy social responsibility of the success of that domestic venture. What wonder that where character is weak, industrial power limited, and social ideals undeveloped, the fathers "desert" when family cares prove unexpectedly heavy, and the mothers fail to keep their children alive because of the too great burden placed upon them? It seems to some of us that the patriarchal type of family with its support and control of the individual parents must have some sort of modern social substitute in order to make the modern type of family, of one father and mother and their children, more successful. It may be that motherhood will be seen to be such an important function that its protection against excessive labor, against poverty below point of health and child-bearing strength, and against immoral and degrading surroundings, may be considered a state duty. It may be that fatherhood will be seen to be such a high civic obligation, and of such vital importance to the common welfare, that its duties and sacrifices shall justly demand some public recognition in proportion to the social value of the service rendered. At any rate we should clearly recognize the fact that the modern type of family places a unique and very heavy responsibility upon men and women in their youth and that it is not strange that many fail to bear it easily and well. Again the tremendous importance of the family life as an agent in the development of human personality should be clearly perceived by us. That mysterious quality or process which gathers universal elements of being into a unity of life which can be known as "you" or "I," that which can be educated as a conscious and purposive creature able to react upon the environment which has shaped it and thus to create an ever-renewed environment—it is well for us to think how difficult a process it has been to develop this human personality. Think of the cosmic cost of will, of unselfish affection, of articulate aspiration! Think how the germinal human being passes rapidly through many of the age-long processes that have thus created human personality; and how many times Mother Nature makes a slip and the human creature becomes but an "unfinished infant" for all its life. And when the baby is fairly born, think how difficult it is for it to keep its footing on this slippery ball and really "be somebody." This achievement of the ages of evolution does not work automatically. Feeblemindedness, physical weakness and degeneracy, moral incapacity in manifold forms, witness that the cosmic struggle to make human beings out of the strain and stress of life is not completed *for* humanity but *by* humanity. Now the family is up to date proved the best and most effective aid in this process of developing personality. It has so far furnished a breakwater against the non-social forces that work against human development. And so far that breakwater has consisted in large part of exclusive affection, reserve of intimacy, and close personal ties between parents and children. The attempt to bring up children, (even a small class for a definite end, as in Sparta), outside of home life has not produced fine personality, although sometimes (as in Sparta) it has produced a few great soldiers. The methods of child care in even good institutions generally result in dulled individuality even if the training for specific kinds of work is effective. The child seems to need as a "buffer" against the world at large a certainty that he is an essential element in the social order, such a certainty as seems seldom given except by the parental partiality of affection.

Moreover, so far in human development, this function of the family in the protection and development of personality as it struggles toward expression in the child has demanded that someone in the family shall have and express a type of individuality which is not primarily concerned with or dependent upon specialization of vocational work, but is rather devoted supremely to the family unity and to the varying wants of the family group. If children are to gather themselves together "out of the everywhere" it seems necessary that someone shall be close at hand when wanted and not leave "hours" and seasons when the child cannot get at anybody to whom it knows it belongs. So far in the organization of the family the mother has been the person so readily at hand when the child's needs, physical or spiritual, demanded the steadying influence of a companionship on which it felt a rightful claim. This has been thought to be a natural arrangement because the child was closest to the mother physically. But there is a deeper reason that underlies both that closer physical relationship and the function of the mother in the development of personality through constant companionship. Speaking generally, the feminine side of humanity is in "the middle of the road" of life. Biologically, psychologically, and sociologically women are in the central, normal, conservative part of the evolutionary process. On the one side and on the other men produce more geniuses, and more feeble-minded; more talented experts, and more incompetents who cannot earn a living; more idealistic masters of thought and action, and more neer-do-weels who shame their mothers. It is because to woman is committed in a peculiar sense this function of development of personality in child-life that they are the practical, teaching half of the race. In the development of individuality it is most essential that the conserving weight of the middle virtues, and the mean of powers, should be nearest the child. It is later, in the more formal educational process, that the highly specialized "variants" which men exhibit, and which directly tend toward human progress on the one side and toward human degeneracy on the other side, have their functional use as example or as warning.

All this has direct bearing upon our subject "How far should the members of the family be individualized?" We have removed from the single pair and their children all the props and discipline of the patriarchal family, and now we are rapidly democratizing the family. This has gone already so far that we are even afraid of controlling effectively our own children lest we check their growth toward self-government. The problems of modern education in respect to moral culture inhere in the fact that we have achieved high ideals of the sacredness of personality and the dignity of individual choice but as yet have not acquired pedagogical technique to work these into character-building. The democratizing of the family, certainly so far as its two adult heads are concerned, is, however, an absolutely essential step in human progress. It is essential especially for that process of making persons to which the family is devoted: for now we need not classes nor castes in the social order but free individuals to make a free and progressive state. It is therefore vital that both parents shall be of the stuff out of which the higher type of human creature is made, and such can only come from a democratic home. The industrial changes, however, which have dominated all recent social movements, have introduced into the modern ideal of individuality an exaggerated demand for highly specialized vocational effort. Men must do some one speciality effectively or they are not considered to achieve success in life. Women are more and more called by education and industrial life to work in the same specialized manner for some definite end of personal achievement. This has given a tendency among some leaders of women's industrial and educational progress to minimize the experience of motherhood, and to magnify the social value of the method of work that suits the prevailing machine-dominated industry. In so far as this tendency implies that motherhood may become a relatively small and rapidly finished task, one which will not interfere with a constant, lifelong pursuit of one speciality of vocation on the same terms as men do their one task, I deplore the tendency. That women should all be educated for self-support at a living wage is a social necessity; that women should be economic factors now as they have always been in the past is also unquestionable; that women must reshape many of their activities to suit that general scheme of modern industry that has created the factory is certain; that women should for their own best good and for the general ends of social progress keep their hands on some specialty, so far as may be, through the years when they cannot follow it as the first obligation, so as to be ready to re-enter their vocation when the children are grown, this is coming to be seen more and more as the wise plan for all women who would do something worth while in life. But that the exigencies of family life can ever be reduced to a perfect system of specialties of work so as to place men and women on the same plane of competitive professional and manual labor, I do not believe. That the majority of women who marry and have children can be the best of mothers and at the same time be as constantly devoted to some particular pursuit as is the average man seems not to be in accordance with facts. There is, it seems clear to some of us looking below the surface, a deep sociological reason for this division of interests and activities in the lives of the majority of women. Personality is not the power to do a specific thing well, although vocational effectiveness is a part of personality; nor is it a capacity to excell all previous achievements of the human race in some one line of endeavor, although great persons may be geniuses of this sort. Personality is above all the quality of unity, some individual wholeness that prevents the human creature from wholly losing himself in the whirl of things. And to develop this in the average life it seems to be necessary that somewhere at the child's first efforts to become a person there shall be some quiet brooding, much leisurely companionship of the beloved, a rich and generous sharing of some larger life always near when needed, and not so much absorbed in its own individual doings as to fail of noting each movement of another toward a truly human existence. For this reason the individualization of women within the family may be often subordinate, so far as vocational effort of the modern industrial type is concerned, to the development of a kind of personality which is effective through its breadth and its normal balance rather than by reason of its technical achievements. In any case the family as a prime factor in the development of personality is the chief concern of all social effort, and therefore the individualization of its members must be controlled by the law of its own supreme function.

CARL E. PARRY, UNIVERSITY OF MICHIGAN

The question of how far the members of the family should be individualized happens to touch upon a very fundamental question of social theory, namely, what is the individual? There is still much difference of opinion among sociological thinkers as to what an individual really is, and over the true relation between the individual and the social order. Perhaps it is a good thing for these questions of fundamental theory to come openly into our discussion, for it can well be maintained that good theory is the most practical thing in the world. Furthermore, it is quite possible that what laboratory training does toward making natural scientists becomingly modest, patient, and sane, can be done for us partly by our wrestling with questions of fundamental theory.

What does it mean to ask how far the members of the family should be individualized? Perhaps it means, especially, how far should wives, mothers, and children be afforded opportunity for freedom of choice. In reality, of course, every individual must individualize himself, because the very essence of human individuality lies in independent judgment, personal, responsible, characteristic, and unique. How can one be a real individual if he does not make up his own mind and carry out his own plans, bearing and expecting to bear most of the consequences himself? All that other persons can do for him, through any kind of social action, is to furnish him with opportunity of some sort. What we are really enquiring into today, therefore, is not *how far,* but rather in what *direction* persons should be individualized—or better, how far unrestricted choice is consistent with their highest personal development, and by whom and in what respects the opportunity shall be afforded. Perhaps it will illustrate my meaning to suggest that it is no more individual for a woman of today to get a divorce under intolerable conditions than it was for the woman of yesterday to throw flatirons under similar provocation. And it is still a debated question between certain manufacturers and social workers whether legislation limiting the hours of working-women is individualizing them or whether it is doing the exact opposite. Would one say that a woman lawyer is more individual than a mother? Or a criminal than a college president? The real question is between different kinds of individuality, as I said before, and different ways of realizing it. If we have the right kind, it is hard to see how the members of the family can be too much individualized, so our question is answered at the very outset; but what *is* the right kind? It seems to me that all social effort is directed toward fostering strong and high individual personality, whatever that may be. If the range of choice for women and children has been recently extended, what we are most concerned to know is whether it has resulted, on the whole, in stronger and better personality or in degeneracy. Of course in judging in this matter we must have in mind some ideal.

It is not established that degeneracy has resulted from the larger opportunities afforded women. Probably there are more good wives and mothers, even, than there ever were before. When before were there so many mothers' clubs, so much interest in child-study, and so many periodicals relating to housekeeping? When before did mothers take so much interest in the education of their children? It is obvious that much depends on what we consider bad effects of enlarged opportunity. The principal speaker of the afternoon has said, "In the making of the home woman renders her greatest social service and finds her highest function." The same thing has often been said before. We can all agree with it, provided it does not imply too much. It should not imply that greater freedom of choice, provided it leads some women to choose not to make homes, is a misfortune. Such an implication would only beg the whole question. What we might better say is that some women, as some men, find their highest function in raising a creditable family, and that some women and some men find their highest function in doing something else that is socially useful, but that neither men nor women serve either themselves or others by choosing to do anything which they cannot do well, or which is narrowly selfish. There are some who seem to think that raising a family is a social service, rather deserving of reward, but nobody has been able to prove that raising a family with bad heredity or bad family training is anything other than a social disservice. All depends on how well one's work is done, and there are more ways of serving heaven and earth than are dreamed of in some men's philosophies. If a woman finds her chief field of self-expression, of individuality, in club life, or some other form of social service, who shall say that this particular woman was not better fitted for this kind of work than for motherhood? Who knows? And who *can* know? Only the most obviously injurious kinds of eccentricity can be safely set down as really bad, for the stone which is rejected of the builders may become the head of the corner. Some results of larger freedom for women have been certainly good, and a great many others we are not yet in a position to pronounce upon.

When we come to discuss the freedom of choice afforded children, we must recognize that there are some limitations which a child cannot escape, simply because he is a child—because of his ignorance and inexperience, and because he must grow up under the eye of whatever parents he may happen to have. In making the recurring choices which fix his habits, and so his character, he must rely upon his parents for almost constant guidance, for good or ill. Yet something can be done for him, and much has already been done for him. We try to enlarge the freedom of the child, for instance, by schools, child-labor laws, playgrounds, etc., and more recently and insistently by industrial education. These help the child, no doubt, but it is not established that the school has grown *at the expense of* the family, as Mr. Hagerty intimated. It is more nearly true to say that both the family and the school have expanded in function. One need only stop to reflect, for instance, to see that the child of working-class parents a few hundred years ago was not taught to read and write by the parents, *instead of* by the school; he simply was not taught to read and write at all. It became necessary as a new demand and was taken over by a new institution. And it is still more certain that the speaker was wrong in thinking that the church has grown at the expense of the family: the fact is that *both* have suffered by the decay in religious thought, feeling, and action. But however that may be, to come back to the question now immediately before us, more and more people are coming to see that compulsory-school-attendance laws and laws against child labor go but a short way toward really enlarging a child's freedom of choice, invaluable though they are. They go no farther than to remove the ignorance and greed of his parents so far as these stand in the way of the child's being in the schoolroom or on the playground. They leave him still subject to the ignorance and greed and incapacity of the parents in a hundred other directions, such as in language, manners, foresight, industry, ideals of conduct, etc., and they leave immediately untouched all the limitations upon his freedom of thought and action which flow from the poverty of the family, from its home and neighborhood surroundings of every kind. It is to remove some of these limitations that housing conditions, playgrounds, etc., are being looked after. Besides, a child may be in the schoolroom or upon the playground and yet be deformed, or sick, or unable to see well or to hear well, or he may be habitually underfed—all conditions preventing him from learning much or indulging much in strenuous play, in which lies the building of character, the foundation of individuality. Here are limitations which challenge society to overcome them.

To this end there are some current proposals of much interest. In addition to furnishing schools and playgrounds and industrial and household and hygienic training, it is proposed by some to emancipate the child still further by furnishing free medical inspection and attention, and also furnishing free meals to school children, and possibly even shoes and clothing. Still more far-reaching is the proposal to give state aid, as by pensions, as a matter of right, to all mothers, from the first coming of their children.[1] In support of this last it is said that state pensions to mothers would set some of them free from the unreasonable domination of their husbands and also from the necessity to go from home to work in factories; the idea is that such freedom would permit women of the working-classes to develop a truer individuality, in caring for their children, than is now possible for them. Such pensions might also result in the children being rescued from neglect, thus coming into larger opportunity and perhaps using it to develop real individuality. All these are

[1] See H. G. Wells, *New Worlds for Old;* also *Socialism and the Family.*

important proposals. Some of them are already being adopted here and there. The distinctive thing about them is that they are directed toward enlarging freedom of choice by furnishing the economic means, instead of depending upon the father to furnish them as has heretofore been done. To indicate where the line shall be drawn upon such methods of "individualizing" the members of the family, in the light of the best sociological theory, would seem to be one of the chief purposes of this discussion. As I have not been able to mature my views on this matter I shall not attempt to answer the question.

Those who attempt to answer it, however, must ask, in regard to all these proposals, What is likely to be their effect upon the standards of family relations? Will they raise and define the standard of what shall be considered by the average community a good husband, a good wife, a good father or mother? Will they lead to stronger and more effectual approval or disapproval, as the case may be, of large families, reckless marriages, neglect of wife or children, the indulgence of children by their parents? And will they lead to greater definition of standards in these and other respects? It is mostly in the light of their effects upon these standards, and thus upon the character of individual fathers and mothers, that these proposals must be judged. It is upon such a basis, it seems to me, that those who feel themselves competent must proceed in answering the question of how far such methods of "individualizing" should be pursued.

As to the general subject of the advantages of freedom of choice, it is only when there is some, but not too much responsibility felt by the person making the choice that the results are good. Increased knowledge of all kinds, including that as to human nature and the social order, increased foresight, including that into the social effects of this kind of conduct and that, such as the treatment of children, increased sense of responsibility for marriage, etc.—in these, of course, lies the hope of the future. But there is nothing very startling or sensational about this, I am very glad to say. All moral effort of everybody—teachers, preachers, social workers, business men, upright citizens—fostering any of these ends just mentioned will foster the true individualization of members of the family.

Dr. Maurice Parmelee, New York City, N. Y.

Professor Hagerty deplores the breaking-up of family solidarity. But, as he himself recognizes, this has been the historical tendency. The early clan and patriarchal organization was based upon the principle of kinship. Since then the basis of social organization has been widening constantly. It is, therefore, not safe to assume that the breaking-up of family solidarity is necessarily an evil. On the contrary, if family solidarity is broken up it may be superseded by a larger social solidarity which will more than compensate for its loss.

I have no far-reaching generalizations as to the future of the family to propose, nor am I so certain as Professor Hagerty that the family will remain the fundamental social institution. I shall therefore limit myself to speaking of a few of the numerous factors which enter into the family life to lessen its value for the members of the family and especially for the children. It has been my good fortune to have the opportunity of studying the careers of several hundreds of criminals and in the case of many of these I have been able to determine what factors there were in their early family surroundings which helped to start them on criminal careers. These same factors serve in the case of many other individuals to make their careers more or less unsuccessful though not necessarily criminal. These factors may be classified in two groups, the first, abnormal, the second, normal. By abnormal factors I mean those which enter into the family life through accidental means and therefore cannot be foreseen and are unusual. By normal factors I mean those which enter habitually into the lives of many families because they arise out of conditions which are now widespread in society.

Among the abnormal factors are the following: The presence of a step-parent in the home lessens very greatly the value of the family life for the children because a step-parent cannot have the same affection for the children that the real parent has. A step-mother is likely to do most harm to young step-children. Though lacking maternal love for these children yet there are imposed upon her the duties of a mother which she is very likely to neglect. She is especially likely to do this if she has children of her own, when her feeling of indifference toward her step-children may become dislike and hatred. A step-father is most likely to do harm to older step-children, especially a boy verging on manhood. Then a step-father is liable to feel that this son of a former husband of his wife is an intruder in his home and this feeling is a prolific cause for dissension.

Incompatibility of temperament between the parents tends to make the family life unwholesome for the children. Dissension between the parents weakens their authority over the children and without parental restraint the children are likely to run wild. In many immigrant families there comes a break between parents and children because the children become Americanized more rapidly than their parents. The knowledge of English and of American customs and ways which the children get so quickly in the public schools and elsewhere gives them a sense of superiority over their parents and makes the parents quite helpless to exercise any authority over them.

In some families undue restrictions are laid upon the children because the moral and conventional standards of the parents are more rigid than those of the surrounding community. This may account for the proverbially bad character of the minister's son. These restrictions are usually upon certain pleasures which the religious or moral prejudices of the parents consider bad. Such restrictions are especially aggravating when these pleasures are countenanced in the vicinity of the home. The time comes when the pent-up desires and energies of the child force him or her to break loose. Frequently the first move is to run away from home.

The principal normal factors which lessen the value of the family life are poverty, and ignorance, which is frequently the result of poverty but sometimes its cause. Poverty frequently causes privation of the necessities of life for some or all the members of the family. It causes a lack of recreational facilities for the children. When the mother has to go out to work it removes restraint from the children at home. Ignorance both in poor and in well-to-do families leads to failure on the part of the parents to feed, clothe, and bring up the children properly.

Society should be ready to step in whenever possible and supply the want when the family fails. The principal social agencies for this purpose are the public schools, children's aid societies, the probation system, etc. Society can supply the want quite frequently when the abnormal factors we have mentioned above enter into the family life, but very little can be done to eliminate these abnormal factors. It can help quite frequently also when the normal factors mentioned above enter into the family. But it should be the ultimate object of society to eliminate poverty and ignorance. The accomplishment of this, however, may not strengthen the family, for the guarantee of well-being which society will then make may be to the individual member of society rather than to the family as a unit. In that case family solidarity will be superseded by a larger social solidarity.

Concluding Remarks of Professor Hagerty

At the outset the question stated was: How far should the state go in individualizing members of the family? The secretary in submitting the subject to me changed it to its present form: How far should the members of the family be individualized? The paper which I read is a discussion of the latter question, which is considered from the view-point of public opinion or the social judgment as well as that of state action.

The writer of the paper labored under the impression that those who were to lead in its discussion were as familiar with the meaning of the subject, as interpreted by the makers of the programme, as he was. On this account an interpretation of the subject was omitted from the paper. If those who discussed the subject had comprehended its intended meaning much that has been said in this discussion would have been omitted. Under the circumstances the writer frankly admits his error in not interpreting the subject without agreeing, however, with much that was said by those who have commented on the necessity for definition of terms.

I dissent entirely from Mr. Parry's criticism of the statement in the paper that "in the household, in the making of the home, woman renders her greatest social service and finds her highest function." I admit with him that *some women* should not marry and that they can be more useful to themselves and to society by abstaining from marriage and by engaging in pursuits suited to their talents. This admission, however, in no wise conflicts with the contention that women as a class render their greatest social service and find their highest functions in the development of homes and in the keeping of homes.

Mrs. Gilman protests against the citation of the failure of the orphanage as indicating the superiority of the home as the normal and proper institution in which children should grow up. While the orphanage deals with an inferior class from the point of view of heredity, when these children are placed in homes, the home deals with precisely the same class securing much better results than the orphanage. Besides, the orphanage frequently has the advantage of expert talent in organizing the work of the institution and also expert talent in training the children.

In spite of these features it is a failure. No other method of rearing children has ever been known which is comparable to home training in the development of efficient and useful citizens.

In institutions organized to reform juvenile delinquents, the cottage system, where the conditions of home life are as far as possible reproduced, furnishes the ideal institution. The smaller the cottage and the fewer the number of children in the cottage making possible imitation of family life, the better is the institution.

HOW FAR SHOULD FAMILY WEALTH BE ENCOURAGED AND CONSERVED?

GEORGE K. HOLMES
U. S. Department of Agriculture

It is understood that this question refers to the encouragement of the accumulation of wealth by the family and to its security, by means of efforts exerted outside of the family—individual efforts, the efforts of associations of individuals, and even of the state.

Hence the discussion seems to invite an examination of some fundamental principles of economics, of politics, and ultimately of biology. Anything of this sort is too large a proposition for this paper, and the endeavor will be mostly to follow lines along which we may not be radically at odds, even though some of us may be state socialists and others individualists and still others occupying various positions between the two extremes.

Why should a family want wealth beyond what is merely sufficient to provide for necessities and comforts? What is called civilization answers the question. There is a minimum standard of living of varying descriptions which, society insists, should be maintained, and this not solely for the betterment of the individual as an individual, nor mostly so, but for his betterment as a member of society and because of the general social elevation in civilization promoted by that of the individual. So society has a legitimate interest in the welfare of every member and in raising the standard of living. Family income, and wealth, too, are closely related to its welfare.

DISTRIBUTION OF WEALTH

In this country, family wealth exists on a high general level, yet inequalities of wealth-distribution are enormous. It seems probable that one-half of the families are almost without wealth, their possessions being mostly confined to household and personal belongings and the implements required by their occupations.

Among the 19,000,000 families there are millions whose property of the descriptions indicated is worth less than $500, and some millions of these, worth less than $200. That is wealth, not income.

Fifteen years ago, favored by exceptional opportunities for exploring the subject of wealth-distribution in ownership, the writer ventured to indicate its character in arithmetical terms. In the meantime great changes have taken place—the multiplication and increase of great fortunes, the accumulation of minor fortunes so common as to fail to attract attention; and, at the other extreme, increasing tenancy of the home, both on the farm and in the town and city, and the continued building-up of the great class of low-wage receivers.

Between these two extremes, another class has been building, what is called the middle class, containing about one-half of the total number of families, and among these the farmers have gained conspicuously. Since 1890 the value of farm capital, including land value, has increased 75 per cent., a gain of three-fourths in 18 years, partly due, however, to extension of cultivated area by new farms.

What the resultant fact of all these diverse movements of the last 18 years upon the character of wealth-distribution is can only be inferred, but it seems probable that inequality has increased. The reference is not to the increased gap between the very poor and the very rich, but to inequality, mathematically expressed so as to measure the effect of the acquisition of say $10,000,000 by one family, and the acquisition of the same amount by 2,000 families at $5,000 each.

It is probably not the growth of large fortunes alone that has caused the increasing inequality of wealth distribution, for there is some indication of a larger hopelessly poor class. We may differ as to the reasons for the existence of this class, but at any rate we shall have to consider among the causes environment, occupation, heredity, and many social efforts to preserve the unfit and enable them to continue their kind.

So it seems probable that the writer's old statement of wealth-distribution made for the conditions of 1890 would not make the

case worse than it is if applied to the present time. The statement was that

about 19 per cent. of the wealth is owned by the poorer families that own
farms and homes without incumbrance, and that these are 28 per cent.
of all of the families. Only 8 per cent. of the wealth is owned by tenant
families and the poorer class of those that own their farms and homes
under incumbrance, and these together constitute 63 per cent. of all families.
As little as 4 per cent. of the nation's wealth is owned by 52 per cent. of the
families, that is, by the tenants alone. Finally, 4,047 families possess about
seven-tenths as much as do 11,560,293 families.

The purpose in quoting this is to call attention to the large
fraction of the families that are poor, really poor; it is about
one-half. It is still to be remembered that the subject is wealth,
not income.

The probate statistics of Massachusetts afford further light
on distribution. If the estates are classified according to amount
and the classes are arranged in order of amount in columns, the
number of estates and the total amount of wealth in each class,
some interesting observations can be made.

The distribution tended to become more even from 1830 to
1860, but more uneven from 1860 to 1890. Analysis localizes
this feature. At the extremes of the scale—in the poor and in
the rich—the distribution becomes more uneven. On the contrary, within the middle class, distribution becomes more even.

Any general plan to encourage family wealth would en-
counter a situation, it would seem, in which wealth-distribution
is becoming more uneven and in which there is an ample quantity
of material to work upon. In one of the richest states, Massachusetts, the inventoried probated estates valued at less than
$500 are 15 per cent. of the total and those valued at less than
$1,000 are 27 per cent.; while, in the whole United States, per-
haps one-half of the families may be regarded as poor in accumulated wealth.

CAUSES OF THIS DISTRIBUTION

Some understanding of the causes of the present deficient
distribution of wealth and of the large fractions of the poor and
very poor, may guide our efforts to encourage family wealth, or
possibly prevent some of them. Wealth is accumulated out of

wealth produced, primarily in the division of the product between labor and capital, and subsequently in the transfer of this wealth from one place and person to another. The process of wealth-accumulation works mostly in favor of the capitalist. If the working-man accumulates much wealth, it is because he has become also a capitalist and mostly because of returns to his capital, either in interest, or rent paid by real-estate tenants, or in un-earned increment to land value, or in pure profit.

Years ago the *New York Tribune* ascertained the sources of the fortunes of all of the reputed millionaires of this country. The results were unavoidably imperfect, but after all they roughly indicated the facts. Over 4 per cent. of the millionaires became such through logging and lumbering, nearly 7 per cent. through mining, and 65 per cent., more or less through increase of land value. All instances in which there is a trace of labor as a source of wealth, and these are confined to the professional kinds, may be segregated. They form but 3 per cent. of the total and in all cases the accumulation out of salaries and fees is qualified by the explanation that these were invested in real estate or other property returning interest and pure profit.

It is possible for a skilled mechanic with wife but no children, abstaining from alcoholic liquors and tobacco and nearly all unproductive expenditures, to accumulate in twenty-five years of good health, unremitting industry, parsimony, and compounding of interest on savings, enough income-returning property to sustain his widow in comfort. This is possible, because it has been done, but the man who did it was a marked man, and he had no children, either to render his feat impossible or to preserve his characteristics for future social good.

Savings banks are often referred to in popular writings as having deposits composed entirely or mostly of the savings of working-people and of the poor. This is a wide-spread fallacy in a large degree. The Massachusetts Bureau of Statistics of Labor, years ago, investigated this subject to ascertain the extent to which working-people were taking advantage of savings institutions, but these people were conspicuously few.

Although working-people may constitute a considerable fraction of depositors, their aggregate deposits are comparatively small and the fact is that these banks are more properly investment institutions than savings banks. A man could be mentioned who had $2,000 in each of twenty savings banks in Massachusetts, and his case was exceptional only in degree. These banks did for him what they did for nearly all depositors—they performed solely the function of an expert investment agent.

Wealth is unevenly distributed because, partly, savings out of wages and salaries play a very small part indeed in comparison with savings out of returns to capital. Then why do not wage and salary receivers strive to build up an income-returning capital? The answer may be given in many forms—circumstances, psychology, defective heredity, public opinion and policy, restrictive, repressive, or subdivided competition, and the social atmosphere.

As we in this country live and as we are agreed that we should live, there is little to be had out of wages and salaries for conversion into income-bearing capital, if a man has wife and children to provide for. The wage-earner is subject to causes that weaken his saving power, both in periods of industrial depression and in times called prosperous. In times of depression he suffers for want of employment and in times of great activity in production, cost of living has increased in a greater degree than wages have. There is a popular inversion of this latter fact due to a misunderstanding of the annual reports of the United States Bureau of Labor concerning wages and retail prices of food.

From 1890 to the latest year, the Bureau has established a series of index numbers standing for relative weekly wage-earnings per employee, and another series representing relative retail prices of food, weighted according to family consumption.

Then, another series of index numbers has been computed to merge the former two into one; that is, to express the purchasing power of full-time weekly earnings per employee measured by retail prices of food weighted according to family consumption. This series of combined index numbers is the decisive one in the matter of wages and cost of food, but it is doubtful that it has attracted the attention of one newspaper writer throughout the length and breadth of the land, and the result is that there is a general misrepresentation of this conclusion of the Bureau of Labor.

The fact is this: The purchasing power of wage-earnings in terms of food from 1890 to 1907 was lowest in 1893, in May of which year a long and severe industrial depression burst upon the country. The purchasing power increased during the period of depression and was highest in 1896, the last year of the depression, and next to the highest in the following year, since which time there was decrease, with oscillations.

The general fact established is that the purchasing power of wage-earnings in terms of food-consumption was on a higher level in the so-called prosperous times of 1897 to 1907 than in the similar sort of times in 1890 to 1892; but also that the workingman's earnings bought more food in the period of depression from 1895 to 1897 than in the preceding fat years for capital; and, again, in the years 1896 and 1897 bought more food than in the periods of great expansion that followed.

It clearly appears that wage-rates are less responsive to elevating and depressing influences than food-prices are.

If the Bureau of Labor's index numbers of weekly wage-earnings are computed into purchasing power of all commodities as shown by Bradstreet's index numbers, the results are of the same sort as those above mentioned, but more boldly expressed than when applied to the prices of food alone.

In the case of all commodities, the purchasing power of wages is conspicuously high in the period of low industrial activity from 1894 to 1898 and decidedly low in the following years of expansion.

The time when productive capital "makes money" is when prices rise faster than wages do; the favorable time for wage and salary earners and persons with fixed or nearly fixed incomes is the period of depression, except in so far as want of employment may reduce wage-earnings.

Attention should be directed to an apparent exception in recent years in the case of the wages of farm labor. There seems to be small mobility and less versatility in the labor of the city man;

but the country man will go to the city and turn his hand to almost anything. If he does not become a conductor on a street car, he will prepare to become the president of the company in a few years; he will operate a delivery wagon, or become a merchant, or a telephone lineman, or a banker, and so on with a long list of occupations. The demand for labor in town and city, increasing from 1897 at an apparent gain over country labor in real wage-earnings, although not properly so in fact since they were only wage-rates, tended to deplete the country of agricultural labor, and the consequent increase of farm wages was greater in degree than the increase in the prices of all commodities. From 1895 to 1906 these prices increased 35.8 per cent., while the wages of farm labor by the month for the year or season without board increased 38.4 per cent. and with board 41.4 per cent.; wages by the day in harvest without board increased 46.5 per cent. and with board 55.4 per cent.; and the wages of ordinary labor by the day without board increased 55.6 per cent. and with board 61.3 per cent. The prices of all commodities increased only 35.8 per cent.

The examination of the causes of low wealth-accumulation by the many may be continued. There is occupation. In 1900, twenty-nine million persons had gainful occupations and a very large fraction of these had occupations of low productivity of wealth or of small personal or professional service—at any rate regarded as low or small on pay day. There were over four and one-half million agricultural laborers, 112,000 clergymen, nearly half a million teachers, nearly three million undescribed laborers, 386,000 persons doing work of washerwomen, more than one and one-half million servants; many soldiers, sailors, and marines, boatmen, hostlers, messengers, porters, and so on; and more than half a million dressmakers and seamstresses, nearly two-thirds of a million clerks and copyists, and about the same number of salesmen and saleswomen.

The unskilled, and poorly remunerative, occupations gave employment to probably more than one-half of all persons having gainful occupations.

What fraction of the persons having gainful occupations shall be assigned to those who are employed under wages or salary? Years ago, the writer worked at this question for all censuses in which occupations were sufficiently described, and it seems probable that the fraction of the employed is increasing.

The question was subsequently propounded to a statistical office in Washington several years ago and a man very competent to answer the question arrived at a percentage differing by about 3 and he did not know that the writer had worked on the problem. The conclusions were 65 and 68 per cent.; that is to say, these are the wage and salary receivers.

Analyze the population of all ages and observe how small a fraction is fitted or disposed, or is in a position, to accumulate wealth after maintaining a family and the required standard of living. The negroes are 11.6 per cent., the foreign-born whites 13.5 per cent., the native white females 36.7 per cent., and the native white males under 30 years of age, 25.2 per cent. Of course there is no sweepng generalization that all of these classes cannot be and are not wealth-accumulators in some degree.

After an allowance of one-half of 1 per cent. for Mongolians and Indians, there remains the chief wealth-acquiring class—the native white males 30 years old and over who constitute only 12.5 per cent. of the population; and how many of these must be rejected as even possible wealth-accumulators?

Still further may be considered the subject of the obstacles to wealth-accumulation. Bradstreet's agency has a record of the failures among nearly a million and a half persons, firms, and corporations engaged in business in the United States. From 1899 to 1907, the mean percentage of annual failure was 0.78 of 1 per cent.; somewhat under 1 in each 100 is the yearly business death-rate.

Unfitness of various descriptions accounts for most of the failures—incompetence for 23 per cent. of them in 1907, inexperience for 5 per cent., lack of capital for 37 per cent., unwise credits for 2 per cent., extravagance for 1 per cent., neglect for 2½ per cent., speculation for 1 per cent., and fraud for 10 per cent. In all, more than four-fifths of the failures were because the responsible persons were not qualified to manage and conserve the capital employed; and yet 90 per cent. of the failures had a capital of less than $5,000.

There are social elements not qualified, or not disposed, to produce enough wealth to afford any surplus as a family possession, or if qualified and favorably disposed to produce the wealth, not disposed to save a surplus away from consumption and expenditure. There is the army of the lazy, another army of the mentally incapable, and the many with criminal natures, the sick, weak, and deformed, the degenerates, the atavists, and the spendthrifts. It requires a mighty good inheritance to enable a man to subordinate present satisfactions to future good and greater future satisfactions; and so income disappears in present consumption.

The wastefulness of our people is a world-wide byword. We have been supplied so prodigally that habits of economy and saving have not been forced upon us. To the Chinese we must seem to have taken hardly our first lesson in getting the greatest utility out of things. All this is destructive to saving out of income.

A cord of wood delivered in a cellar in Washington costs $8, and the same cord delivered in little bundles in the kitchen, one at a time, costs $20. As an untried proposition, the cord would cost only two-fifths of the bundles, but upon trying it there will often be found an unexpected factor. When buying by the cord and having an abundance of wood on hand, it is burned unnecessarily and so wastefully that two and one-half cords will not last as long as one cord delivered by the little bundle.

Two pounds of sugar in a single purchase may last as long as five pounds do in kitchen experience. An exhibition of a plentiful supply of butter, soap, and other things will incite the cook and laundress to a riot of waste.

These are illustrations of a widespread and prevalent waste, found not only among servants, but perhaps among your next friends.

So it is often found that the most economical way to live in affairs of the kitchen, where about one-half of the working-man's income is consumed, is the costly one of small purchases at the highest prices, instead of large quantities at wholesale prices. Experience of a similar general nature with a wide range of application is very common in American life.

Now, take the families that are able to accumulate some wealth for investment. How many of them in 100 can invest it so as to keep it from getting away? And how many, or better how few, are competent to use their savings as productive capital and conserve it? The fractions of the competent in these cases are small. A majority of men can work for others better than for themselves; only exceedingly small fractions are organizers and managers even on a small scale.

A few words must be said about income, or there may be some false impressions derived from what has been said about wealth-distribution and the large element of the poor. A family may be poor—that is, have little or no wealth but personal and household belongings and the implements of occupation—and still have a good-sized income. The family may prefer to raise the level of its living and expense to the height of the income rather than to keep the living and expense down and let a surplus remain for building up the stock of family wealth. This is the favorite policy in the United States. The preference is to raise high the standard of living and expense and let the comparatively few provide the nation's capital.

So when we observe the general appearance of well-being throughout the land, the inference is that wealth is well distributed; and, on the other hand, when we are confronted with the probable distribution in fact, we are horrified at the dreadful condition of humanity that it is assumed to indicate.

It is time to put the brakes on our unproductive consumption. Much of this is of no benefit to the family and some of it is detrimental. This topic needs considerable time for its treatment and only a general protest can be entered here. With a reduction of this sort of consumption, there would be available for building up the family wealth, a portion of family income that is now practically wasted.

ENCOURAGEMENT

From whence shall a family get its encouragement? Shall it be from the state? Shall the state treat the family as a child, enforce saving, invest its wealth, guarantee the deposits, establish postal savings banks, the solvency of which will be protected by the wealth of the nation? These questions need not be answered in the affirmative until great social necessity requires such answers, and need not receive consideration at all until self-help, with neighborly encouragement, has failed.

In the meantime degrading conditions should receive attention. Not from the point of view of social welfare, but from that of social preservation, it may be demanded of the state that it shall remove such conditions. This is justification of such legislation as that for improving tenement houses and the conditions of labor in them.

There are many things that we cannot do, or at any rate, will not undertake to do, unless associated with others. By means of co-operation the building and loan association provides loans to its members and at the same time stimulates family savings. Co-operative investment of capital in small contributions by many persons will establish and sustain a co-operative store, or a co-operative laundry, or a co-operative coal yard, or a co-operative printing office, or a co-operative milk-buying and delivery service. The field for economic co-operation is very large, and it may be carried on in many directions.

Co-operation has been enormously developed by farmers in this country and successfully established, and it is working in favor of accumulating the wealth of farmers' families and of conserving it. The magnitude of this movement deserves some words, because of the demonstrations that it presents. Eight or nine years ago, there were obtained from 35,000 crop correspondents of the United States Department of Agriculture, representing all of the townships of the country, the names of the farmers' co-operative economic organizations, and afterward statements of their business were obtained. One who has kept in touch with this co-operative movement of the farmers during the intervening years may risk the statements that follow.

Farmers' economic co-operation in the United States has developed enormously, and it is safe to say that at the present time more than one-half of the 6,100,000 farms are represented in economic co-operation; the fraction is much larger if it is based on the total number of medium and better sorts of farmers, to which the co-operators mostly belong.

The most prominent object of co-operation is property insurance, in which about 2,000 associations have probably 2,000,000 members. This kind of insurance costs the farmers only a few cents per hundred dollars of risk above the actual losses.

The co-operative creameries number more than 1,900, and the cheese factories about 260, the membership of the two classes being very large and representing an immense number of cows.

With the exception of insurance, the greatest success in the farmers' co-operative movement is in selling. Associations to regulate, promote, and manage the details of selling the products of co-operating farmers are found in all parts of the United States. There is co-operation for selling by fruit growers, vegetable growers, nut growers, berry growers; by live-stock men, by the producers of cotton and tobacco, wheat, sweet potatoes, flax, oats, eggs, poultry, and honey. Farmers co-operate to sell milk for city suppy, to sell wool, cantaloupes, celery, cauliflower, citrus fruits, apples, and so on with a long list.

Co-operative buying is conducted by about 350 stores in this country, a majority of which are mostly owned by farmers. This is chiefly the result of a very recent movement. Another form of co-operation for buying is based on the discount plan, as carried on by the granges, farmers' clubs, and various other associations of farmers with co-operative buying as either a primary or secondary object. Things bought in this way are all sorts of store goods: potatoes, wheat, etc., for seed; coal and wood; and a great variety of farm and family supplies.

Warehousing is conducted by farmers on the co-operative plan with success, particularly for the storage of wheat and corn. A co-operative cotton-warehousing movement is of recent date.

Co-operative telephone service has permeated vast regions,

and the co-operative feature has kept the expense at the lowest figure, both of equipment and of service.

Co-operative irrigation is carried on by many thousands of associations in the arid and semi-arid regions, and there is co-operative drainage for reclaiming swamp land.

The progress of farmers in forming and expanding associations of an educational and semi-economic character has made great advances. These associations are national in their scope, or are confined to state lines or to sections within states, and are devoted to the interchange of ideas and experiences, the assembling of information for common benefit, the holding of competitive exhibitions of products, the devising of plans for the common good, and business of a like character; and are concerned with special subjects, such as horticulture, floriculture, dairying, plant breeding, live-stock breeding, poultry breeding, the scientific aspects of breeding, forestry, agricultural education, fraternal association with incidental educational and economic features, seed-breeding, agriculture, vegetable-growing under glass, and the nursery business.

Important associations of the social sort, with incidental economic features, are farmers' clubs, of which there are a great many.

Altogether the number of farmers' co-operative economic associations must be fully 75,000, and may easily be many more, with a membership rising above 3,000,000, without counting duplicates.

Contrary to his reputation, the farmer is a great organizer and he has achieved remarkable and enormous successes in many lines of economic co-operation in which the people of other occupations have made no beginning.

Economic co-operation is a feasible proposition in scores of directions, each of them making at least a small demand for wealth-saving and offering opportunity for investment. If you are engaged in encouragement, you do not wait for fellow-co-operators to come to you, but you go to them and so you are incidentally doing missionary work along lines suggested by the question now under discussion. You may be sure that the co-operator in the successful association will not let go.

The highest form of social co-operation is the voluntary sort. All co-operators are willing, and not a minority of them unwilling as in politico-economic co-operation. Another thing in its favor is that it reacts upon its members to enlarge, or at any rate to strengthen, their individuality. It is a scheme for promoting both socialism and individualism, and it leaves and preserves the largest degree of liberty consistent with the social compact.

In the work of encouraging family wealth, as in other matters, co-operation is selective. Only the suitable ones can become co-operators and remain such. The unsuitable ones will not respond to suggestion and offers of help.

The writer was spending the summer on a farm in Virginia a few years ago, the guest of the owner of 250 acres. 150 of which were nominally improved, and producing a gross return of only $3 or $4 per acre. Partly because it was painful to behold such poor agriculture, and partly from friendly feelings, the services of some of the most talented practical agriculturists in the United States were enlisted to direct the farmer. They promised a gross return of say $75 per acre within five years upon the adoption of their plans, and no doubt their promise was good, but the farmer neglected to accept the offer. He was one of the unimprovable incompetents, irresponsive to social stimulus.

If efforts in behalf of such a farmer or in behalf of your neighbor, to encourage him to add to his family wealth by suggestion, by offer of opportunity, by invitation to co-operate with you and others, are unfavorably received, let that end the matter. Nothing further can be done, unless the state takes charge of him. If it does, the state, and not he, will practically be the saver and conserver; and neither Spencer's nor Weismann's theory of heredity perceives in such procedure the creation of a transmissible habit of saving.

Family in *America*

AN ARNO PRESS / NEW YORK TIMES COLLECTION

Abbott, John S. C. **The Mother at Home:** Or, The Principles of Maternal Duty. 1834.

Abrams, Ray H., editor. **The American Family in World War II.** 1943.

Addams, Jane. **A New Conscience and an Ancient Evil.** 1912.

The Aged and the Depression: Two Reports, 1931–1937. 1972.

Alcott, William A. **The Young Husband.** 1839.

Alcott, William A. **The Young Wife.** 1837.

American Sociological Society. **The Family.** 1909.

Anderson, John E. **The Young Child in the Home.** 1936.

Baldwin, Bird T., Eva Abigail Fillmore and Lora Hadley. **Farm Children.** 1930.

Beebe, Gilbert Wheeler. **Contraception and Fertility in the Southern Appalachians.** 1942.

Birth Control and Morality in Nineteenth Century America: Two Discussions, 1859–1878. 1972.

Brandt, Lilian. **Five Hundred and Seventy-Four Deserters and Their Families.** 1905. Baldwin, William H. **Family Desertion and Non-Support Laws.** 1904.

Breckinridge, Sophonisba P. **The Family and the State:** Select Documents. 1934.

Calverton, V. F. **The Bankruptcy of Marriage.** 1928.

Carlier, Auguste. **Marriage in the United States.** 1867.

Child, [Lydia]. **The Mother's Book.** 1831.

Child Care in Rural America: Collected Pamphlets, 1917–1921. 1972.

Child Rearing Literature of Twentieth Century America, 1914–1963. 1972.

The Colonial American Family: Collected Essays, 1788–1803. 1972.

Commander, Lydia Kingsmill. **The American Idea.** 1907.

Davis, Katharine Bement. **Factors in the Sex Life of Twenty-Two Hundred Women.** 1929.

Dennis, Wayne. **The Hopi Child.** 1940.

Epstein, Abraham. **Facing Old Age.** 1922. New Introduction by Wilbur J. Cohen.

The Family and Social Service in the 1920s: Two Documents, 1921–1928. 1972.

Hagood, Margaret Jarman. **Mothers of the South.** 1939.

Hall, G. Stanley. **Senescence:** The Last Half of Life. 1922.

Hall, G. Stanley. **Youth:** Its Education, Regimen, and Hygiene. 1904.

Hathway, Marion. **The Migratory Worker and Family Life.** 1934.

Homan, Walter Joseph. **Children & Quakerism.** 1939.

Key, Ellen. **The Century of the Child.** 1909.

Kirchwey, Freda. **Our Changing Morality:** A Symposium. 1930.

Kopp, Marie E. **Birth Control in Practice.** 1934.

Lawton, George. **New Goals for Old Age.** 1943.

Lichtenberger, J. P. **Divorce:** A Social Interpretation. 1931.

Lindsey, Ben B. and Wainwright Evans. **The Companionate Marriage.** 1927. New Introduction by Charles Larsen.

Lou, Herbert H. **Juvenile Courts in the United States.** 1927.

Monroe, Day. **Chicago Families.** 1932.

Mowrer, Ernest R. **Family Disorganization.** 1927.

Reed, Ruth. **The Illegitimate Family in New York City.** 1934.

Robinson, Caroline Hadley. **Seventy Birth Control Clinics.** 1930.

Watson, John B. **Psychological Care of Infant and Child.** 1928.

White House Conference on Child Health and Protection. **The Home and the Child.** 1931.

White House Conference on Child Health and Protection. **The Adolescent in the Family.** 1934.

Young, Donald, editor. **The Modern American Family.** 1932.